BRITISH BRUTALITY IN IRELAND

JACK O'BRIEN

Foreword by
Paul O'Dwyer

THE MERCIER PRESS
CORK & DUBLIN

The Mercier Press Limited
4 Bridge Street, Cork, &
24 Lower Abbey Street, Dublin 1

Copyright © Jack O'Brien, 1989

All rights reserved. No part of this publication may be reproduced, stored in a retrieval system, or transmitted in any form or by any means, electronic, photocopying, recording or otherwise, without the prior permission in writing from the publisher.

British Library Cataloguing in Publication Data:
O'Brien, Jack
    British Brutality in Ireland
    1. Great Britain. Foreign relations, 1171-1988 with
       Ireland.
    2. Ireland. Foreign relations, 1171-1988 with
       Great Britain.
    I. Title
    327.410415
    ISBN 0 85342 879 4

Typeset in Palatino by Seton Music Graphics Ltd., Bantry, Co. Cork
Printed and bound in Ireland by Litho Press Co., Midleton, Co. Cork

Acknowledgements
The author and publisher gratefully acknowledge the following publishers and individuals for their kind permission to reprint extracts from their work in this text:
Anvil Books, Dublin, for permission to quote from
    Guerrilla Days in Ireland by Tom Barry.
Olivia Durdin-Robertson for permission to quote from
    Crowned Harp by Nora Robertson.
Jack Fitzpatrick for permission to quote from the diary
    of Captain Seán Fitzpatrick.
Thomas Kinsella and Peppercanister for permission to
    quote from *Butcher's Dozen*.
Methuen & Co, London, for permission to quote from
    A History of Ireland by Edmund Curtis.
Weidenfeld and Nicolson, London, for permission to
    quote from *Ireland since the Famine* by F.S.L. Lyons

Great efforts have been made to check the copyright of all material quoted. One or two items proved impossible to trace, despite extensive research; if copyright has been infringed the matter will be rectified in future editions

Contents

Foreword *by* Paul O'Dwyer	vii
Introduction	1
Chapter 1: Physical Occupation 12th to 15th centuries	7
Chapter 2: Genocide 16th and 17th centuries	19
Chapter 3: The Final Solution 18th century	36
Chapter 4: No Republic Here 18th century	45
Chapter 5: Century of Union Rule 19th century	56
Chapter 6: 'We the People' 20th century	68
Chapter 7: British Army: Instrument of Terror I War of Independence: 1919-21 II Revolt in Northern Ireland: 1969 to date III Gibraltar 1988	83 99 109
Chapter 8: So What?	122
Select Bibliography	133
Chapter Notes and References	135
Biographical and Explanatory Notes	139
Historical Chart	160
Index	169

Foreword

Jack O'Brien's historical masterpiece could not be more appropriately timed. It comes when the spotlight has been turned on the flaws in the British judicial system, flaws which have been uncovered as a result of the efforts of Margaret Thatcher and her colleagues in the House of Commons to eliminate from the law the right of silence of an accused and the denial to the media of their right to interview dissenters. These were rights written into previous court decisions which were accepted as sacred by judges, barristers, solicitors and bailiffs. It was believed by many that basic civil liberties were protected by the Magna Carta.

It has come as a shock to people on both sides of the Atlantic that there was no bar to the draconian laws undermining the people's liberties which Prime Minister Thatcher caused to be enacted. Furthermore, that the Magna Carta was a paper tiger which provided no protection against a neurotic ruler or an hysterical parliament.

Up to the present day, the British criminal justice system has operated under a cloak of fairness. At every opportunity, a majority of its barristers and judges and their media exhibit the Great Charter as if it constituted the emancipation of the, so-called, lower classes. As late as two years ago, Mrs Thatcher boasted to the American Bar Association about the firm foundations on which British law rested. In point of fact, the Great Charter was no more than an arrangement imposed on a despotic monarch which resulted in a guarantee that the Feudal System would remain intact, but the Royal privileges would henceforth be shared by the equally avaricious Barons.

This year, Mrs Thatcher's petulant action has resulted in opening a virtual Pandora's Box and an ancient document, the pride of England, has been held up for public scrutiny and its weakness has become apparent.

The present polite revolt by a group of intellectuals made up of judges, journalists, novelists and academics, coming together under one banner known as 'Charter '88', hopes belatedly to establish a written constitution for Great Britain. I venture to predict that many moons will pass before the Tory Government of Mrs Thatcher will provide the people of Northern Ireland with a written constitution, which would halt their assault on a subject people.

The Magna Carta was honoured in England during the reign of Elizabeth I and William and Mary, but as Jack O'Brien points out, quoting the much-respected Anglo-Irish historian, William Edward Hartpole Lecky: 'The slaughter of Irishmen was looked upon as literally the slaughter of wild beasts ... even the women and children who fell into the hands of the English were deliberately and systematically butchered.'

Edmund Spenser, Elizabethan poet and wealthy land-owner in Ireland, describing the conditions that existed in the country in his time, wrote: 'Out of every corner of the woods and glens, they came creeping forth upon their hands, for their legs could not bear them ... they spoke like ghosts crying out of their graves ...'

The story of murder, rapine and plunder is told in this account of the British occupation of Ireland from 1171 up to the killings in Gibraltar in 1988. The physical harm done to the people of Ireland was so extensive that their survival is one of the great wonders of the world. But those centuries of servitude left a disabling legacy to many of its survivors. Seán MacBride described it as a slave mentality. MacBride is gone and great is the loss, but Captain O'Brien is left to fill the void. It is to be hoped that his talents will go a long way to restore the mental health of the inheritors of a great and ancient culture, and a courageous and spirited people.

Paul O'Dwyer
New York, December 1988

Paul O'Dwyer (1907-), born in Bohola, Co Mayo, has had a distinguished career at the American Bar. For over fifty years, he has successfully defended in the American courts the inalienable constitutional rights of American citizens of all races and creeds, and has acquired a worldwide reputation in the field of human rights. He has acted as defence counsel in many well-known cases, including the trial of the 'Harrisburg Seven' (Fr Philip Berrigan, Sr Elizabeth McAlister and others), initiated in 1971 by the FBI's J Edgar Hoover and the Justice Department, and the trial of the 'Fort Worth Five'. He was elected President of New York City Council in 1973. His autobiography, Counsel for the Defence, *was published in 1979.*

Acknowledgements

The list of authors on whose researches and writings I have drawn extensively in preparing this work is practically endless. Those from whom I have quoted directly are named in the Bibliography. I freely acknowledge the incalculable debt I owe to all of them. In recording what they wrote, I have tried to be scrupulously accurate and if any mistakes have been made by me they are entirely unintentional.

I wish to thank particularly Jack Fitzpatrick for permission to quote from his father's diary and Olivia Durdin-Robertson for permission to quote from her mother's book, *Crowned Harp*. My thanks are due also to: Paul O'Dwyer who wrote the Foreword; Kevin Boland who gave constant encouragement; General Seán MacEoin who read the manuscript and advised on several points; my colleagues in the National Commemoration Day Association for their advice — especially to the late Lt General M J Costello; Seán MacBride, SC; Col A T Lalor; Col H McNamee; Comdt Pat Cahalane; and two very active officers who were always available for any job — Comdts Martin McEvoy and Jim Lavery.

For the work in bringing out the book, I thank Capt Seán Feehan, a man who blazed a trail in Irish publishing 40 years ago when there was a great dearth of such facilities in Ireland; Carole Devaney, his capable and painstaking Dublin editor, and the other members of the staff of The Mercier Press.

Finally, I thank all who were involved in the typing and photocopying of the original manuscript — Bill O'Brien, Nora O'Reilly, Mary O'Brien, Catherine Duggan and, in particular, my daughter Marguerite, whose input can never be adequately acknowledged.

Jack O'Brien
Dublin, January 1989

THIS BOOK IS DEDICATED TO

*The millions who were tortured and murdered
and robbed and forced to emigrate
or suffered in countless other ways
under British rule in Ireland
from the Norman Conquest to Gibraltar 1988*

Magna est veritas et prevalebit
Truth is mighty and it will prevail

— ESDRAS, IV 41

Introduction

'One word of truth shall outweigh the whole world.'
— SOLZHENITSYN
Nobel Lecture in Literature, 1970

Simple lessons cut most deep.
This lesson in our hearts we keep:
Persuasion, protest, arguments,
The milder forms of violence,
Earn nothing but polite neglect.
England, the way to your respect
Is via murderous force, it seems;
You push us to your own extremes.
You condescend to hear us speak
Only when we slap your cheek.
And yet we lack the last technique:
We rap for order with a gun,
The issues simplify to one
— Then your Democracy insists
You mustn't talk with terrorists!
— THOMAS KINSELLA
Ninth ghost in *Butcher's Dozen*

The principle that freedom is the birthright of every nation, and that every nation has 'full power to levy war' to defend its freedom[1], is now generally conceded the world over. These basic tenets are clearly stated in the American Declaration of Independence and similar charters of liberty everywhere. But when conflict between large and small nations arises in the application of such principles, it is unfortunately, more often than not, the rule of force which prevails. Nowhere is this truth better illustrated than in the still unfinished struggle for Irish freedom against British imperialism.

Ireland is a small island nation which has never been at war with other peoples outside of its own shores. It has never had any foreign possessions — colonies or dependant territories. It has never had any desire for territorial expansion and it has never sought to undermine, enslave or conquer other peoples. Until 1922, it had no organised permanent army, navy or air force. Yet throughout most of the past 800 years, it has been involved in wars brought to its shores by a larger neighbouring country with a continual lust for power and conquest, a country led by an upper class recently described, by a British MP, as 'arrogant beyond belief'.[2]

As a result of having to take up arms regularly to resist subjection and to establish their freedom, the Irish people have been repeatedly described by their attackers as murderous, rebellious and savage, in much the same way as European immigrants spoke of the American Indians, the Aborigines and other indigenous peoples. It is an image that persists to this day among certain sections of the British public, particularly in the Tory Party and the Establishment press. Rebellion by the Irish is referred to in terms which would never be used about rebellion by, say, the American colonists, the French Maquis or the Polish underground. Even a figure who won world recognition and was awarded the Nobel *and* Lenin peace prizes, together with numerous other distinctions for his international work in the cause of human freedom and justice — the late Seán MacBride — was described after his death in the editorials of Britain's leading newspapers *The Times* and *Sunday Telegraph* as 'infamous' and 'evil' respectively[3], because of his unceasing defence of the cause of Irish freedom.

British politicians are, of course, long-time specialists in political propaganda and in presenting to their own people what Dick Crossman (former Labour Minister and Lord President of the Council) so vigorously condemned as 'the establishment version of events — not the truth'.[4] In the light, therefore, of the well-established ignorance and prejudice of such politicians and of many English commentators, and indeed of some of their opposite numbers in Ireland, there is clearly a need for a brief and truthful account of the efforts made by England to impose its rule on this country and the effect of these efforts on the course of current events.

Drawing extensively on various public records, on the original researches and writings of the distinguished historian William Edward Hartpole Lecky for the period up to the Act of Union in 1800, on numerous published and unpublished works relating to contemporary events and on the opinions of many people still living — the aim throughout the present text has been to tell the truth and to record the facts as accurately as possible. The same set of facts, naturally, have different significance for different people. It is a matter for individual readers to draw their own conclusions and to take their own moral stance. It is hoped, however, that this study will go some way to explaining why the majority of the common people of Ireland today are distrustful of politicians and why they are convinced that the British Establishment cannot be believed. They view the British pretence — that they are in Northern Ireland primarily in the role of 'honest broker' between the remnant of the British settlers in Ireland and the rest of the population — as so much window-dressing.

Two important questions arise at every step throughout the record and they call for special mention. The first relates to the question of murder and terrorism as a political weapon. Throughout all history, the taking of human life by conquering powers in the course of conquest, either in the field or by judicial process, is not, according to the conqueror, 'murder'. It can be justified in the name of civilization or religion or some other high-sounding motive. It is carried out in the name of law — the conqueror's law. It is therefore legal. But the taking of life by the victims of conquest — be they Indian, Irish, Palestinian or Mujahedin — even where entirely justifiable in self-defence is, according to the conqueror, 'murder' and is punishable accordingly.

The second question relates to religion — not to religious doctrine as such, which was never a source of conflict in Ireland, but to the way in which religion was used to secure or to deprive others of material benefits in land, money, power and privilege. Under the feudal system introduced by the Norman Conquest, title to all land depended ultimately on the King of England. After Henry VIII made acceptance of the Act of Supremacy a condition of full loyalty, adherence to the King's brand of religion became a *sine qua non* to continued possession of one's estates. Henceforth, religion became an economic factor — an excuse for greed, a cover-up for discrimination, oppression and exploitation.

'The common people' is an all-embracing description used regularly throughout this story. Who were they? In Ireland, they comprised the vast majority, at least 80 per cent of the population: workers of all sorts, 'men of no property' — tenant farmers, labourers, artisans and craftsmen. At the trial of Robert Emmet in 1803, the Crown and the press referred to them as 'the lower classes', comprising 'an outlawed bricklayer and such contemptible creatures as an outlawed clerk, hodmen, hostlers, old clothes men, etc'.[5]

The remaining 20 per cent of the population owned up to 90 per cent of the nation's wealth. They constituted 'the upper classes', 'the nobility', 'the landed gentry', 'the professional classes', together with their supporters.

At the time of the Conquest of Ireland in the late 12th century, the number of the common people outside the principal coastal towns (Dublin, Wexford, Waterford, Cork, Limerick and Galway) must have been quite small and scattered. Despite some growth during the Middle Ages, following expansion in agriculture, forest reclamation and commerce, the population remained small. Petty estimated that even as late as 1652, the total population of Ireland — urban and rural — was only about 850,000, having lost about 616,000 in the previous eleven years of war.[6] It was not until 1672 that the population again topped the million mark, reaching an estimated total of 1.1 million.[7]

The real population explosion occurred in the 18th and 19th centuries.[8] During the period of the Penal Laws, numbers actually quadrupled and by 1788 the population was stated to be 4,040,000. In the next half-century, it had doubled again, reaching 5,395,456 in 1805 (Major Newenham's calculation); 6,801,827 in 1821 (official census); 8,175,124 in 1841 (official census); and 8,295,061 in 1845 (Registrar-General's official estimate). If the Great Famine had not struck during the years 1845-49, and had the population continued to increase at its normal rate, the Census Commissioners claimed that it would have reached 9,018,799 by 1851.[9]

This huge increase in population — tenfold in two centuries — occurred almost entirely among the common people.

England's policy of placing 'possession of the whole property and power of the country'[10] in the hands of the few (whose only title to it was confiscation), its subsequent economic policy of *laissez-faire* and its refusal to face the problems of population growth in a non-industrialising country or to maintain the food supply for the common people — such policies turned rural Ireland during these centuries into a vast concentration camp from which the only exit gates were the ports of call of the emigrant ships.

Between 1851 and 1910, according to the Registrar-General's reports, 4,187,000 people emigrated from Irish ports.[11] It is stated by Professor Lyons that for the period 1841 to 1925 'gross overseas emigration' to the USA, Canada and Australia reached a total of 5,190,000.[12] To appreciate the full implications of this population upheaval, one must add equivalent numbers to cover those who died at home from starvation and famine-related diseases — typhus, cholera and tuberculosis. The gross loss would be more than twice the total population of all Ireland today. In an European context, it would be equivalent to a cataclysm involving some 600,000,000 people today.

The efforts — ultimately futile — of the British Crown and government to suppress freedom in Ireland over the centuries is the subject of this brief record. It is significant that the loudest critics of these efforts, and of the evils of British imperialism in Ireland, and the most fervent supporters of the cause of Irish freedom were themselves of English or hybrid origin. To name a few:

THEOBALD WOLFE TONE (1763-98): born a Protestant, but regarded the Established Church as part of the privileged injustice of his time. Became a Deist.
LORD EDWARD FITZGERALD (1763-98): born of Anglo-Irish Protestant parentage.
THOMAS RUSSELL (1767-1803): son of an officer in the British army. Himself an officer in the British 64th Regiment of Foot. A member of the Established Church.
ROBERT EMMET (1778-1803): son of Dr Robert Emmet and Elizabeth Mason, both Protestants.
THOMAS DAVIS (1818-45): son of a surgeon in the British army and an Irish mother (Mary Atkins) of Cromwellian stock, both Protestants.

JOHN MITCHEL (1815-75): son of an Unitarian minister from Dungiven, Co Derry.

THOMAS CLARKE LUBY (1822-1901): Fenian. Son of a Church of Ireland rector.

CHARLES STEWART PARNELL (1846-91): son of an Anglo-Irish Protestant land-owner. Great grandson of Sir John Parnell, opponent of the Union of Great Britain and Ireland in 1800.

DOUGLAS HYDE (1863-1947): son of a Protestant rector.

ROGER CASEMENT (1864-1916): son of a Co Antrim Protestant. Knighted for his work in the British consular service in the Congo and South America.

WILLIAM BUTLER YEATS (1865-1939): poet with Fenian sympathies; of Anglo-Irish Protestant parentage.

MAUD GONNE (1866-1953): daughter of an English mother and an Irish father, Colonel Gonne of the British army (Cavalry). Married Major John MacBride in 1903.

COUNTESS MARKIEVICZ (1868-1927): born Constance Gore-Booth, daughter of a Protestant land-owner. She was second in command to Michael Mallin in Dublin's College of Surgeons during the Easter Rising of 1916.

ERSKINE CHILDERS (1870-1922): son of an English father and an Irish mother (Anna Barton), both Protestants.

PATRICK HENRY PEARSE (1879-1916): son of an English father and an Irish mother.

ONE
Physical Occupation
12TH TO 15TH CENTURIES

'a rude and ignorant people ...'
— POPE ADRIAN IV (1154-59)
describing the Irish in the
Bull Laudabiliter (1155)

'It is no more sin to kill an Irishman than a dog, or any other brute, and some monks affirm that if it should happen to them, as it does often, to kill an Irishman, they would not on that account refrain from saying mass, not even for a day.'
— THE REMONSTRANCE OF THE IRISH PRINCES
to Pope John XXII in 1317

To acquire undisputed control of land where men can settle and prosper is the first objective of all colonial effort. It inevitably involves subjugation, assimilation or expulsion of the people already in possession. It is the story of colonial expansion in all ages and in all parts of the world — the Americas, both North and South, Africa and Asia. It is, in large part, the story of Britain in Ireland.

WITH PAPAL APPROVAL
When Henry II of England landed in Waterford on 17 October 1171, he had with him an army of some 4000 men and the authority of an important papal document known to history as the *Bull Laudabiliter*. Henry clearly meant business: he intended to secure control of the land of Ireland and to keep it. He was properly armed and his 'papers' were in order. So far as the papacy was concerned, Ireland lay within the legitimate 'sphere of influence' of England and, despite the Reformation, that view has been demonstrated time and again, up to modern times.

Under the *Bull Laudabiliter* of 1155, Henry was given title to the land of Ireland by Pope Adrian IV in the following terms — and they are worth quoting in full:[1]

> 'ADRIAN, bishop, servant of the servants of God, to our well-beloved son in Christ the illustrious king of the English, greeting and apostolic benediction.
>
> Laudably and profitably does your majesty contemplate spreading the glory of your name on earth and laying up for yourself the reward of eternal happiness in heaven, in that, as becomes a Catholic prince, you purpose to enlarge the boundaries of the Church, to proclaim the truths of the Christian religion to a rude and ignorant people, and to root out the growths of vice from the field of the Lord; and the better to accomplish this purpose you seek the counsel and goodwill of the apostolic see. In pursuing your object, the loftier your aim and the greater your discretion, the more prosperous, we are assured, with God's assistance, will be the progress you will make: for undertakings commenced in the zeal of faith and the love of religion are ever wont to attain to a good end and issue. Verily, as your excellency doth acknowledge, there is no doubt that Ireland and all islands on which Christ the sun of righteousness has shone, and which have accepted the doctrines of the Christian faith, belong to the jurisdiction of the blessed Peter and the holy Roman Church; wherefore the more pleased are we to plant in them the seed of faith acceptable to God, inasmuch as our conscience warns us that in their case a stricter account will hereafter be required of us.
>
> Whereas then, well-beloved son in Christ, you have expressed to us your desire to enter the island of Ireland in order to subject its people to law and to root out from them the weeds of vice, and your willingness to pay an annual tribute to the blessed Peter of one penny from every house, and to maintain the rights of the churches of that land whole and inviolate: We therefore, meeting your pious and laudable desire with due favour and according a gracious assent to your petition, do hereby declare our will and pleasure that, with a view to enlarging the boundaries of the Church, restraining the downward course of vice, correcting evil customs and planting virtue, and for the increase of the Christian religion, you shall enter that island and execute

whatsoever may tend to the honour of God and the welfare of the land; and also that the people of that land shall receive you with honour and revere you as their lord: provided always that the rights of the churches remain whole and inviolate, and saving to the blessed Peter and the Holy Roman Church the annual tribute of one penny from every house. If then you should carry your project into effect, let it be your care to instruct that people in good ways of life, and so act, both in person and by agents whom you shall have found in faith, in word and in deed fitted for the task, that the Church there may be adorned, that the Christian religion may take root and grow, and that all things appertaining to the honour of God and the salvation of souls may be so ordered that you may deserve at God's hands the fullness of an everlasting reward, and may obtain on earth a name renowned throughout the ages.'

This papal document states clearly that in view of Henry's acknowledgement that Ireland, and all islands which have accepted the doctrines of the Christian faith, belongs to the jurisdiction of the Blessed Peter and the Holy Roman Church, and that he, Henry, proposes to enter Ireland:
- to enlarge the boundaries of the Church;
- to proclaim the truth of the Christian religion to a rude and ignorant people;
- to subject the people to law; and
- to root out from them the weeds of vice,

he, Pope Adrian, agrees to the proposed invasion. The English pontiff also declares that the people of Ireland should receive the invading king with honour and revere him as their lord, provided always that the rights of the Church remain whole and inviolate, and that an annual tribute of one penny from every house (Peter's pence) be paid to the Vatican.

The blessing and approval of Adrian IV for the proposed invasion of Ireland was of vital importance to Henry in a century when the temporal power of the papacy was at its height. In a document entitled *Dictatus Papa*, published a century before the invasion and attributed to Pope Gregory VII (1073-85), it is proclaimed:[2]

'The Roman Pontiff alone is properly called universal. He alone may depose bishops, and restore them to office. He is the only person whose feet are kissed by all princes.

> He may depose emperors. He may be judged by no one. He may absolve from their allegiance the subjects of the wicked. The Roman church never has erred, and never can err as the Scriptures testify.'

One of Gregory's successors — Pope Innocent III (1198-1216) — reiterated these claims in even more uncompromising terms:[3]

> 'As the moon receives its light from the sun, and is inferior to the sun, so do Kings receive all their glory and dignity from the Holy See ... God has set the Prince of the Apostles over kings and kingdoms, with a mission to tear up, plant, destroy, scatter and rebuild.'

When, therefore, Pope Adrian's immediate successor, Alexander III, wrote in October 1172 (six months after King Henry's departure from Ireland) to the Irish bishops, to King Henry himself and to the kings and princes of Ireland,[4] he was merely giving expression to papal thinking on the recent invasion of Ireland in the context of these most dogmatic claims of the papacy in temporal matters. To the bishops of Ireland Pope Alexander wrote:

> 'Understanding that our dear son in Christ, Henry, illustrious King of England, stirred by divine inspiration and with his united forces, has subjected to his dominion that people, a barbarous one, uncivilized and ignorant of the Divine law ... We command and enjoin upon you ... that you will diligently and manfully ... assist the above said King ... to maintain and preserve that land and to extirpate the filthiness of such great abominations. And if any of the kings, princes or other persons of that land shall rashly attempt to go against his due oath and fealty pledged to the said King ... you shall lay ecclesiastical censure on such a one ...'

In his second letter, addressed to King Henry, the pontiff wrote:

> 'We have been assured how ... you have wonderfully and gloriously triumphed over that people of Ireland ... and over a kingdom which the Roman emperors, the conquerors of the world, left (so we read) untouched in their time, and ... have extended the power of your majesty over the same people, a race uncivilized and undisciplined ... and it appears that the aforesaid people ... marry their stepmothers and are not ashamed to have children by them; a man will live with his brother's wife while the brother is still alive; one man will live in

concubinage with two sisters; and many of them, putting away the mother will marry the daughters ... We understand that you, collecting your splendid naval and land forces, have set your mind upon subjugating that people to your lordship and ... extirpating the filthiness of such abomination, we hold your purpose good and acceptable in all ways. And so we exhort and beseech your majesty and enjoin upon you that you will even more intently and strenuously continue ... and earnestly enjoin upon your majesty that you will carefully seek to preserve the rights of the see of Saint Peter.'

In his third letter, addressed to the kings and princes of Ireland, Pope Alexander said:

'Whereas you have received our dear son in Christ, Henry, the illustrious king of England as your king and lord, and have sworn fealty to him ... and you have of your free will submitted to so powerful and magnificent a king ... we commend your wise forethought as most worthy of praise. We moreover warn and admonish your noble order to strive to preserve the fealty which by solemn oath you have made ... and may you so show yourselves in all humility and meekness, submissive and devoted towards him that you may be able ever to win his abundant favour ...'

The temporal power of the papacy has, of course, long since disappeared, but it was very real in 1171 and for some centuries later. Almost every king had at one time or another become liegeman to the Pope or at any rate held his crown with the Pope's approval. Even William the Conqueror carried a banner consecrated by Alexander II on his expeditions. Under Henry II, England became a fief of the Holy See and the King made full submission to the Pope in September 1173 rather than incur the risk of interdict for his part in the murder of the Archbishop of Canterbury — Thomas Becket. Henry's successor in Ireland — King John — refused to accept Pope Innocent's nominee as Archbishop of Canterbury. For his disobedience the Pope replied by excommunicating him and laying his kingdom under interdict until he submitted.

All over Europe for another three centuries, the popes gave their blessings to the military ventures of warring kings and princes, and promulgated laws binding on conquered peoples. Even as late as 1493, Pope Alexander VI issued a Bull granting

Ferdinand and Isabella exclusive rights over the new lands discovered by Columbus the year before. Alexander, in fact, laid down an imaginary line of demarcation in the Atlantic — 300 miles west of the Azores — and declared all new lands discovered west of the line were to belong to Spain and all those east of it to Portugal.

These documents are more than papal warrants for warrior kings bent on conquering fresh territories for themselves. They are masterpieces in contemporary political propaganda and false representation. Henry II is described as a God-fearing son in Christ, illustrious King of England stirred by divine inspiration, and so on. In reality, he was an ambitious Norman conqueror, determined to subjugate the new territory of Ireland by force of arms — as evidenced by the size of the army he brought with him (4000 men). That he was a ruthless destroyer of those who opposed him is clear from his involvement in the murder of Thomas Becket.

'A RUDE AND IGNORANT PEOPLE'

The Irish people are described in these papal documents as a rude and ignorant people, uncivilized and undisciplined. Yet the literary, artistic and architectural survivals from the period — illuminated manuscripts, artistic works in gold, silver and precious stones, large churches such as Cashel and small pre-Norman stone churches — would suggest a high level of civilization and Christian practice, comparable with the rest of Europe at the time.

The accusation that the people were steeped in vice — in the habit of marrying their stepmothers and not ashamed to have children by them, living with one another's wives and living in concubinage with two sisters — is probably a gross exaggeration. Irish habits were most likely no worse than those of the invading Normans themselves. The behaviour of the Welsh Princess Nesta, often described as the 'queen bee' of the whole Norman-Welsh swarm, is a case in point. By her love affairs with King Henry I and with Stephen, Constable of Cardigan, and by her genuine marriage with Gerald of Windsor, this lady was said to be the mother and grandmother of the Fitzgeralds, Barrys, Carews and other partners in the conquest of Ireland.

As is usual with all propaganda, breaches of the eighth

commandment (Thou shalt not tell lies) are no subject for rebuke when the objective is the enlargement of the boundaries of the power and influence of the body issuing it — whether it be Church or State. Distortion of the truth is the essence of brainwashing.

In any event, the papal letters gave full moral sanction to Henry's invasion as they did, in later times, to the conquest of the Americas by Spanish and Portuguese conquistadores. By thus weakening Irish opposition, such papal approval greatly facilitated the physical occupation of the country. It was the beginning of the subjugation of the Irish people, with the sword in one hand and the Bible in the other. This disastrous combination has led to many centuries of bloodshed, because of Ireland's continued resistance to England's efforts to gain control of its lands. The papal blessing discredited the Christian message by giving support to the use of force by an invading power to achieve naked political ends.

Within a few generations of Henry's arrival, the English colony had become firmly established over the greater part of Ireland. The limits of the old Gaelic kingdom had everywhere been pushed back to make room for the new settlers. The submissions to the English king, which the Pope had advised and praised, were general. The feudal theory of land-ownership, which gave undisputed control of all land to the king, was introduced and accepted. The British tradition, which has survived to the present day, had begun.

VASSALS OF THE CROWN

There are few detailed manorial records (such as leases or account books) available to illustrate the social and economic changes that the English invasion brought about in Ireland. The broad developments that did occur are, however, well known. Giraldus Cambrensis reported that at the time of the invasion 'Ireland is well-wooded and marshy' and 'the plains are of limited extent compared with the woods'.[5] From 1171 onwards, increasing demand for timber and for agricultural produce generally (particularly corn, wool and hides) from royal purveyors purchasing supplies for military campaigns abroad, and from merchants engaged in the export trade, led naturally to progressive reclamation of wooded and marginal land, multiplication of holdings, rising population and so on.

Production appears to have been on the lines of the mixed farming described by Arthur Young in the 18th century and as practised generally in most areas even up to the early decades of this century. There is little tradition of the 'open-field' system or 'labour service' to the Lord of the Manor, or of any other features associated with classical feudalism practised on the continent of Europe. Apart from some military obligations, most other duties were probably met by payment of charges. The increased trade due to greater production would, in the normal way, call for trading centres — fairs, pig markets, shops, merchants — and it is probably as such centres that many of Ireland's smaller inland towns came to be established in the vicinity of the first Norman castles.

The most important and lasting changes which feudalism brought to the Irish, however, were legal and political. Prior to the invasion, the people owed allegiance to the elected kings of their area and to the elected chiefs and sub-chiefs of the clan, or sept, to which they belonged. Obedience to the law meant obedience to the Brehon laws, which governed nearly all aspects of their lives. Land was held mostly in collective ownership.

Under the feudal system introduced by the invader, all this was to change. Election of chiefs and sub-chiefs ceased. Ownership of land was removed from the people and vested in the king of England, following the voluntary submissions made to Henry II and his successors by Norman barons and Gaelic chiefs alike. Henceforth, therefore, all land and titles depended ultimately on the king and as supreme landlord he could grant or recover them as 'Dominus Terrae' or 'Dominus Hiberniae'. Under these powers, the king confirmed Gaelic chiefs in parts of their traditional kingdoms and made grants of land to various Norman magnates — Fitzgeralds, Butlers, Burkes, to name a few. They, in turn, sub-infeudated by making grants to sub-tenants. All grants and lettings were subject to tight feudal contracts, which meant forfeiture of lands and titles if not kept.

It was thus that the tillers of the soil, 'the common people', got stitched into involuntary loyalty to the usurper of the land (*viz* the king of England) and were subjected to English law. Under the same system in other countries, the people owed loyalty to their sovereign, but he was sovereign of their own country — not an alien king. The new system generally was foreign to the Irish mind and experience. It was undemocratic and laid the foundation of a class-orientated society. It inevitably led to the two-nations idea, associated with landlordism, ground rents and control by a minority of owners over a majority of non-owners. It gave rise to real divisions in society which deepened with time and led to the growth of distinctly separate classes which never did, or could, assimilate.

Altogether, this was a colossal upheaval in the traditional position and rights of the common Irish people, equivalent to the change created for the Kulaks in Russia when the Communist government decided in the 1930s to proceed in the opposite direction and abolish private ownership of land in favour of collectivised public ownership.

In the same way, a vicious propaganda war was waged against the native population by those who favoured the change. Pope Alexander III in his letter to Henry II (*above*) described the Irish as uncivilized and undisciplined. Giraldus Cambrensis, historian of the Normans, summed up the Irish in 1185: they were a rude people, a barbarous people, adulterous and incestuous, illegitimately born and married; they lived like beasts, knew nothing of the very rudiments of faith and were the most filthy people and the most ignorant on the face of the earth.

Some centuries later, Edmund Spenser and other Elizabethans in various dispatches home described the Irish as 'vile caitiffs', 'rascal rout' and a 'herd of wild rogues'.[6]

THE REMONSTRANCE

Notwithstanding all the pious platitudes attending the establishment of the sovereignty of Henry II of England over Ireland — with the full approval of the Pope — things did not go as envisaged. Within a century and a half, the operation of the English colony had run into trouble and become the subject of complaint to the then Avignon Pope, John XXII, from some descendants of the original chiefs. (These men had failed to oppose Henry II at the appropriate time, to the detriment of their own interests subsequently and the interests of the common people who lost their stake in the land.) In 1317 the Irish princes, under the leadership of Donald O'Neill, wrote a long letter in Latin to the Pope, entitled *The Remonstrance*. In their indictment they complained bitterly about English oppression. They charged that, contrary to the promises given to the Pope by Henry II before the invasion:[7]

- The English have striven 'to wipe our nation out entirely and utterly to extirpate it' and 'have compelled us to seek mountains, woods, bogs, barren tracts and even caverns in the rocks to save our lives'.
- More than 50,000 of both races in addition to those who died from 'famine, distress and prison' have perished as a result of the invasion.
- The boundaries of the church have been restricted rather than expanded.
- The English have deprived us of our ancient written laws [Brehon Laws] and have enacted new ones for the extermination of our race, which provide that:
  (a) any person who is not an Irishman may sue an Irishman, but no Irishman may sue an Englishman;
  (b) when an Englishman kills an Irishman no punishment is inflicted — the more eminent the murdered, the more the murderer is honoured;
  (c) every Irishwoman who marries an Englishman is deprived at his death of the third part of his lands and possessions precisely because she is Irish;
  (d) on the death of an Irishman the English seize his property.
- Monasteries may not receive into their orders any except those that are English by nation — friars, preachers, minorities, monks, canons and other English religious have been behaving thus even where the monasteries were founded by the Irish.
- The English in Ireland who call themselves the middle nation differ in character from the English of England and from other nations that they may be called a nation not of the middle (medium) but of the utmost perfidy.
- The English invite Irish noblemen to a banquet and during the feast or while they are asleep, they mercilessly murder their unsuspicious guests, cut off their heads and sell them for money to their enemies. For example:
  (a) Baron Bermingham, at a banquet given on Trinity Sunday, had his guests murdered when they rose from the table (along with twenty-four of their following) and sold their heads dear to their enemies;
  (b) Sir Thomas de Clare, Earl of Gloucester, tore his guest Brian Ruadh, Prince of Thomond, from his feast table and had him dragged at horses' tails and having cut off his head had the headless corpse hung by the feet from a beam.

- To the English these acts appear honourable and praiseworthy for not only their laymen and secular clergy, but some of their regular clergy dogmatically assert that it is no more sin to kill an Irishman than a dog, or any other brute, and some monks affirm that if it should happen to them, as it does often, to kill an Irishman, they would not on that account refrain from saying mass, not even for a day.
  (a) the monks of the Cistercian order of Granard, or the monks of the same order at Inch, fulfil in deed what they proclaim in word; for bearing arms publicly, they attack the Irish and slay them, and nevertheless they celebrate their masses;
  (b) Friar Simon of the Order of Friars Minor, brother of the bishop of Conor, chief formulator of this heresy, boasted in the court of Edward Bruce that it is no sin to kill a man of Irish birth and if he were to commit it himself he would none the less for that celebrate mass.
- The English assert that it is lawful to take from us by force of arms whatever they can of our lands and possessions without scruple, even when at the point of death ... All the land they hold in Ireland they hold by usurpation in this way.
- Since in way of life and speech the English are more dissimilar from us than many other nations, there is no hope whatever of our having peace with them. For such is their arrogance and excessive lust to lord it over us, and so great is our natural desire to throw off the yoke, there cannot now or ever henceforward be established sincere good will between them and us. For we have a natural hostility to each other, arising from the mutual malignant and incessant slaying of fathers, brothers, nephews and other near relatives and friends.

Having unsuccessfully sought redress for these injustices from King Edward II, the Irish princes end their letter by saying that they have transferred their allegiance to Edward Bruce, whom they have set up as King and Lord, and that they will wage deadly war against the English to the end. They seek the approval of the Pope for their action.

However, it was too late to complain — the days of supreme papal power were over. In the words of Lord Acton, 'supremacy over the states was at an end'. The Pope himself was an absentee from Rome, a captive of the French King, with a sort of government in exile at Avignon. All Pope John XXII was prepared to do was to acknowledge the letter and make representation to Edward II of England, urging him to attend to the complaint. Nothing happened.

The whole thrust of the Irish princes' complaint in *The Remonstrance* is about themselves and what they suffered following the submission of their forebears to the King of England. There is nothing in it about the common people — the labourers, craftsmen, tenant farmers who tilled the soil — and how *they* lost out as a result of the introduction of the feudal system. Such a reference would not, of course, have made any difference, because the papacy itself had long since changed from being the messenger of the Nazarene — whose work and identity was with the poor and oppressed — into a powerful feudal overlord with enormous temporal power, identifying mainly with kings and princes.

Under the feudal system, the role of the common man was that of hewer of wood and drawer of water, and an entire armoury of controls was invented by kings and popes alike to tie him mind and body to his spiritual and temporal masters. It was a system that produced an involuntary obedience to authority, based on the arbitrary power of the few, and because of the corrupting effect of such power on those who exercised it, it led inevitably and inexorably to the exploitation of the majority by the minority, a system which could only result in violent efforts to break it.

TWO
Genocide
16TH AND 17TH CENTURIES

'The war, as conducted by Carew, by Gilbert, by Pelham, by Mountjoy, was literally a war of extermination. The slaughter of Irishmen was looked upon as literally the slaughter of wild beasts.'

— LECKY

During the centuries following Donald O'Neill's complaint to the Pope in 1317, the general objective of the English Crown was, in the words of that famous Attorney-General Sir John Davies — 'to root out the Irish from the soil', to confiscate the property of the septs and plant the country systematically with English tenants.[1]

Those who were required for cultivation work (tenant farmers, ploughmen and labourers) were in the main suffered to stay in the areas confiscated, but former owners were progressively forced out. By the late 16th century, Irish princes such as Desmond, O'Neill, O'Donnell and many others, who felt that their estates had been marked out for confiscation, were in open rebellion as a result of this policy. Until the end of the next century, war between land-owners and the Crown was the order of the day.

Driven by hunger for land and the prospect of easy pickings, armies of English adventurers swarmed into Ireland from about the start of the reign of Elizabeth I, in 1558, to the close of the reign of William and Mary, in 1694. It was during this period, of less than a century and a half, that the land of Ireland, which in pre-Norman times had been held collectively by Irish chieftains and their clans, passed by stages almost entirely into the possession of a minority of individual owners, nearly all of them eventually Protestant and comprising no more than 20 per cent of the total population. The common people — the other 80 per cent — were totally deprived of such collective rights as they had had under the pre-feudal system of ownership. In the rural areas, they were reduced to the level of serfs and slaves of the landlords. Such was their lot until at least some of them — the renting occupiers — were enabled to buy out their holdings under the land acts at the turn of the present century.

Expulsion of existing owners without compensation and the resettlement of confiscated lands with new owners on the scale embarked upon by the English in Ireland could have been accomplished only by a series of military campaigns which removed all opposition by force. The record of how these campaigns were carried out by Elizabeth's generals (men like Carew, Gilbert, Pelham and Mountjoy) in the 16th century and by Cromwell and his lieutenants (Ireton, Ludlow, Coote and others) in the 17th is based almost entirely on the writings of the historian William Edward Hartpole Lecky. Although a Protestant and a Unionist member of parliament for Trinity College Dublin, Lecky was a devastating critic of the savage, Pol Pot methods consistently employed by the British Crown and parliament to put the Davies policy into effect ('to root out the Irish from the soil') and of the penal laws enacted to crush the Irish people to the dust, centuries before Hitler invented the term 'final solution' for another group of people. From the start, Lecky asserts that:[2]

> 'The slaughter of Irishmen was looked upon as literally the slaughter of wild beasts. Not only the men, but even the women and children who fell into the hands of the English were deliberately and systematically butchered. Bands of soldiers traversed great tracts of country, slaying every living thing they met. The sword was not found sufficiently expeditious, but another method proved much more efficacious. Year after year, over a great part of Ireland, all means of human subsistence were destroyed, no quarter was given to prisoners who surrendered, and the whole population was skilfully and steadily starved to death.'

Such conduct was warmly encouraged and richly rewarded by the British government. Lecky goes on to say:[3]

> 'The idea that it was possible to obtain at a few hours' or days' journey from the English coasts, and at little or no cost, great tracts of fertile territory, and to amass in a few

years gigantic fortunes, took hold upon the English mind with a fascination much like that which was exercised by the fables of the exhaustless riches of India in the days of Clive and Hastings.'

Many contemporary accounts record the state of the country following these operations. In his book *View of the Present State of Ireland*, Edmund Spenser, who had been secretary to Lord Deputy Grey and who had been given a grant of 4000 acres and the castle of Kilcolman near Doneraile, Co Cork, wrote:[4]

'... out of every corner of the woods and glens, they came creeping forth upon their hands, for their legs could not bear them. They looked like anatomies of death; they spoke like ghosts crying out of their graves; they did eat the dead carrion, happy when they could find them; yea, and one another soon after, in as much as the very carcases they spared not to scrape out of their graves; and if they found a plot of watercresses or shamrocks there they flocked as to a feast for the time, yet not long able to continue therewithall, that in a short space there were none almost left, and a most populous and plentiful country suddenly made void of man or beast.'

Holinshed tells how the people were 'not only driven to eat horses, dogs, and dead carrions, but also did devour the carcases of dead men ... The land itself ... is now become so barren, both of man and beast, that whoever did travel from the one end of all Munster, even from Waterford to the head of Smeereweeke, which is about sixscore miles, he would not meet any man, woman or child saving in towns and cities.'[5]

The *Annals of the Four Masters* record how in 1580 the bands of Pelham and Ormond 'killed blind and feeble men, women, boys and girls, sick persons, idiots and old people'; how in Desmond's country, 'even after all resistance had ceased, soldiers forced men and women into old barns which were set on fire and if any attempted to escape they were shot or stabbed'; and how in 1582 'from Dingle to the Rock of Cashel, not the lowing of a cow nor the voice of the ploughman was that year to be heard.'[6]

Pacata Hibernia, which is reputed to have been written by Sir George Carew, states that:[7]

'The troops of Sir Richard Percie left neither corn, nor horn, nor house unburnt between Kinsale and Ross ... The troops of Sir Charles Wilmot entered without resistance an Irish camp, where they found nothing but hurt and sick men, whose pains and lives by the soldiers were both determined ... The Lord President himself [Sir George Carew] assures us that having heard that the Munster fugitives were harboured in certain parts of that province, diverted his forces thither, "burnt all the houses, and corn, taking great preys ... and harassing the country, killed all mankind that were found therein." From thence he went to other parts, where "he did the like, not leaving behind him man or beast, corn or cattle except such as had been conveyed into castles".'

Archbishop Usher described how women were accustomed to lie in wait for a passing rider and to rush out like famished wolves to kill and to devour his horse.[7] According to Froude, 'The slaughter of women as well as of men, of unresisting peasants as well as of armed rebels, was openly avowed by the English commanders.'[8] It was boasted that in all the wide territory of Desmond [Munster], not a town, castle, village or farmhouse was unburnt. A high English official, writing in 1582, computed that in six months more than 30,000 people had been starved to death in Munster, besides those who were 'hung or who perished by the sword'.

On 26 October 1569 — at the very early stage in this campaign of genocide — the Lord Deputy Sidney reported to the Privy Council that, 'From the Cahir I departed into the Whyte Knight's country burning all the corn that was gathered and spoiling the rest. I raised one of his castles, burnt and spoiled all his other houses.'[9]

Almost twenty years later, when the war was nearly over, Sir Edward Phyton reported to Elizabeth's chief minister, Lord Burghley, on 30 July 1587, 'The country generally is wasted, but yet not a pile in any place but full of the poorest creatures that ever I saw, so lean for want of food ... so idle they will not work because they are descended either of Kerne, horsemen or gallowglass, all three the very subversion of this land. Sermon not once in seven years. The churchmen collect their tithes with most rigour, and neither give food, temporal or spiritual.'[10]

In his *History of Ireland*, Leland wrote, 'Long before the war ended, Elizabeth was assured that she had little left to reign over but ashes and carcases.'[11]

'In Ulster', states Lecky, 'the war was conducted in a similar spirit. An English historian, who was an eye-witness of the subjugation of the province, tells us that "Lord Mountjoy never received any to mercy but such as had drawn the blood of some of their fellow rebels." Thus "McMahon and McArtmoyle offered to submit, but neither could be received without the other's head." The country was steadily subdued by starvation. "No spectacle was more frequent in the ditches of towns, and especially in wasted countries, than to see multitudes of these poor people dead, with their mouths all coloured green by eating nettles, docks, and all things that could rend above ground." In the single county of Tyrone 3,000 persons in a few months were starved ... at last, hunger and the sword accomplished their work; Tyrone bowed his head before the storm, and the English ascendancy was supreme.'[12]

'In Munster', continues Lecky, 'after Desmond's rebellion, more than 574,000 acres were confiscated and passed into English hands. One of the conditions of the grants was that none of the native Irish should be admitted among the tenantry of the new proprietors. It was intended to sweep those who had survived the war completely from the whole of this enormous territory, or at least to permit them to remain only in the condition of day-labourers or ploughmen, with the alternative of flying to the mountains or the forests to die of starvation, or to live as savages or as robbers.'[13]

In Ulster, no less than six counties — Donegal, Derry, Tyrone, Fermanagh, Cavan and Armagh — were confiscated by the Crown after the flight of the Earls O'Neill and O'Donnell in 1607. Some 500,000 acres of 'profitable' land were planted under the initial Ulster plantation scheme with English and Scottish colonists. Concerning these colonists, Stewart (the son of one of the ministers who came over with them) wrote:[14]

> 'From Scotland came many and from England not a few, yet all of them generally the scum of both nations, who from debt, or breaking or fleeing from justice, or seeking shelter, came hither, hoping to be without fear of man's justice, in a land where there was nothing, or but little as yet, of the fear of God ... Going to Ireland was looked on as a miserable mark of a deplorable person; yea, it was turned into a proverb, and one of the worst expressions of disdain that could be invented was to tell a man that Ireland would be his "hinder end".'

Another Presbyterian writer, by the name of Reid, adds that 'among those whom Divine Providence did send to Ireland, there were several persons eminent for birth, education and parts, yet the most part were such as either poverty, scandalous lives or, at the best, adventurous seeking of better accommodation, had forced thither.'[15]

The wars of extermination of the 16th century and the plantations which followed them did, as intended, wipe out great numbers of Irish land-owners and common people, while great tracts of confiscated lands in Munster and Ulster were granted to English settlers. However, it is nevertheless true to say that many of the common people were able to escape the marauding soldiery and take refuge in woods and mountainous areas from which, as Spenser complained, they were later to emerge to compete with English tenants. Such experience shows that total displacement of a rural population is extremely difficult, even where the most barbarous methods are employed.

Many of the new owners — such as the London corporations who received substantial grants of lands in Derry — were absentees and found that they had no other option but to retain thousands of the common people as small tenants or cultivators, notwithstanding the prohibition against such practice in their grants. Gradually, plantation terms were found impossible to operate literally and wholesale expulsion of the common people from the planted areas became a dead letter. Over a period, there was increasing intermarriage between the indigenous population and those who came as immigrants to work lands that had been newly sub-infeudated, or as soldiers to fight in various military campaigns and remained on after the wars were over, or who came in other ways. Between them they formed the basic hybrid stock of the subsequent Irish population. Of these, Curtis writes:[16]

> 'In the common people we see a blended race who in the long run have proved to be the characteristic Irish people, feeling a sense of common history and a common Faith, with an intense passion for the land which nothing has been able to shake, and speaking that Gaelic language which was the speech of the majority up to 1800. Milesian or Old English, Danish or Norman, whatever their origin, they have all accepted the Irish legend as against the English legend.'

It is clear that 'religious zeal' did not at first play any part in the struggle. All sixteen English kings, from Henry II to Henry VIII, were Catholics, as were all the Irish land-owners. Past efforts of the Crown were directed simply towards securing control over more and more Irish land and the revenues from them. It was not until Henry VIII fell out with the Pope over his divorce from his Catholic queen that religion became an additional weapon in the fight to secure that control. Loyalty to the King as superior feudal land-owner was no longer sufficient to secure a man's title. Under the Act of Supremacy, Henry VIII assumed a new title in 1534 — 'supreme head on earth of the church of England'; two years later, he was declared by the Irish Parliament 'the only supreme head on earth of the church of Ireland', on the grounds that 'this land of Ireland is depending and belonging justly and rightfully to the imperial crown of England'.

Henceforth, full allegiance to the King demanded acknowledgement of this 'fact'. At first, no more than a handful of Irish land-owners subscribed to the Oath, but as time passed and more pressure, direct and indirect, was applied, most of the large land-owners, who after all held their titles at the pleasure of the King, complied and became members of his church. For them, it was a question of economics and politics — not religion. When Sir Thomas More was being urged to take the Oath on the grounds that all the important families in England had already done so, he is alleged to have replied, 'The nobility of England would have snored through the Sermon on the Mount.'

In Ireland, some land-owners and the majority of the common people did not subscribe to Henry's Reformation. To the common people in particular, the new religion meant nothing: it was in English and the Book of Common Prayer had not been translated into Irish, which was the only language they understood. The new religion as represented by a Carew or an Essex was far from prepossessing in their eyes. Naturally, under such circumstances, they maintained their traditional convictions and practices; the Pope and new theories about religion were far-off things in their work-a-day world. None of the causes that had produced Protestantism in England — royal succession, royal authority and the like — was of the slightest concern to them.

Although the Elizabethan wars were undoubtedly savage and deliberate wars of extermination, they were only a prelude to the much bloodier times to come. In a single decade of the 17th century wholesale massacres halved the population of Ireland and resulted in the transfer of practically the entire land of the country into the hands of a religious minority, the Protestants. The appetite for Irish land grew by what it fed upon and in the words of Lecky:[17]

> 'During the whole of the reign of James [1603-25] a perpetual effort was made to deprive the Irish of the residue which remained to them. The concessions intended in the plantation scheme were most imperfectly carried out. "The commissioners", writes a temperate Protestant historian [Leland] "appointed to distribute the lands scandalously abused their trusts, and by fraud or violence deprived the natives of the possessions the King had reserved for them." In the small county of Longford, twenty-five members of one sept were all deprived of their estates, without the least compensation, or any means of subsistence assigned to them. All over Ireland the trade of the Discoverer now rose into prominence. Under pretence of improving the King's revenue, these persons received commissions of inquiry into defective titles, and obtained confiscations, and grants at small rents for themselves ...
>
> 'Everywhere, discoverers were at work finding out flaws in men's titles to their estates ... Every man's enjoyment of his property became precarious, and the natives learnt with terror that law could be made in a time of perfect peace, and without any provocation being given, a not less terrible instrument than the sword for rooting them out of the soil.'

In the case of a family named O'Byrne in Co Wicklow, it was found impossible to secure dispossession by any legal chicanery. So the Lord Justice, Sir William Parsons, and his accomplices trumped up a false criminal charge against the proprietors. They induced men of infamous character to give evidence against them and tortured others into compliance by burning on a grid iron. Lord Justice Parsons was described by Lecky — 'one of the most unprincipled and rapacious of the land-jobbers who had, during the last generation, been the curse of Ireland ... Parsons ardently desired and purposely stimulated rebellion in order to reap a new crop of confiscations.'[18]

REBELLION

Rebellion was bound to come, sooner or later. Roused by the memory of the Elizabethan wars, the wholesale confiscations that ensued, the suppression of the religion of the majority of the common people, the plantation among them of an alien and hostile element, ever-anxious to root them out and goaded on by officers of the law like Sir William Parsons — the Insurrection of 1641 was inevitable. It began in Ulster on the night of 22 October and subsequently spread to other provinces. It was the dispossessed O'Byrne sept *(above)* that first rose to arms in Leinster. The rebellion continued until a truce was signed with the Crown in 1643.

Borlase, Carte and other English historians of the day confirm that the rebellion was essentially about land. Lecky also records:[19]

> 'From the very beginning the English Parliament did the utmost in its power to give the contest the character of a war of extermination. One of its first acts was to vote that no toleration of the Romish religion should be henceforth permitted in Ireland, and it thus at once extended the range of the rebellion and gave it the character of a war of religion. In the following February, when but few men of any considerable estate were engaged in the rebellion, the Parliament enacted that 2,500,000 acres of profitable land in Ireland, besides bogs, woods and barren mountains, should be assigned to English adventurers in consideration of small sums of money which they raised for the subjugation of Ireland. It thus gave the war a desperate agrarian character, furnished immense numbers of persons in England with the strongest motive to oppose any reconciliation with the Irish, and convinced the whole body of the Irish proprietary that their land was marked out for confiscation.'

The public utterances of many of the principal political figures illustrate the fanaticism of the times. Lecky reports it was said that Sir John Clotworthy had declared in Parliament that the conversion of the Irish Papists could only be affected with the Bible in one hand and the sword in the other; that Pym had boasted that the Parliament would not leave one priest in Ireland; that Sir William Parsons predicted at a public banquet that within a twelvemonth not a Catholic would be seen in Ireland.[20] Lecky also records:[21]

> 'The Parliaments, both in England and Scotland, passed ordinances in 1644 that no quarter should be given to Irish who came to England to the King's aid. These ordinances were rigidly executed, and great numbers of Irish soldiers being taken prisoners in Scotland were deliberately butchered in the field or in the prisons. Irishmen taken at sea were tied back to back and thrown into the waves. In one day eighty women and children in Scotland were flung over a high bridge into the water, solely because they were the wives and children of Irish soldiers.
>
> 'If this was the spirit in which the war was conducted in Great Britain, it may easily be conceived how it was conducted in Ireland. In Leinster ... the orders issued to the soldiers were not only "to kill and destroy rebels and their adherents and relievers, but to burn, waste, consume, and demolish all the places, towns, and houses where they had been relieved and harboured, with all the corn and hay therein; and also to kill and destroy all the men there inhabiting capable to bear arms". But, horrible as were these instructions, they but faintly foreshadowed the manner in which the war was actually conducted ... The soldiers of Sir Charles Coote, of St Leger, of Sir Frederick Hamilton, and of others, rivalled the worst crimes that were perpetrated in the days of Carew and Mountjoy.'

Carte, the biographer of Ormond, confirms these atrocities: 'The soldiers, in executing the orders of the justices, murdered all persons promiscuously, not sparing the women, and sometimes not children. Whole villages, as well as houses of the gentry, were remorselessly burnt even when not an enemy was seen. In Wicklow, in the words of Leland, Coote committed "such unprovoked, such ruthless and indiscriminate carnage in the town as rivalled the utmost extravagance of the Northerns".'[22] According to Nalson, the saying 'nits will make lice' then came into use, being constantly employed to justify the murder of Irish children.[23]

'Sir William Parsons', writes Sir Maurice Eustace to Ormond at a later stage of the rebellion, 'has, by late letters, advised the Governor to the burning of corn, and to put man, woman and child to the sword; and Sir Arthur Loftus hath written in the same strain.'[23] According to Curry, the Catholic nobles of the Pale, when they at length took arms, solemnly accused the English soldiers of 'the inhuman murdering of old decrepit people in their beds, women in the straw and children of eight days old; burning of houses, and robbing of all kinds of persons without distinction of friend or foe'.[23]

Carte confirms that 'in order to discover evidence or to extort confessions, many of the leading Catholic gentry were, by order of the Lords Justices, tortured upon the rack'. Lord Castlehaven accuses the men in power in Ireland of having 'by cruel massacring, hanging, and torturing, been the slaughter of thousands of innocent men, women, and children' and he states that orders were issued 'to the parties sent into every quarter to spare neither man, woman nor child'.[23]

'Scarce a day passes', writes Lord Clanricarde from Galway, 'without great complaints of both the captain of the fort and ship sallying out with their soldiers and trumpet and troop of horse, burning and breaking open houses, taking away goods, preying of the cattle with ruin and spoil ... killing and robbing poor people that came to market, burning their fishing boats and not suffering them to go out, and no punishment inflicted on any that commit outrages.'[24] He describes how on one occasion, under his own eyes, four or five poor innocent creatures, women and children, were inhumanly killed by the soldiers of Lord Forbes. General Preston speaks of the soldiers destroying by fire and sword men, women and children without regard to age or sex.[25]

Leland reports that General Monroe and his soldiers killed in one day near Newry 700 country people — men, women and children — who were driving away their cattle; while the parties he sent into Westmeath and Longford burnt the country and put to the sword all the country people that they met. In the island of Maggee thirty families were butchered in their beds by the Scotch garrison of Carrickfergus.[26]

'The scenes of horror that took place over Ireland', continues Lecky, 'almost defy description and crime naturally engendered crime. Thus a party of English prisoners were waylaid near Naas, and many of them, were murdered. The English at once resolved upon the destruction of the whole population of the district. Sir Arthur Loftus ... with a party of horse and dragoons came to the place where the murder had been committed, killing such of the Irish as they met. But the most considerable slaughter was in a great strength of furze seated on a hill, where the people of several villages had sheltered themselves. Now Sir Arthur, having invested the hill, set the furze on fire on all sides, when the people (being a considerable number) were all burnt or killed.'[26]

Carte records that when Sir Henry Tichborne drove O'Neill from Dundalk, the slaughter of the Irish was such that for some weeks after 'there was neither man nor beast to be found in sixteen miles between the two towns of Drogheda and Dundalk; nor on the other side of Dundalk, in the county of Monaghan, nearer than Carrickmacross.'[27] Lecky describes how the soldiers were 'accustomed to spread themselves out over the country in long, thin lines, burning every cabin and every cornfield in their way. Sir William Cole thus burnt completely thirteen miles about him in the North. Ormond himself burnt the Pale for seventeen miles in length and twenty-five in breadth.'[28] One of the items of Sir William Cole's own catalogue of the services performed by his regiment in Ulster gives a graphic picture of how the war was conducted: 'starved and famished of the vulgar sort, whose goods were seized on by this regiment, 7,000.'[28]

Lecky is careful to stress that what he has written of the suppression of the rebellion of 1641 represents only a fraction of 'the long catalogue of the crimes of the English'.[29] He says he has restricted himself to 'a few testimonies taken from the very best authorities' and he cites striking evidence from contemporary publications such as Prendergast's *Cromwellian Settlement of Ireland*, Clarendon's *History of the Rebellion* and Curry's *History* among others. He states: 'What I have written will be sufficient to enable the reader to form his own judgment of those writers who, by the systematic suppression of incontestable facts, have represented the insurrection of 1641 as nothing more than an exhibition of the unprovoked and unparalleled ferocity of the Irish people.'

The quarter the rebels at first undoubtedly gave to their prisoners in Ulster seems seldom to have been reciprocated. The Lords Justices gave strict orders to their officers to refuse it and a large proportion of the atrocities committed by the rebels were committed after the wholesale and promiscuous slaughter reported by Lecky.[30] He emphasises that in Ulster 'the rebellion was chiefly an agrarian war and a war of race. The confederation of the Catholic rebels in the other provinces comprised a large proportion of the English families of the Pale, who drew the sword for the purpose of defending their religion ...'[31]

Although a truce between the rebels and the Crown was signed in September of 1643, final reconciliation was not achieved until 1649. By then, however, the Crown itself had been overthrown, with the execution of Charles I on 30 January 1649. On 15 August that same year, Oliver Cromwell, Lord Lieutenant and General for the Parliament of England, arrived in Dublin to deliver the *coup de grâce* to the policy of genocide, which had now been in operation in Ireland for almost a full century.

CROMWELL'S MODUS OPERANDI
Commanding an army of about 20,000 men, Cromwell's first moves were against Drogheda and Wexford, where he proposed to demonstrate how he intended to impose his will upon the country. Lecky takes up the story:[32]

> 'The sieges of Drogheda and Wexford, and the massacres that accompanied them, deserve to rank in horror with the most atrocious exploits of Tilly and Wallenstein, and they made the name of Cromwell eternally hated in Ireland. At Drogheda, there had been no pretence of a massacre and a large proportion of the garrison were English. According to Carte, the officers of Cromwell's army promised quarter to such as would lay down their arms; but when they had done so, and the place was in their power, Cromwell gave orders that no quarter should be given. Ormond wrote that "the cruelties exercised there for five days after the town was taken would make as many several pictures of inhumanity as are to be found in the Book of Martyrs or in the relation of Amboyna".'

It is stated that some 3500 people in all — both soldiers and townsfolk, women and children — were slaughtered on 11 and 12 September 1649. Sir Arthur Aston, the governor, had his brains beaten out and his body hacked to pieces in what Cromwell declared to be just vengeance for innocent blood. About 1000 were put to the sword in St Peter's church, having fled there for safety. According to the Oxford historian Anthony Wood, whose brother Thomas was one of those who took part in the storming of the church, the soldiers made their way up to the tower where the enemy had fled; 'each of the assailants would take up a child and use it as a buckler of defence when they ascended the steps, to keep themselves from being shot or brained.'[33] 'All their friars', wrote Cromwell in his letters, 'were knocked on the head promiscuously but two, who were taken prisoners and killed ... I wish that all honest hearts may give the glory of this to God alone, to whom indeed the praise of this mercy belongs.'[34]

After Drogheda, Cromwell turned south to Wexford, which he dealt with in a similar fashion.

The Cromwellian campaign ended in 1652 and according to Sir William Petty's calculations, at least 616,000 people — almost half of the total population — had perished by the sword or by plague or by famine, artificially produced, since 1641.[35] Other calculations place the total losses much higher and some say that as a result of eleven years of war and ravage, the population of the country had fallen to roughly half a million.

'TO HELL OR CONNAUGHT'

The military effort to exterminate the Irish people had certainly gone a long way towards achieving full success. It was now to be followed by a huge plantation scheme 'to root out' the residue of the population, in accordance with the keystone policy enunciated by Britain's Attorney-General Sir John Davies nearly half a century before.

Under the Cromwellian Act of Settlement of 1652, all Irish land-owners whose lands were confiscated were now ordered out of their homes and holdings. These confiscations were made to meet the claims of the Adventurers in England who had advanced money to finance the recent war and to pay the arrears to Cromwell's officers and soldiers in the huge British army involved in the campaign (numbering some 34,000 at the close of hostilities). The dispossessed could, in the words of Cromwell, 'Go to Hell or Connaught'. As Curtis points out, 'the common people were too valuable as labourers and cultivators to be expelled; the fate of transplantation beyond the Shannon was reserved for the upper classes.' [36]

The level of property transfer was truly enormous. Petty reckoned that some 11,000,000 (English) acres out of the whole 20,000,000 acres in Ireland were confiscated and planted, and that nearly 8,000,000 of these acres were 'profitable'.[37] For all

GENOCIDE 33

that, the colonisation under the Settlement was not entirely successful. Large numbers of the soldiers who were given lands sold out to officers and speculators for whatever they could get and returned to England.

'Nevertheless', Curtis states, 'many thousands of the common soldiery were planted on the land and with their families formed a new and considerable element in the Protestant and English population of Ireland. The real result was to create a new landlord class in Ireland: for the Adventurers, and also great numbers of army officers, were installed in Irish estates. The Catholic land-owners were reduced to a minority, and the new English element in the towns never again lost their dominance in the civic and industrial life of the country.'[37]

The final decades of the 17th century witnessed the consolidation of the new position created by the Cromwellian Settlement. Charles II, after his restoration as king of England in May 1660, did nothing to disturb the status quo. His son, James II, used Ireland simply as a base for the continuance of his struggle to retrieve his crown from William III ('King Billy'). The contests between the forces of these two rival kings — composed mainly of continental mercenaries and allies, together with some ill-armed, raw Irish levies — at Derry, the Boyne, Limerick and elsewhere were of no concern whatever to the overwhelming majority of Irish people. In his book *The Anglo-Irish: Three Representative Types — Cork, Ormonde, Swift — 1602-1745*, Brian Fitzgerald contends that:[38]

> 'So far as Ireland was concerned the Williamite war was essentially one between an English Protestant king and an English Roman Catholic king; more accurately, between the English capitalists and the English feudal land-owners. And the Irish people stood to lose whichever side won. The Irish people stood to lose because both sides regarded Ireland as a colony of England to be exploited in the English interest. William of Orange won; the Irish people suffered. But the Irish people would have suffered no less had James II been victorious. Small nations invariably do suffer when they become inadvertently dragged into the power-politics shimozzle. And the Boyne war was but an incident in the tremendous tussle then being waged on the Continent between Louis XIV and his allies, on the one side, and a European coalition (which included the Pope

as well as William of Orange) on the other. This brings us to another remarkable fact: the defeat of the Papist James at the hands of Protestant William of Orange was greeted with undisguised enthusiasm in certain Roman Catholic states of Europe. In Catholic Vienna, for example, a *Te Deum* was sung in thanksgiving; and in Rome itself, we may take it that the Pope's feelings were... mixed.'

When the 18th century dawned, the majority of former landowners were either sunk in poverty or scattered as exiles throughout Europe. The common people who survived the slaughter continued, as Young states, as slaves and labourers for a rising arrogant breed of landed despots.[39] In the words of Lecky, 'the last spasm of resistance had ceased and the period of unbroken Protestant ascendancy had begun.'[40]

Concerning these policies Nora Robertson, of Elizabethan stock, remarks in her book *Crowned Harp*:[41]

> 'Whilst the Munster wars have unending fascination for historians, their toll of misery was intense. What one has learnt to call "guerrilla" warfare and "genocide" led to "scorched earth", and for a generation blood and starvation cried out to God ... The Irish Desmond's own Palatinate had not fallen into their lap as manna from Heaven; it had been grabbed by the mighty from the less mighty at the expense of the still more helpless and obscure. Admitting this, it would still be difficult, if not impossible, today to present the Elizabethan argument in such a way as to be excusable to an Irish descendant of those who were victimised by the policy. The situation was basically unnatural and unworkable. Neither full collaboration between the two peoples, nor complete settlement by Englishmen, was a feasible project ... Fear, as the father of cruelty, echoed down our history through the wholesale massacres of Cromwell to the complete conquest of William III ...
>
> 'It was the forcing of the establishment of a minority rule, which persisted for 400 years after them, that constituted the Elizabethan fallacy in Ireland, and by which their descendants are still circumscribed today.'

In *Bowen's Court* Elizabeth Bowen, also descended from Anglo-Irish stock (Cromwellian), writes, 'The structure of the great Anglo-Irish Society was raised over a country in martyrdom ...

My family got their position and drew their power from a situation that shows an inherent wrong.'[42]

That other great Elizabethan, Edmund Spenser — who had been given a grant in 1590 of 4000 acres, along with the castle and lands of Kilcolman (where he wrote part of *The Faerie Queen*) — had no such misgivings. By his lights, Ireland was held solely by right of conquest and every barbarity of fire and sword and famine that was used to hold it while the interest of England so required was justifiable.[43]

In the end, of course, it all goes back to the hypothesis that the same set of facts have a different significance for different people. In England, men like Spenser, Sir Walter Raleigh, Sir Philip Sydney, Sir Richard Boyle and other big land-owners are regarded as distinguished courtiers and men of culture, while to persons descended from the dispossessed and subjugated Irish of the 16th and 17th centuries, they are regarded as land-robbers, gangsters and exploiters of the common people.

THREE

The Final Solution

18TH CENTURY

'The law does not suppose any such person to exist as an Irish Roman Catholic.'
— THE LORD CHANCELLOR BOWES
and CHIEF JUSTICE ROBINSON,
laid down from the Bench

As intended, the ultimate effect of the confiscation policies of Elizabeth I, James I and Cromwell was to place the ownership of almost the entire profitable land in Ireland in the hands of a small conquering class, which represented less than 20 per cent of the population. That class was so placed as to be able, in conjunction with their English masters, to enact legislation which gave them absolute control over the lives of the other 80 per cent of the island's people.

A tiny number of land-owners of 'the old faith' continued to hold their lands on sufferance because of their declared loyalty to the Crown. But since they were not prepared to take the Oath of Supremacy (declaring the king of England head of the church in Ireland) and to concede that the sacrifice of the mass was damnable, they could not participate in the political life of their country. They were accordingly excluded from the first parliament held in Ireland since the ending of the wars between the rival English kings — James II and William III. When that parliament opened in 1692, it was exclusively Protestant.

'Here then', writes John Mitchel, 'ended the last vestige of constitutional right for Catholics; from this date, and for generations to come, they could no longer consider themselves a part of the existing body politic of their native land; and the division into two nations became definite. There was the dominant nation consisting of the British colony, and the subject nation, consisting of five-sixths of the population, who had thereafter no more influence upon public affairs than have the Red Indians in the United States.'[1]

'UNPARALLELED CODE OF OPPRESSION'

The conditions of the common people under the laws enacted by such a tyranny — variously referred to as 'The Ferocious Acts of Anne' (the English Queen) or 'The Penal Laws' — has been adjudged by many writers as considerably worse than that of the negroes in the United States; certainly they could only have been worse had the people been bought and sold as slaves. Clearly, their condition was infinitely worse than that of the common people of France prior to their Revolution or of the colonists in America prior to their rebellion against the British Crown over simple commercial matters, such as stamp duty.

It is, says Mitchel, 'an irksome and painful task to pursue the details of that terrible penal code'.[2] It is, nevertheless, the history of Ireland for most of the 18th century and its effects were appalling. Lecky gives an extended account of those days in his *History of Ireland in the 18th Century*, writing:[3]

> 'There was a large element of melancholy truth in the assertion of Burke that "all the penal laws of that unparalleled code of oppression were manifestly the effects of national hatred and scorn towards a conquered people whom the victors delighted to trample upon and were not at all afraid to provoke. They were not the effect of their fears, but of their security ... Whilst that temper prevailed, and it prevailed in all its force to a time within our memory, every measure was pleasing and popular just in proportion as it tended to harass and ruin a set of people who were looked upon as enemies to God and man, and indeed, as a race of savages who were a disgrace to human nature itself."'

All attempts to acquit the English government of blame in this matter, by throwing the responsibility of the penal laws on Irish parliaments, are 'wholly sophistical', according to Lecky, because:[4]

- an English Act of Parliament made the Irish Parliament an exclusively Protestant body;
- the Royal Veto, which could have arrested any portion of the penal code, was still in full force;
- no Irish Bill could be laid before the Irish Parliament which had not received the approval of the English Privy Council;
- no Irish Bill could become law except in the precise form which the English Privy Council had sanctioned.

The broad objectives of the penal code were to copperfasten the fruits of the various confiscations, by depriving Catholics (who constituted 80 per cent of the total population) of four basic human rights: any place in the civil life of their country; education; ownership, even on an extended leasehold, of any property, particularly land; and, finally, the right to practise their religion.

All of these objectives were closely integrated and were obviously meant to provide 'the final solution' to the Irish problem — by wiping out the majority of the Irish people and making the residue useful to Britain.

The first objective — denial of any place in civil life — meant that Catholics were excluded from participating in the parliament of their country. They were deprived of the right to vote and were excluded from the corporations, magistracy, bar, bench, grand juries and vestries. They could not be sheriffs, solicitors or constables, or even gamekeepers (lest they should learn the use of firearms). They were forbidden to possess any arms, not even a fowling piece. They were excluded from the army and navy. They could not possess a horse with a value of more than £5 and should any Protestant tender that sum he could appropriate the animal. Lecky records:[5]

> 'The whole tendency of the law was to produce in the dominant minority, already flushed with pride of conquest and with recent confiscations, all the vices of the most insolent aristocracy ... The law gave the Protestant the power of inflicting on the Catholic intolerable annoyance ... and even under the most extreme wrong it was hopeless for him [the Catholic] to look for legal redress. All the influence of property and office was against him, and every tribunal to which he could appeal was occupied by his enemies. The Parliament and the Government, the Corporation which disposed of his city property, the vestry which taxed him, the magistrate before whom he carried his complaint, the solicitor who drew up his case, the barrister who pleaded it, the judge who tried it, the jury who decided it, were all Protestants.'

The position of the Irish Catholic was summed up in a nutshell by The Lord Chancellor Bowes and the Chief Justice Robinson — 'The law does not suppose any such person to exist as an Irish Roman Catholic.'[6] Small wonder that the mass of the people would have an inveterate hostility to what passed for law.

The second objective — denial of the right to education — ensured that the people were kept in total ignorance of the injury being done to them. As Burke put it, 'To render men patient under such deprivation of all the rights of human nature everything which would give them a knowledge or feeling of these rights was rationally forbidden.'[7]

The provisions of the penal code regarding education amounted to universal, unqualified and unlimited proscription. Catholics were forbidden to keep a school, to act as ushers or private tutors or to send their children to be educated abroad. They were not permitted to be guardians of a child and they were excluded from the university.

The provisions in relation to property and land — the central and overriding objective of the penal code — were designed to place total control of all tangible material wealth, particularly land, fully in the hands of the Protestant minority. This was simply a continuation of the Elizabethan policy of two centuries before — 'to root out the Irish from the soil'. Accordingly, a summary of Lecky shows that:[8]

- No Catholic was allowed to buy land, to inherit it or to receive it as a gift from a Protestant. Nor was he allowed to hold life annuities, mortgages on land or leases of more than 31 years; indeed any lease which yielded profits from the land that exceeded one-third of the rent was forbidden.
- If a Catholic leaseholder so increased his profits that they exceeded this proportion and if he did not immediately make a corresponding increase in his rent, his property passed to the first Protestant who made the discovery.
- If a Catholic secretly purchased either his own forfeited estate or any other land owned by a Protestant, the first Protestant who informed against him became the proprietor.
- When a Catholic land-owner died, his estate was divided equally among his sons, unless the eldest became a Protestant, in which case he got the lot.
- The law by which the eldest son could thus become heir-at-law to his father's estate ('upon apostatising', as Lecky puts it) reduced the father to the position of a mere life tenant and prevented him from selling, mortgaging or otherwise disposing of his property.

- Under a similar law, a wife who became a Protestant was immediately freed from her husband's control and the Chancellor was empowered to assign to her a certain proportion of her husband's property.
- If any child, however young, professed to be a Protestant, it was at once taken away from the father. The Chancellor (or the child itself if an adult) could then compel the father to produce the title deeds of his estate and such proportion as the Chancellor determined was given to the child.
- Any Protestant woman who was a land-owner and who married a Catholic was at once deprived of her inheritance, which passed to the nearest Protestant heir.

The fourth objective of the penal code was to suppress the Catholic religion. The laws make it plain that despite the ferocity of some of the measures, the whole object of the Ascendancy was not so much to convert Catholics to Protestantism as to convert the goods of Catholics to Protestant use. A keen observer of the situation commented that enlightened Protestants only made a pretext of religion, taking no thought of what became of Catholic souls if only they could get possession of their lands and goods. Thus:[9]

- Apostasy (becoming a Protestant, in this context) was encouraged because it meant the automatic transfer of property from Catholic to Protestant ownership.
- Minor children of a deceased Catholic had to be brought up as Protestants and Catholic property thereby passed into Protestant hands in due course.
- Anyone who provided shelter or protection for an unregistered priest or a banished dignitary was liable to fines; a third offence meant confiscation of all goods and in certain cases death as a felon.

A SINFUL OATH

The Oath of Abjuration was enacted by the Irish Parliament in 1709. It empowered any two magistrates to summon before them any Irish layman and to tender to him the Oath which pledged the swearer to perpetual loyalty to the Protestant line. Refusal meant imprisonment. If the Oath was tendered three times and still refused, the Catholic was guilty of praemunire (*see explanatory notes, p. 156*) and liable to life imprisonment and the confiscation of all his property.

It was well known that the Catholic authorities had declared that this Oath was sinful. Thus the whole purpose of the provision in the 1709 Act was to enable the Crown to come by any property still held by a Catholic who would not, or could not, take it on grounds of conscience. Lecky asserts that:[10]

> 'The oath contains three clauses which, in the opinion of the writer [Lecky] must necessarily offend a Catholic conscience. It asserts that the Late Prince of Wales, who was now the Pretender, had no right or title whatever to the crown of England, and thus passes a judgement on the Revolution which cannot be accepted by anyone who believes in the divine right of hereditary monarchy, and who denies that the measures of James in favour of Catholicism invalidated his title to the throne. It restricts the allegiance of the swearer to the Protestant line, and therefore implies that if the existing sovereign were converted to Catholicism, the Catholic on that ground alone would be bound to withdraw his allegiance from him. It contains the assertion that the oath was taken "heartily, freely and willingly", which in the case of a sincere Roman Catholic would certainly be untrue ...
>
> 'It was scarcely conceivable that any sincere and zealous Catholic could look upon the Revolution as a righteous movement, or could believe that James had justly forfeited his crown ... or that his son had "no right or title to it whatsoever" ... The Catholics well knew that he had lost his crown mainly on account of his Catholicism, that the last great unconstitutional act with which he was reproached was an attempt to suspend the penal laws against themselves, that the object of the Act of Settlement [1701] was to secure that no Catholic should again sit upon the throne.'

For all these reasons, it was obvious that the lands of a conscientious Catholic could, without much difficulty, be confiscated, as intended under the 1709 Act.

It is a measure of the extent to which religion was then, and can still be, used to secure and consolidate material wealth, power and privilege in one class when we find Enoch Powell, former MP for South Down, publicly warning Charles, the Crown Prince, in 1978 against marrying the Catholic princess Marie Astrid of Luxembourg, because the 1689 Bill of Rights had declared that the King of England could not be a Roman Catholic or marry a person of that religion.[11]

There are some appalling instances of barbaric inhumanity and sadistic cruelty in the penal code. For example, there was the proposal inserted by the Irish Privy Council in 1719, in a Bill being sent to England for approval, that unregistered priests should be castrated rather than branded on the cheek with a red-hot iron, as proposed by the Irish House of Commons. Lecky, nevertheless, considered that the code 'was inspired much less by fanaticism than by rapacity, and was directed less against the Catholic religion than against the property and industry of its professors. It was intended to make them poor and to keep them poor, and to crush in them every germ of enterprise, to degrade them into a servile caste who could never hope to rise to the level of their oppressors. The division of classes was made as deep as possible, and every precaution was taken to perpetuate and embitter it.'[12]

A letter sent by Burke to Sir Hercules Langrishe indicates the depth of the contempt in that class division:[13]

> 'Sure I am that there have been thousands in Ireland who have never conversed with a Roman Catholic in their whole lives, unless they happened to talk to their gardener's workmen, or to ask their way when they had lost it in their sports; or, at best, who had known them only as footmen or other domestics of the second and third order; and so averse were they some time ago to have them near their persons, that they would not employ even those who could never find their way beyond the stable. I well remember a great, and in many respects a good man, who advertised for a blacksmith, but at the same time added, "he must be a Protestant."'

The general attitude towards the great majority of the Irish people is revealed by the phrase 'common enemy', which was the habitual term by which the Irish Parliament described them throughout the penal century. (It is a term often heard today in relation to the revolt in Northern Ireland.) Lecky records[14] that in 1706, Lord Pembroke referred to them as 'domestic enemies'. In 1715, the Lords Justices urged upon the House of Commons such unanimity in their resolutions 'as may once more put an end to all other distinctions in Ireland but that of Protestant and Papist'. In 1733, the Duke of Dorset called on Parliament to secure 'a firm union amongst all Protestants, who have one common interest and the same common enemy'. In a similar speech, Lord Carteret said, 'All the Protestants of the Kingdom have but one common interest, and have too often fatally experienced that they have the same common enemy.'

'PERVERTED INGENUITY'

Lecky's criticism of the penal code, and of the bigotry and greed which motivated its framers, was accurate and far-seeing. He saw its evil and lasting effects not only on the vast majority of the population who suffered under it, but on the entrenched Protestant minority which made up the bulk of the British tradition in Ireland and which profited from it. He saw the deep fissures it sent through Irish life and society which ran on through the 19th century and whose last cracks can still be seen and felt in Northern Ireland. He showed that when power is placed in the hands of a greedy minority on a sectarian basis by a stronger neighbouring power (as happened again under the Partition of Ireland Act 1920) the inevitable consequence must be discrimination, injustice and, ultimately, violence. He anticipated the great saying of Acton, that 'all power corrupts and absolute power corrupts absolutely'. It is worth quoting Lecky's final assessment of the penal code:[15]

> 'It [the penal code] was intended to degrade and to impoverish, to destroy in its victims the spring and buoyancy of enterprise, to dig a deep chasm between Catholics and Protestants. These ends it fully attained. It formed the social condition, it regulated the disposition of property, it exercised a most enduring and pernicious influence upon the character of the people, and some of the worst features of the latter may be distinctly traced to its influence. It may be possible to find in the statute books both of Protestant and Catholic countries laws corresponding to most parts of the Irish penal code, and in some respects surpassing its most atrocious provisions, but it is not the less true that that code, taken as a whole, has a character entirely distinctive. It was directed not against the few, but against the many. It was not the persecution of a sect, but the degradation of a nation. It was the instrument employed by a conquering race, supported by a neighbouring power to crush to the dust the people among whom they were planted. And, indeed, when we remember that the greater part of it was in force for nearly a century, that

its victims formed at least three-fourths of the nation, that its degrading and dividing influence extended to every field of social, political, professional, intellectual, and even domestic life, and that it was enacted without the provocation of any rebellion, in defiance of a treaty which distinctly guaranteed the Irish Catholics from any further oppression on account of their religion, it may be justly regarded as one of the blackest pages in the history of persecution. In the words of Burke, "It was a complete system, full of coherence and consistency, well digested and well composed in all its parts. It was a machine of wise and elaborate contrivance, and as well fitted for the oppression, impoverishment, and degradation of a people, and the debasement in them of human nature itself, as ever proceeded from the perverted ingenuity of man."'

When George III mounted the throne of England in 1760, positive persecution under the penal code had more or less ended. Some toleration had come about, but this merely meant connivance at specific breaches. It did not mean repeal of the main disabilities under which the majority of the people still lived; some 70 years would pass before Catholics could sit in the Irish Parliament. George was the 29th successor to the throne since Henry II gave his promise to Pope Adrian IV 'to proclaim the truth of the Christian religion to a rude and ignorant people, and to root from them the weeds of vice'.

The penal laws mark the climax of that Royal promise not only to root out vice, but to finally ruin and crush to the dust the breeders of vice 'who were looked upon as enemies to God and man, and indeed as a race of savages who were a disgrace to human nature itself' — the common people.

FOUR
No Republic Here
18TH CENTURY

*'I met murder on the way,
He had a mask like Castlereagh.'*
— SHELLEY, *The Mask of Anarchy*

*'If it were possible to collect all the innocent blood
that you have shed in your unhallowed ministry
in one great reservoir, your Lordship might swim in it.'*
— ROBERT EMMET, addressing Lord Norbury
from the dock in 1803

At the outbreak of the French Revolution in 1789, the population of Ireland was estimated to be 4,040,000 — roughly half that of England, Scotland and Wales, and about the same as the newly formed United States of America.[1] The rural poor made up the greater proportion of the total — certainly well over 3,000,000. Dublin city accounted for about 172,000, Cork for 70,000, and Belfast (still quite a small place) for 25,000. A minority, considerably less than 20 per cent, owned all the profitable land in the country and the large city estates. Ownership was almost entirely in the hands of Protestants.

The social divide was clear-cut. The upper classes comprised the land-owners, those involved in the government, courts, administration of what passed for justice, the higher clergy, a handful in the upper echelons of the professions (mainly legal and medical) and a small number of Establishment-minded businessmen (builders, manufacturers and commercial people). The lower classes comprised the vast army of the people — tillers of the soil, labourers and the general body of craftsmen, carpenters, masons, shoemakers, bakers — the kind of people referred to by the Crown at the trial of Robert Emmet in 1803, and subsequently in the *Dublin Evening Post*, as 'such contemptible creatures as an outlawed clerk, hodmen, hostlers, old clothes men, etc'.² Outside of Belfast, there appears to have been no sturdy middle class, even among those who were not denied education. Certainly, there was nothing like what existed in Paris before the Revolution or among the colonists in America.

The Catholic Committee was founded in 1760 to work for the cause of civil rights, denied to Catholics under the penal laws. Thus it had overwhelming grounds for vigorous pleading of the cause of those it represented, but it remained a supine and ineffective body given to presenting inoffensive addresses and genuflecting to authority. It never pursued its aims with the vigour shown by either the French or the Americans.

In Belfast and elsewhere in Ulster, a strong middle class was developing among the Presbyterians. Not belonging to the established Episcopalian church, they were, like the Catholics, victims of some of the provisions of the penal code. As early as 1730, they were crowding to America to escape high rents, tithes to Episcopalian clergy or insecurity of tenure. The descendants of these emigrants played an important part in the fight for American independence. News had come back from them about a free country and their contemporaries in Ulster were imbued with ideas of liberty and democracy.

THE UNITED IRISHMEN

Political clubs to advance American and French democratic and republican sentiments were accordingly being founded and one such was formed in Belfast under the guidance of a 'secret committee'. In September 1791, this club noted that a pamphlet had been published in Dublin under the title *An argument on behalf of the Catholics of Ireland,* by 'A Northern Whig'. Enquiries were made. The author was not a Northern Whig at all: he was a young Dublin Protestant barrister named Theobald Wolfe Tone. He was also a friend of one whom they in Belfast knew well already, because he had been an associate of their club the previous year while stationed in Belfast — one Thomas Russell, late ensign in the British 64th Regiment of Foot. The Presbyterians were impressed with the reasoning in Tone's pamphlet and had 10,000 copies printed for circulation throughout Ulster. They invited Tone and Russell to visit them and on 11 October 1791, the two friends arrived in Belfast for their historic meeting with the secret committee of eleven, all businessmen in Belfast and all Presbyterians: Samuel Neilson,

William Sinclair, William McCleery, Henry Haslett, William Tennant, Samuel McTier, Thomas McCabe, Gilbert McIllveen, Campbell, William Simms and Robert Simms.

After a week's discussion and drafting by members of this small group, a public meeting was held in Belfast on 18 October 1791, at which they stated their case:[3]

> 'We have no national government. We are ruled by Englishmen and the servants of Englishmen, whose object is the interest of another country, whose instrument is corruption and whose strength is the weakness of Ireland: and these men have the whole of the power and patronage of the country as means to seduce and to subdue the honesty and the spirit of her representatives in the legislature.'

On this basis, a society to be known as 'The Society of United Irishmen' was formed. The following resolutions were adopted:[3]

> (1) That the weight of English influence in the Government of this country is so great as to require a cordial union among all the people of Ireland, to maintain that balance which is essential to the preservation of our liberties and the extension of our commerce.
> (2) That the sole constitutional mode by which this influence can be opposed is by a complete and radical reform of the representation of the people in Parliament.
> (3) That no reform is just which does not include Irishmen of every religious persuasion.

Three weeks later, on 9 November 1791, a branch of the Society was founded in Dublin; its first meeting was held at the Eagle Tavern in Eustace Street, with the Honorable Simon Butler in the chair, James Napper Tandy as Secretary and an attendance of 18. The declaration and resolutions of the Belfast branch were adopted. A constitution was also agreed upon, the first sentence of which explains in plain and moderate terms that:[4]

> 'This society is constituted for the purpose of forwarding a brotherhood of affection, an identity of interests, a communion of rights, and an union of power among Irishmen of all religious persuasions, and thereby obtaining an impartial and adequate representation of the nation in Parliament.'

In December of that year, a public letter was issued to all sympathisers, asking them to organise similar societies all over the country. Part of the circular read, 'The object of this society is to make an United Society of the Irish nation; to make all Irishmen citizens — all citizens Irishmen.'[5]

At the beginning of 1792, a newspaper called *The Northern Star* was established in Belfast to advocate the Society's views. Its editor was one of the founder members of the Society in Belfast — a woollen draper named Samuel Neilson, the son of a Presbyterian minister. The Society expanded rapidly and had about 150,000 members within a few years.

The Society of United Irishmen was clearly established for the simple purpose of obtaining a measure of parliamentary reform and the securing of voting rights for Catholics, the bulk of the island's population. The easing of the economic oppression arising from the massive confiscations of land and the penal laws was for another day. Had these modest reforms been granted, even progressively, the subsequent course of Irish history, up to today, would have been entirely different.

In 1795, the Lord Lieutenant, Fitzwilliam, was withdrawn suddenly from Ireland, only months after his appointment, by the British Prime Minister, Pitt. Fitzwilliam's plans to grant Catholic emancipation were unacceptable. Only then did it become clear to the United Irishmen that their modest proposals for reform would never be granted. Timidly and reluctantly, they were led into republicanism. A minority in the Society, however — including Wolfe Tone and Napper Tandy — never had any illusion that reforms would be granted; they saw that revolution was to be the natural end issue of their movement.

Tone frankly acknowledged from the beginning that the desire to break the connection with England was one of his prime objectives and that hatred of England was so deeply rooted in his nature that 'it was rather an instinct than a principle.'[6] In his autobiography, he states his policy:[7]

> 'To subvert the tyranny of our execrable government, to break the connection with England, the never-failing source of all our political evils, and to assert the independence of my country — these were my objects. To unite the whole people of Ireland, to abolish the memory of all past dissensions, and to substitute the common name of Irishman, in place of denominations of Protestant, Catholic and Dissenters — these were my means.'

Elsewhere, Tone wrote, 'My unalterable opinion is that the bane of Irish prosperity is in the influence of England. I believe that influence will ever be extended while the connection between the countries continues.'[8]

The government, however, would have nothing to do with reform and braced itself for the job of crushing the Society of United Irishmen and its power. It was not, of course, a government in the normal sense, but rather a junta comprising the Viceroy (always an Englishman representing the King), the Chief Secretary and the British-appointed Lord Chancellor (John Fitzgibbon at the time). It was the latter's job to rule Ireland in the British interest with the aid of the British army, militia and an oligarchy of Protestant land-owners and prelates. To this ruling body, the ideas being promulgated by the Society of United Irishmen reeked of 'French Principles': the concept of 'brotherhood' in their constitution was the equivalent of 'fraternité' and 'civil, political and religious liberty' simply meant 'égalité'. Thus the Society and its aims would have to be put down by force.

For a long while, government spies had been closely watching the Presbyterians, whom they regarded as riddled with French ideas and dangerous to the British monarch's rule in Ireland. What they feared most was co-operation between them and the oppressed Catholics. They moved quickly on two fronts — political and military. In 1793, an Act had provided some minor reliefs for Catholics. It enabled them to bear arms, take commissions in the army below the rank of General, take degrees in Dublin University, vote as forty-shilling free-holders and become members of corporations. But they were still debarred from sitting in Parliament and from taking offices in the government and state.

Early in 1796, an Insurrection Act was passed which compelled arms to be given up and imposed the death penalty for administering the United Irishmen's oath. In November of that year, the *Habeas Corpus* Act was suspended.

Believing that rebellion was imminent and that its back must be broken rapidly if British rule was to survive in Ireland, the authorities determined to beat any thought of rebellion out of the people. Floggings, burnings, tortures, shootings and hangings were administered freely by the hordes of soldiery living at 'free quarters' on the people; those who were not thereby goaded into rebellion were cowed into submission.

Ulster was regarded as the most dangerous province since the Presbyterians there were to a large extent sworn United Irishmen. Between May and October 1797, the province was disarmed; some 50,000 muskets and 70,000 pikes were taken in and the popular Presbyterian leader, William Orr, was hanged under the 1796 Insurrection Act for administering the United Irishmen's oath.

Repression brought the inevitable reaction — a general insurrection was planned for 23 May 1798. But the government was well informed; through its many spies, it was able to act swiftly and arrest at the very outset the principal leaders and organisers of the rebellion. It was over quickly, after savage and barbarous fighting in many places. The dead were numbered in thousands throughout Leinster and it is calculated that over 2000 rebels, armed generally with nothing better than pikes, fell at New Ross alone before the artillery, muskets and mounted cavalry of the regular troops and militia. The Presbyterians in Ulster would have put up the most effective fight by far if they had not been disarmed the previous year. As it was, they came out in thousands in Antrim and Down under the leadership of Henry Joy McCracken and Henry Monroe, both of whom were captured and executed. Munster and Connaught remained for the most part quiet.

UNION — AN IMPERIAL NECESSITY

A huge British army of some 137,590 troops was now put in position to hold Ireland down.[9] This left Britain's Prime Minister Pitt and Ireland's Lord Chancellor Fitzgibbon free to get on with their political plans for the further subjugation of the country.

To Pitt, a full union between Britain and Ireland was an imperial necessity. The rebellious elements in Ireland had sought aid from France and could do so again. If they had secured such help for the rebellion of '98, it would not have been possible, in Pitt's opinion, to hold the country. In an Imperial Parliament of Great Britain and Ireland, however, Irish Catholics and Presbyterians, even if they combined, would be submerged by the Protestant majority and England would no longer be menaced by Irish nationalism, whether extreme or moderate. England would then be free to use the whole force of Great Britain and Ireland against France.

To Fitzgibbon, union with Britain was necessary for another reason — the protection of the garrison. He knew that landed property in Ireland was generally based on centuries of confiscations, royal grants, submission to the Crown and dispossession of older inhabitants (now mainly the common people). Unlike the Indians in America, the native Irish had not moved away; they still remained on the confiscated lands as small farmers, tenants-at-will and labourers. Fitzgibbon recognised that the situation was outrageous; he said as much in a speech in 1785, when as Attorney-General he stated:[10]

> 'I am very well acquainted with the province of Munster, and I know that it is impossible for human wretchedness to exceed that of the miserable peasantry in that province. I know that the unhappy tenantry are ground to powder by relentless landlords. It is impossible for them any longer to exist in the extreme wretchedness under which they labour. A poor man is obliged to pay £6 for an acre of potatoes, which £6 he is obliged to work out with his landlord at 5d. per day ... The lower order of the people of Munster are in a state of oppression, abject poverty, sloth, dirt, and misery, not to be equalled in any other part of the world.'

Despite these emphatic words, Fitzgibbon, according to Lecky, looked back with absolute and unqualified approval on the penal laws. He admitted that they had one disadvantage — 'they lowered the value of landed property in Ireland, but they were essential to the security of the titles of the owners.'[11] He knew that the people would react violently against such treatment as soon as they were strong enough to do so and it was his firm belief that to concede any rights to people that had been wronged so grieviously was to put them in a position to attack and destroy the 'offender'. He said this in his speech on the Catholic Relief Act 1793: no better explanation of the British tradition can be given. Lecky reports on Fitzgibbon's speech:[12]

> 'The people of this country consisted of "two distinct and separate castes, the one with a short intermission in possession of the whole property and power of the country, the other expelled from both in consequence of unremitted and inveterate rebellion and resistance to English Government and English connection" ... The Protestants were "an English colony settled in an enemies' country. The natives had contracted a rooted

and incurable aversion to them." The obvious policy, the vital interest of "that body of people in whom the power and property of the nation had centred", was to remain strictly united among themselves and closely connected with England, and to guard jealously every avenue of political power from encroachments by Papists ...

'"Great Britain must maintain her connection with Ireland, and she can maintain it only by maintaining and supporting the old English interest here. She must look for support in Ireland by maintaining and defending the old English settlers who, with a very few exceptions, constitute the Protestant interest in this country; and they must know and feel that they can maintain their present situation only by a close adherence to Great Britain."'

Other prominent figures were arguing along the same lines. Lecky gives an account of a letter from the Duke of Richmond to his sister, Lady Louisa Connolly, on 27 June 1795.[13] The Duke's purpose was that the contents should be laid before Louisa's husband, an important member of the Irish Commons.

'The duke expressed his deep conviction that the existing bond between the two countries was utterly precarious, and could not possibly be permanent, and that the full admission of the Catholics to political power in the independent Parliament of a country in which they are the great majority must lead, in time, to their ascendancy, to the ruin of the Protestants, to the ruin of the British Empire. Its first consequence, he said, would be the downfall of the Protestant Establishment. The next would be the ruin of the landlords, for the Protestant ownership of land which had been established by the Act of Settlement, the confiscations, and the penal laws, could not long survive a political revolution ... All these calamities seemed impending in the near future, and the only possible way of averting them was the speedy enactment of a legislative union of the two countries. Under such a union, the Catholics would "only become a partial majority of a part of the Empire, and their claims must give way to the superior ones of the majority of the whole ... The whole argument and justice of the case, which was before in their favour, becomes against them, and the Protestant King, religion and government may be maintained in Ireland ... England may subsist without Ireland, but the Protestant interest in Ireland can be preserved, in my opinion, by no means but an union."'

THE CHURCH'S PART

Although it was no time since the penal laws had been in full force and the whole thrust of pro-Union policy was anti-Papist (against letting Catholics into Parliament or taking jobs from Protestants), nevertheless, the Catholic bishops, and under their guidance priests and 'respectable Catholics', were also in wholehearted support of the Union. Whatever their reasons, one may have been their fear that 'the common people' might, in their justifiable wrath at the wrongs inflicted on them, rise up and wreak a bloody revenge — as they had in France. According to Lecky:[14]

> 'The Catholic bishops appear to have been unanimous in favour of the Union ... Archbishop Troy of Dublin was indefatigable in procuring signatures to addresses, and in urging his brother prelates to depart from the neutrality which they appear at first to have desired to maintain ... In July [1799] the Catholic Archbishop of Cashel wrote to Archbishop Troy, expressing his decided good wishes for the measure, and promising to exert his influence "discreetly" in the counties of Tipperary and Waterford, to procure the signatures of respectable Catholics ... Dr Moylan, the Bishop of Cork, was in the close confidence of the Government ... He wrote in September, "The Roman Catholics in general are avowedly for the measure. In the South, where they are the most numerous, they have declared in its favour."'

Similarly, Bishop Caulfield of Wexford presided over a great Catholic meeting in favour of the Union and received 3000 signatures for his address. Others were persuaded; the Archbishop of Tuam, for example, although in favour of the Union, did not wish to take an active part in the political movement, but 'the advice of Archbishop Troy and of the Archbishop of Armagh decided him.'

Finally, through the efforts of the priests, other, purely Catholic addresses in favour of the Union were obtained. Lord Cornwallis firmly believed that, 'although the numerical superiority of the Catholics might be indifferent or seditious, the preponderance of opinion in the guiding, educated and respectable portion of that body was in favour of his policy.' Thus, continues Lecky:[15]

> 'The combined pressure of a Government which had so much to give in this world, and of a priesthood which

was believed to have so much influence over the next, was enormously great. It is indeed surprising that, with such a weight of influence, the signatures in favour of the Union were so few ...

'The fact that the Orange party were in general vehement opponents of the Union, and the strong reason the Catholics already had to believe that their emancipation would be one of the first acts of the United Parliament, all influenced their judgements ...

'A very important section of them [the Irish Catholics], including their whole hierarchy, the vast majority of their landed gentry, and many if not most of their lower priests, decidedly and consistently favoured it [the Union].'

In his final speech in support of the Union to the House of Lords, Fitzgibbon stated in the clearest terms why a free and independent Ireland should not be tolerated:[16]

'"What was the situation of Ireland at the Revolution and what is it at this day? The whole power and property of the country has been conferred by successive monarchs of England upon an English colony, composed of three sets of English adventurers who poured into this country at the termination of three successive rebellions. Confiscation is their common title, and from their first settlement they have been hemmed in on every side by the old inhabitants of the island, brooding over their discontents in sullen indignation ... What was the security of the English settlers for their physical existence at the Revolution? And what is the security of their descendants at this day? The powerful and commanding protection of Great Britain. If by any fatality it fails, you are at the mercy of the old inhabitants of this island."'

'In accordance with these views', Lecky adds, 'his [Fitzgibbon's] uniform object was to represent the Protestant community as an English garrison planted in a hostile country, to govern steadily, sternly and exclusively, with a view to their interests, to resist to the utmost every attempt to relax monopoly, elevate and conciliate the Catholics, or draw together the divided section of Irish life.'[17]

In a nutshell, then, Fitzgibbon's advice to the landed gentry of Ireland was — close ranks, become part of the British Empire, join the British army and the British army will protect you and your property against any future Jacquerie which surviving republicans might call forth.

The Union of the two countries was effected on 1 January 1801. Thus was the United Kingdom of Great Britain and Ireland brought into existence, without the slightest reference to the five million Irish people. The combination of George III, the Catholic hierarchy, Pitt, Fitzgibbon and the land-owning oligarchy ensured that the common people — mainly Catholic and Presbyterian — would be kept under foot and that there would be 'no republic here' for many generations to come.

Although the rebellion of 1798 was over, the United Irishmen were not all dead and the ideas of the French Revolution, about justice and equality, continued to inspire all who loved freedom. The final effort in 1803, by that young idealist Robert Emmet, to continue the fight for liberty, was doomed to failure in a military sense from the start. His trial and execution, and the vile pursuit of his character and reputation after his departure from this world, mark the abysmal depths to which the British Government could sink.

FIVE
Century of Union Rule
19TH CENTURY

*'Between a small nation and a great,
between a conquered people and its conqueror,
there can be but a sham union
— the union of a boa constrictor with its prey.'*
— LORD BYRON

The hopes of the United Irishmen were put to rest on the day in 1803 that Robert Emmet was executed. The struggle for a free country in Ireland was over — for the time being. A democracy based on the American model that the Presbyterian emigrants from Ulster had been writing home about, or on the lines of the more recent model evolving in France, had been sought. Democracy would have to wait.

For more than a century under enforced union with Britain, Ireland was the negation of a free country — a slave colony in all but name. It experienced military and police domination; a corrupt legal system; coercion and class oppression; economic exploitation; famine, emigration and depopulation; elimination of republican principles among the Presbyterians in the North; and loss of the national language.

Another thirty years were to go by before Catholics could enter Parliament, following the Catholic Emancipation Act in 1829, passed at the enormous price of disfranchising the forty-shilling free-holders. This provision restricted the right to vote to a mere 14,000 out of a total population of 7,000,000. It took another 100 years before the Irish tenant farmer could have security of tenure in his rack-rented and underdeveloped holding, and was given the right to buy back the land which had been confiscated from his ancestors in the first instance.

AN INVOLUNTARY UNION

The union between Great Britain and Ireland had not been a voluntary union of peoples or states (such as the union of the separate colonies in America), but rather a full annexation of Irish territory by Britain, dictated, in the opinion of Prime Minister Pitt, by 'imperial necessity'. Britain's primary accomplices in this annexation were the landed interests, described by Fitzgibbon as 'an English colony, composed of three sets of adventurers who poured into the country at the termination of three successive rebellions'.[1] Given these facts, it was inevitable that the whole thrust of British administration in Ireland throughout the 19th century would be directed towards maintaining that interest rock-solid.

The interests of the landlords meant only one thing — profit. The tenantry were important only in so far as they contributed to rental totals and profits; where this was not the case, they were expendable. The tenants and their families were part of the livestock, removable at will when economic considerations so required. Thus, when at various times during the century it became more profitable to let land for grazing due to falling prices for tillage crops, large areas of cultivated land were cleared of tenants by the landlords and converted to pasture for letting to graziers. Under the various 'clearance schemes' operated on such occasions, whole counties were often almost entirely depopulated. Following the repeal of the Corn Laws in 1846 and the availability of cheap corn from America, it is recorded that some 373,000 families (numbering some 2,000,000 people) were evicted within a decade. 'In one union [administrative district] alone at the time of the famine, within one year', according to Sir Robert Peel, '15,000 persons were driven from their homes.'[2] 'I do not think', he added, 'the records of any country, civilized or barbarous, ever presented such scenes of horror.' Speaking in the House of Commons about the clearances after the collapse in agricultural prices in the 1870s, the then Prime Minister Gladstone remarked, 'The notices to quit keep falling as thick as snow flakes.'[2] It should be remembered that both of these gentlemen, Peel and Gladstone, were speaking about a country of which they were prime ministers under the Act of Union, not about some part of Czarist Russia for which they had no responsibility.

Under the conqueror's law, 'clearances' were perfectly legal.

Tenants had no rights, few if any had leases. They held land by the year or at the discretion of the landlord. In his capacity as proprietor, judge and administrator, he held the power of life and death over them. He imposed rules, fines and other penalties. His power was still the same as when Young wrote in his *Tour of Ireland* a century before, 'The landlord in an Irish estate inhabited by Roman Catholics is a sort of despot who yields obedience in whatever concerns the poor to no law but that of his will.'[3]

When, therefore, the landlord decided that he needed to get back his land, he merely sent in his agents to level the fences, demolish the cabins, evict the occupants and generally sweep out the entire population from whatever area he required for whatever purpose he had in mind. In the words of Lord Normamby, he had 'the monopoly of the means of subsistence, together with a power that exists nowhere else, the power of starvation.'[4] He made full use of it to refuse leases, to levy rack rents and to evict tenants at will.

This was the beleaguered English garrison in Ireland, hemmed in on every side, according to Fitzgibbon, 'by the old inhabitants, brooding over their discontents in sullen indignation' and who required 'the powerful and commanding protection of Great Britain'.[1] The land-owners were, indeed, very well protected — by an enormous military presence, estimated at 137,590 personnel in 1798 and higher again by 1800.

Over the whole period of the Union between Great Britain and Ireland, the entire country was like a vast concentration camp, where the landlords were the area camp governors and the British army and police the camp guards. Early on in the century, new military regiments were raised and existing ones reinforced. The country was dotted with new barracks to house them; even small places with a population of no more than a couple of thousand got their barracks and detachment of troops. Bigger concentrations grew up in the cities and at provincial centres such as the Curragh, Kilworth, Fermoy and Athlone. The dispersion of units throughout the country greatly facilitated enlistment to the British army, since the rank and file were largely recruited from the towns and villages convenient to garrison towns. Loyalty to the Crown and the opportunity to participate in the building of Empire were great attractions for the younger members of the landed families, who provided most of the officers, but sense of adventure and the lure of the King's shilling were the driving motives for the ordinary private.

The regimental records of the principal Irish units — The Royal Irish Regiment, The Royal Munster Fusiliers, The Royal Dublin Fusiliers and others — show that, in addition to their periods maintaining imperial rule in Ireland, they also saw active service in every part of the world where the British flag flew — such colonies as India, China, Burma, Africa, the West Indies, New Zealand and Australia. In the unforgettable words of Field Marshal His Royal Highness Arthur William Patrick Albert, brother of the King (Edward VII), Duke of Connaught and Colonel-in-Chief of The Royal Dublin Fusiliers, his men 'played an honourable part in all the great battles that assured us the conquest of these places'.[5]

Coupled with this formidable occupation force was a supplementary military presence in Ireland — euphemistically called 'the police'. This comprised some 12,000 able-bodied men, armed with carbines and bayonets, and organised in every parish of the country in some 1500 to 1600 strategically sited posts, or 'police stations', though they looked more like fortified blockhouses, with iron doors and shutters.

Introduced in 1836 by Under-Secretary Thomas Drummond, the chief business of the police (called the 'Irish Constabulary'), in conjunction with the British army, was to uphold landlordism. They gave direct protection to landlords, their agents and land-grabbers, as well as lending military support to bailiffs involved in seizures, evictions and tithe collections. The rank and file of the force was drawn from among the Catholic population, which made it ideally suited to operating among the general public. Its officers were mainly from England, which ensured the British interest. Its training on counter-subversion and on how to keep down the people — disrupting gatherings, taking notes at meetings, prosecuting and securing convictions of nationally minded people — made it totally amenable to all orders emanating from its political masters, such as Balfour's notorious 'Don't hesitate to shoot' instruction at the time of the Land League in 1887.[6]

By skilled espionage, inquisition and bullying, the police intimidated the common people in much the same way as the German Gestapo intimidated those in occupied Europe during the last war. As a reward for their role in suppressing the Fenian rising of 1867, the force was awarded the prefix 'Royal'. Without doubt the Royal Irish Constabulary (RIC) was highly successful in maintaining British rule in Ireland.

THE RULE OF LAW
Such were the twin military arms of British oppression that ensured a practically continuous form of martial law from the very start of the Union. They enforced an unending series of repressive laws, designed to facilitate and expedite evictions, land clearances and collection of church tithes. These measures embraced every conceivable form of coercion of the people; a few examples will suffice:[7]

- The Act of 1800, which removed court martial decisions from review by the ordinary courts and which meant removal of the existing right of appeal against a conviction.
- The Act of 1817, which gave the justices (ie the landlords) power to try without the right of appeal and to award punishment of up to 7-years transportation of any person in a disturbed district who was adjudged to be 'idle and disorderly', especially anyone found in possession of arms or in a tavern after 9pm.
- The Act of 1881, passed by a Liberal Government, which authorised imprisonment for an indefinite period without trial of any person regarded as an object of 'legitimate suspicion'.
- The Act of 1882, which empowered the police in disturbed districts to make 'domiciliary visits' at night and to arrest any persons found outside their homes. It also established special courts of Summary Jurisdiction.
- The Act of 1887, carried by the Conservatives, which substituted trial by Resident Magistrates for trial by jury in the case of certain offences and which gave the Lord Lieutenant power to proclaim disturbed districts, dangerous associations, and so on.

Under these 'laws', people were sent to jail for shouting 'Hurrah for Mr Gladstone' or whistling *Harvey Duff*. A girl of twelve was convicted for obstructing the Sheriff's bailiffs in the course of a seizure and a young boy was convicted of intimidation for looking at a policeman 'with a humbugging sort of smile'. At the beginning of the century, whipping was still the punishment prescribed in many Acts and was of daily application. 'I have known men', said Daniel O'Connell, 'whipped almost to death.' In three years, Balfour as Chief Secretary for Ireland was able to proceed against 5000 people under the 1887 Act alone.

Throughout the century of the Union the economic condition of Ireland was without parallel. Gustave de Beaumont, who visited the country before the Famine, wrote that though he had seen the Red Indian in his forests and the Negro in his chains, in Ireland he had seen the very extreme of human wretchedness.[8] In his evidence before the Primrose Committee (set up to inquire into the financial relations of Ireland and Great Britain, for the purpose of the 1912 Home Rule Bill), Sir Anthony McDonnell, who had been Under-Secretary for Ireland from 1902-8, testified that Ireland had been severely over-taxed since the date of the Union, while the people were becoming gradually enfeebled and their taxable capacity growing less and less.[9] 'A number equal to the whole population of the country has been', he said, 'cleared out and that, I submit, is a result which is a scandal to British administration. They would not have gone if they could have lived in their own country.'

The prevailing economic theory of free trade had inevitably brought about untold poverty for the agricultural producer who comprised the mass of the population. Prices for agricultural goods fell to the lowest world levels and there was little or no industrial production in Ireland from which it could earn an alternative income. The consequences were unemployment, starvation and the poor house. When the Great Famine of the 1840s struck, it merely aggravated the existing economic disease that stemmed from the continuous outflow and investment abroad, via the landlords, of such limited amounts of capital as were generated under the appalling circumstances at home. The only solution which the British administration could think of was to get rid of the surplus people somehow — anyhow. The Devon Commission proposed state-aided emigration and a scheme to settle people on reclaimed wastelands, mountains and bogs.[10] The landlords themselves simply turned their backs on the problem and evicted the poor when they could no longer pay their rents.

Then the Famine came and providentially solved the problem for the authorities. From 1845-51, it is estimated that over 1,500,000 people died from starvation and hunger-related diseases — famine-fever, dysentery and cholera among others. In the remaining half century, the deaths from tuberculosis and other diseases brought on by post-famine poverty were of the same order. Any wonder then that those who could fly that charnel-house did so in their droves? In his history of *Ireland since the Famine*, Lyons states, 'There is no doubt about the strength of the current that flowed to the far corners of the earth, and it is beyond dispute that between 1841 and 1925 gross overseas emigration included 4.75 million going to the USA, 70,000 to Canada and 370,000 to Australia.'[11]

It was a matter of enormous relief then to the British Government that it was spared the problem of having to do anything about getting rid of the surplus population of Ireland. The British press went wild with joy: 'In the short term', wrote *The Times*, 'a Catholic Celt will be as rare on the banks of the Shannon as a Red Indian on the shores of Manhattan.'[12] The paper had earlier advocated organised emigration in its editorial of 22 February 1847: 'Remove Irishmen to the banks of the Ganges or the Indus or to Delhi, Benares, or Trincomalee — and they would be far more in their element there than in a country to which an inexorable fate has confined them.'[13]

THE ORIGINAL MULTINATIONAL

In its long struggle to gain and keep control over the Irish people, England has persistently sought to win and hold the support of the Catholic Church. It has every reason to be proud of its successes. The original letter of approval for the invasion of Ireland by Henry II — the *Bull Laudabiliter* of 1155 — came from the only Englishman ever to become Pope, Adrian IV (*see Chapter 1*). The Act of Union, uniting Ireland with Great Britain, had the support of the whole Irish hierarchy and many, if not most, of the lower clergy. So long as the Church had got free from the restrictions placed on it as an institution in the past, it was not much concerned about political liberty for the people. Indeed, in the struggle for political liberty, the Church — when it was not indifferent — was usually on the side of the British, as shown at the time of the Union (1801), the Repeal Movement (1842-44), the Fenians (1867), the Plan of Campaign (1887) and in 1916-21. Even when Catholics were given the right to enter Parliament in 1829 at the price of almost total disfranchisement, the Church did not object. It could be called the original multinational.

Throughout the Famine period, the Church preached the rights of property as vigorously as the most ruthless landlords or capitalists. On the advice of their bishops and clergy, the poor paid their rents while their families were allowed to starve to death. It is related that, at a meeting in the Conciliation Hall in Dublin in 1847, John O'Connell, MP, son of the 'Liberator', read a letter from the Catholic bishop in West Cork, in which the bishop states, 'The famine is spreading with fearful rapidity, and scores of persons are dying of starvation and fever, but the tenants are bravely paying their rents.'[14] To which O'Connell exclaimed, 'I thank God I live among a people who would rather die of hunger than defraud their landlords of the rents.'

Commenting on the whole situation in *The Fall of Feudalism in Ireland*, Michael Davitt writes:[14]

> 'There is possibly no chapter, in the wide records of human suffering and wrong, so full of shame — measureless, unadulterated, sickening shame — as that which tells us of (it is estimated) a million people — including, presumably two hundred thousand adult men — lying down to die in a land, out of which forty-five millions worth of food was being exported in one year alone, for rent — the product of their own toil — and making no effort, combined or otherwise, to assert even the animal's right of existence — the right to live by the necessities of its nature. It stands unparalleled in human history, with nothing approaching to it, in the complete surrender of all the attributes of manhood by almost a whole nation in the face of an artificial famine ... Nothing explains, or excuses, the wholesale cowardice of the men who saw food leave the country in shiploads, and turned and saw their wives and little ones sicken and die, and who "bravely paid their rents" before dying themselves.'

Davitt maintained that: 'The mass of the people — the peasants of the country — were under all but the absolute leadership of the bishops and priests ... The bishops' pastorals proclaimed the general obligation of obeying magistrate and masters, as carrying authority from a divine source ... The responsibility for what happened — the holocaust of humanity which landlordism and English rule exacted from Ireland in a pagan homage to an inhuman system — must be shared between the political and spiritual governors of the Irish people in those years of a measureless national shame. One power ruled the material interests of the people, the other their religious and moral convictions. Both preached law and order ...

'Both, too, agreed in fathering upon the Almighty, the cause of the famine. It was the visitation of God! Hundreds of thousands of women, children and men were, on this hideous theory, murdered by starvation, because of some inscrutable decree of the God of the poor, who, two thousand years before, had died to rescue them from the actual slavery of the Roman Empire, and of other pagan powers, by his Gospel, teaching and life among the working people. No more horrible creed of atheistic blasphemy was ever preached to a Christian people than this, and looking back with a shudder upon that time, one can well understand now how and why it was that myriads of human beings, into whose soul this moral poison had been instilled, should have laid down and died "in obedience to the will of God", after having "bravely paid their rents".'[15]

Mitchel, too, blames the priests, primarily for persuading the people not to fight: 'When the final scene opened, however, and the whole might of the empire was gathering itself to crush us, the clergy, as a body, were found on the side of the enemy. They hoped more for their Church in a union with monarchical and aristocratic England than in an Ireland revolutionised and republicanised, and having taken their part they certainly did the enemy's business well.'[16]

Two senior churchmen, however, joined with Mitchel in condemning the general attitude of the clergy. Dr Maginn, Catholic Bishop of Derry, in a letter addressed to Lord Stanley, said, 'If the Irish priesthood have anything to answer for to God it is for the tameness and the silence and the patient submission with which most of them looked upon the wrongs and the ruin of their country.'[17]

In a lecture delivered in New York on 20 March 1847, Archbishop Dr John Hughes of that diocese said:[18]

> 'I fear there is blasphemy in charging on the Almighty the result of human doings ... The soil has produced its usual tribute for the support of those for whom it is cultivated. But political economy, finding Ireland too poor to buy the products of its own labour, exported that harvest to a "better market" and left the people to die of famine or live by alms ... There is no law of Heaven

— no law of nature — that forbids a starving man to seize on bread wherever he can find it ...

'I say to those who maintain the sacred and inviolable "rights of property", if they would have them respected, to be careful also, and scrupulous, in recognising the rights of humanity ... Let us be careful, then, not to blaspheme Providence by calling this God's famine.'

ROTTEN TO THE CORE

Despite the fact that Catholics had recently obtained the right to sit in Parliament, following their so-called emancipation in 1829, the common people (80 per cent of the population) still had no say on matters that affected their daily lives. Basic human rights, justice, living conditions — in all of these concerns they were the victims of the stringent application of the political and economic theories of their day and of the attitude towards Ireland of whatever political party happened to be in power in England at the time. Free trade, Britain's imperial wars, laws about education, health, taxation — all these decisions, of course, affected them, yet they had no input whatever on such matters.

So far as the British Parliament and the colonial interest in Ireland was concerned, it was important that the common people should continue in the erroneous belief that there was nothing they could do about these things. They should be taught to accept that it was in their own interests to remain peaceful and satisfied with their lot, as hewers of wood and drawers of water, pay their rents and resign themselves to 'the will of God' in all matters. It was particularly important that doctrines which disturbed the status quo (such as sovereignty of the people or breaking the connection with England) should not take root among them. Accordingly, the teachings of Tone and Emmet, the Young Irelanders, the Fenians and all forms of radical political thought were roundly condemned at every opportunity by both Church and State.

The legal system, however, touched everybody at local level and was therefore a matter which was well understood. In it, the people saw the blatant injustice of British rule in Ireland. It was totally biased in favour of the landlords and property, and against the common people. Between 1829 and 1867, for example, the English Parliament threw out or strangled 23 Bills in favour of tenants. Between 1800 and 1900, it passed 87 Coercion Acts designed to make it easier, quicker and cheaper for landlords to evict, clear whole areas and seize goods. The illegalities of the administration knew no bounds.

The rule of force was supreme. Arthur Balfour, Chief Secretary for Ireland, gave his blessing to the order 'Don't hesitate to shoot' during the Plan of Campaign in 1887. All over the country the RIC did *not* hesitate. On 9 September 1887, for example, they opened fire in broad daylight on a public meeting of tenant farmers at Mitchelstown and murdered three innocent, unarmed members of the crowd — Lonergan, Shinnick and Casey. Although a coroner's jury found that four named policemen 'did wilfully kill and murder the three victims'[19] and a warrant was issued for their arrest, no one was ever brought to trial. Juries were 'packed' by ordering jurors whose religion was known or suspected to 'standby' when their names were called. Protestants were thus tried by their friends and Catholics by their enemies. Peter O'Brien, the Attorney-General (nicknamed 'Peter the Packer'), though a Catholic himself, refused to allow Catholics to serve on juries; for his loyalty, he won high favour with Mr Balfour and in due course was made Lord Chief Justice of Ireland.

It was evident to all that the system was rotten, from the Crown down to the humble policeman, and that its defenders were deliberate liars. According to them, no government official, high or low, could do wrong — the judge who spoke like a crown prosecutor was 'impartial'; the magistrate who inflicted a savage sentence was merely 'doing his duty'; the police officer who gave a reckless order resulting in riot and bloodshed was a 'conscientious official'.

Ordinary people saw the evil by-products of such conditions since the start of the Union — the families of evicted people at the poorhouse gates, the greedy 'gombeen' man, the landgrabber, the subservient church and the time-serving politicians (like Sadlier and Keogh) who climbed to eminence and wealth on the backs of the poor. It was only natural, therefore, that such awareness should beget a violent reaction when, as Thomas Jefferson put it a century before, 'a long train of abuses and usurpations, pursuing invariably the same object, evinces a design to reduce them under absolute despotism'.[20] The train of abuses in Ireland which produced the Fenian rebellion in 1867 was infinitely worse than that which incited the American colonists to revolt in 1775. Although the Fenian rebellion was not successful in the military sense, it put the British on notice that there was a substantial proportion of the Irish people that had had enough of oppression and, seeing the futility of constitutional effort, were prepared to use whatever force they could to put an end to it.

In the circumstances few people, then or since, paid any serious attention to the pronouncement of His Lordship the Most Reverend Dr Moriarty, Bishop of Kerry, when on 9 March 1867 in Killarney Cathedral he said that the Fenians 'had resisted the ordinance of God and by so doing, they purchased for themselves damnation'.[21] Still fewer heeded his apocalyptic outburst:

> 'O God's heaviest curse, His withering, blasting, blighting curse is on them ... When we look down into the fathomless depth of this infamy, of the heads of the Fenian conspiracy, we must acknowledge that eternity is not long enough, nor hell hot enough, to punish such miscreants.'

The prelate's words fell on ears deafened by centuries of abuse. They were regarded merely as what might be expected from an overweening, 19th-century churchman, intoxicated by his own verbosity and whose political sympathies were entirely with the British — a fact which shines out through all of his sermon. In his long admonition, Dr Moriarty refers on several occasions to the common people — the overwhelming bulk of his congregation — as 'the peasants' and to the owners of property as 'the gentry'.

Thus derided by Church and State, and by many obsequious Catholic business and professional people, who joined with Dr Moriarty in scoffing at the apparently futile attempt to 'destroy the British Empire with a few rifles', it is testimony to the character of the Fenians — nearly all poor men — that none of them ever 'bent the knee'.

At the end of a century of Union rule, a great part of Ireland was indeed on its knees. 'By long bending', wrote Dr Wyse, 'they [the people] had become bent.'[22] It was to this bowed-down Ireland that Hyde and the Gaelic League, W B Yeats and the Anglo-Irish literary crowd, Cusack and Croke, and later Pearse, the Irish Republican Brotherhood (IRB), Sinn Féin and the Volunteers addressed themselves.

SIX

'We the People'

20TH CENTURY

*'Whatever Ulster's right may be, she cannot
stand in the way of the whole of the rest of Ireland.
Half a province cannot impose a permanent veto
on the nation. Half a province cannot
obstruct forever the reconciliation between
the British and Irish democracies.'*
— WINSTON CHURCHILL
proposing the second reading
of the 1912 Home Rule Bill

*'What Irishmen all over the world most desire
is not hostility against this country,
but the unity of their own.'*
— WINSTON CHURCHILL
Speaking in House of Commons, 16 February 1922

In her book *Life and the Dream*, Mary Colum (wife of the poet Padraic) tells of her life and experiences in Ireland at the turn of this century. She writes, 'The country I grew up in had all the marks of a conquered country and some of the habits and manners of an enslaved country.'[1] Other contemporary accounts confirm that this is an accurate description of Ireland at that period. The growth in the number of people who had succumbed to the scorn poured by Dr Moriarty and other clerical as well as lay pundits on the efforts of the Fenians *(see pp. 66-7)* meant that not only was Ireland a conquered country, but that even nationally minded people appeared to have accepted silently the inevitability of conquest.

The education system introduced by the British in 1831 further helped the enslavement process. In the words of Dr R Whately, the Anglican Archbishop of Dublin and one of the first commissioners of education, it aimed at making every Irish pupil 'a happy English child'.² The teaching of Irish history and the Irish language was forbidden. Anglicisation began in the classroom with the inclusion of such material in school texts as:

> 'I thank the goodness and the grace
> That on my birth have smiled,
> And made me in these Christian days,
> A happy English child.'

The attitude of the Irish hierarchy generally towards Irish nationalism, together with their willing co-operation with the British under the school management system, were also powerful factors in inducing resigned acceptance of the conquest by millions of poor people, who were asked to accept the blasphemy that their enslavement was the 'will of God'.

It is small wonder that when Queen Victoria paid her 22-day visit to Dublin in April 1900, she was greeted with fulsome speeches and addresses of welcome by a host of loyalists in reception committees, schools and hospitals — Catholic as well as Protestant. Everywhere she went, the crowds lined the streets in their thousands to greet her. She was met at the city boundary in Leeson Street on her way in from Dun Laoire (then Kingstown) by the Lord Mayor and 31 members of Dublin Corporation (29 members stayed away), who begged to offer 'on behalf of ourselves and our fellow citizens a hearty welcome on your arrival in the capital city of your majesty's Kingdom of Ireland'.³ While she was in Dublin, prominent loyalists were invited to dine with her each evening in the Viceregal Lodge and came regularly to after-dinner parties in the Drawing Room. On one of these occasions his Eminence Cardinal Logue, the Catholic Primate of Ireland and Archbishop of Armagh, was her dinner-guest. It was as if the Cardinal Primate of France, or of any other occupied country of Europe, had agreed to dine with Hitler while he was on a visit to their country during the last war.

The only dissenting voices came from the small group led by W B Yeats, Maud Gonne, John O'Leary and the few Fenians who still remained. On the eve of the visit, Yeats wrote to the newspapers:⁴

> 'Whoever is urged to pay honour to Queen Victoria tomorrow morning should remember the sentence of

Mirabeau, "The silence of the people is the lesson of Kings." She is the official head and symbol of an Empire that is robbing the South African Republics of their liberty as it robbed Ireland of theirs. Whoever stands by the roadway cheering for Queen Victoria cheers for that Empire, dishonours Ireland and condones a crime.

But whoever goes tomorrow night to the meeting of the people and protests within the law against the welcome that Unionists and time-servers will have given to this English Queen honours Ireland and condemns a crime.'

Three years later, the *Irish Times* reported on another important reception — this time for the Royal Dublin Fusiliers on their return to Dublin 'after a long and arduous service under the British flag in foreign lands'.[5] 'There was', the report says, 'quite a contest for places in the great Central Hall of the Royal Dublin Society's buildings in Ballsbridge to see the heroes of a regiment which had gained undying laurels in Burma, India and South Africa ... A great crowd of people watched the men detraining and several hearty rounds of cheering greeted their appearance ... The departure from Ballsbridge occasioned unbounded enthusiasm on the part of thousands of eager spectators who ... had patiently waited for a couple of hours to catch a glimpse of the "old toughs" ... The appearance of the fêted warriors was the signal for an astonishing ovation at Ballsbridge ... At different points, like Baggot Street Bridge, Stephens Green and Grafton Street, the reception was of a most cordial nature, while an immense crowd in College Green raised deafening cheers as the sturdy warriors marched past. Enthusiasm reached its height when the tattered colours of the battalion, borne by two young ensigns, came into view ...' And so on.

In 1907 a memorial arch was erected at the north-west corner of St Stephen's Green to the memory of those Royal Dublin Fusiliers who had died in the Boer War. At the unveiling the Earl of Meath addressed the Colonel-in-Chief of the Regiment (Field Marshal HRH, AWSA, Duke of Connaught and Strathearn, KG, KP, KT, GCB, GCMG, GCIE, GCVO):[6]

'We meet today for the purpose of honouring the memory of the gallant men belonging to the Royal Dublin Fusiliers who sacrificed their lives for King and Country ... As the only surviving brother of the gracious and mighty sovereign whose uniform these heroes wore *when they died in the defence of their country's interests* [author's emphasis] ... it is fit and proper that you, Sir, should be invited to perform the ceremony ... This memorial ... will be an ever-present reminder to coming generations of the citizens of Dublin of the obligations of loyalty, of faithfulness to duty and to honour which Ireland demands of her sons.'

'Loud cheers', we are told, 'were raised as the soldiers involved in the unveiling ceremony passed out into Grafton Street and proceeded down that thoroughfare which was thickly lined on either side with spectators.'

Such unfortunate men were the original mercenaries — soldiers of a conquered people going out to deprive other people of their freedom in many parts of the world on behalf of their conquerors, simply for the few shillings pay they received. They took their orders from officers of the King and Country class, who had a vested interest in Empire-building.

CONQUEST — A NEAR-TOTAL SUCCESS

These simple accounts give an idea of public attitudes in the capital city of Ireland during the first decade of the 20th century. From the British point of view, the conquest was regarded as a near-total success. The native population had been decimated. Some 5,000,000 had emigrated in less than 60 years; an equivalent number had died from famine and famine-related diseases. The greater part of those left had been either cowed into submission or corrupted into collaboration. The remnant of old Fenians, who would never submit, and the rising group of Irish Irelanders (associated with such activities as the promotion of the Irish language, Gaelic games and Anglo-Irish literature) offered no political threat as yet and thus could be ignored. The Catholic and Protestant churches, the police force (RIC), the press, law, business community and the rest of the Establishment supported the conquest. Over all stood the 'landed gentry' — backbone of the British tradition in Ireland — and the British army itself.

Attitudes in rural Ireland at the time were not significantly different from those in the cities, as the following extract from a statement written in 1953 by Seán Moylan, TD, confirms:[7]

'There was a grovelling outlook on the part of the so-called Nationalist population quite different to that of the Unionist population. To be a Unionist was to be a superior being who owned of right the fruits of the earth and the fullness thereof. A substantial intelligent Nationalist farmer was "Mickeen Murphy". His dull-witted Unionist neighbour was "Master William Brown". The local bank manager and his assistants were Unionists; so also were the local stationmaster, the petty sessions clerk, the postmaster. There were no other white-collar jobs. All of these people were possessed by a perfervid loyalty to England.

The Nationalists seemed to have no loyalties. Once or twice a year we had a concert to raise funds for the support of the local foxhounds. They were poor performances and invariably finished with the singing of *God save the King*. The ascendancy occupying the front seats stood bareheaded. A few respectable shopkeepers then arose shamefacedly, but, like the rest of the audience, with an unquiet feeling that they were not entitled to participate in the ceremony. The last of these concerts was a riotous affair. The usual programme was carried out. The Colonel spoke a few words of thanks to the audience and at length on the benefits bestowed on the locality by the foxhunters. Then we had *God save the King*. As it went on its quivering way a small boy ... at the back of the hall, started to sing *God save Ireland* and the King and his minions had to make way for the nation. The gallery shouted the song and immediately we were all singing. As we surged into the street there were cheers and laughter and a general feeling of elation.'

TORY CHICANERY, LIBERAL COWARDICE

To this servile Ireland the Liberal Government of 1910 decided to throw a political crumb, euphemistically called 'Home Rule'. This was designed to give limited control over certain domestic matters. It was a harmless measure, under which an Irish Parliament would be set up, consisting of the King of England and two houses, with little more than the power of a county council. The head of the government would not be the head of the party, or combination of parties, with the most seats; he would be the Lord Lieutenant, appointed by the King of England. He would choose his own ministers, senators and judges. Matters concerning the army, navy, peace and war, foreign affairs, treaties, extradition, treason, external trade, navigation, merchant shipping, coinage and legal tender, customs and excise (with minor exceptions) and taxation — all such powers would remain with the British Parliament. Ultimate, or supreme, power in relation to all matters to be delegated was also to remain with the British Parliament, so that in effect that body was to have the power to alter or repeal any act of the proposed Irish 'Parliament'.

After a century of union with Great Britain (described as 'the union of a boa constrictor with its prey' by Lord Byron), the common people of Ireland — as distinct from the time-serving politicians of Westminster — were not interested in such an obviously worthless measure. The basic tyranny of the enforced annexation of Ireland by Britain — the power and privilege of the ascendancy classes, the British army, the RIC, the legal system — all would remain as before, loaded against them and in the hands of their enemies. However, Patrick Pearse and the other spokesmen of the new freedom movement of Sinn Féin were prepared to allow John Redmond, leader of the Irish Party, a last chance to get the proposed measure enacted as a stage on the way to full independence. This was stated publicly by Pearse on 31 March 1912. [8]

In England, the Tories saw 'Home Rule' as a tempting opportunity to oust their political opponents, the Liberals, from power. So for their own political ends, they played the 'Orange Card', once again effectively blocking the road to even this minor instalment of freedom. The 'Orange Card' was a phrase first used by Lord Randolph Churchill to describe Tory policy in relation to Home Rule after the indecisive General Election of 1885. 'I decided some time ago', he wrote on 16 February 1886, 'that if the GOM ['grand old man', ie Gladstone] went for Home Rule, the Orange Card would be the one to play. Please God it may turn out the ace of trumps and not the two.' [9] In reality, playing the Orange Card meant inciting the Ulster Orangemen to revolt, described by Lord Randolph to Lord Salisbury as 'resistance beyond constitutional limits'.

As with Hitler and the Jews in the 1930s, the opportunity for propaganda was superb, playing as it did on popular fears and leaving general political mayhem in its wake. The Tories knew that many of the property classes in Ireland feared, or pretended to fear, even such an innocuous measure as Home Rule as an attack on their centuries-old ascendancy position; they also knew that the once rabid republicanism of the Orangemen was long dead and that it was now an easy matter to play upon their prejudices.

What British politicians really thought about the Orangemen, however, is clear from the House of Commons' *Report of the Select Committee on Orange Lodges* (1835): [10]

> 'It is notorious that the Orange Lodges exist under the patronage of men high in rank in England, Ireland and Scotland, and the countenance given, in consequence of all the orders of the Orange institution being issued by and under the authority of such men as His Royal Highness the Duke of Cumberland, as Imperial Grand Master, and of His Grace the Duke of Gordon, Deputy Grand Master for Scotland, will be found to have a greater effect on the *poor and ignorant — of which the Orangemen chiefly consist* [author's emphasis] — than might be expected.'

Winston Churchill (then First Lord of the Admiralty in the Liberal Administration) accused the Tories of hypocrisy in their 'concern' for minority rights in Ireland.[11] 'They', he added, 'have always been straining for some short-cut to office and they now seek to utilise the fanaticism of the Orangemen ... Behind every sentence of Bonar Law's speeches on the Ulster question, there was the whispering of the party [Tory] manager, "We must have an election. Ulster is our best card. It is our only card. This is our one chance."'

Having accurately gauged the minds of those whom they wanted to influence, the Tories proceeded in 1912 to undermine the Liberal Government — with a thoroughness which can only be explained by their overweening lust for political office. They assembled a galaxy of Lords and former senior office-holders: ex-Ministers of State, field marshals, generals, admirals and scores of British MPs were all chosen to go on an American-style electioneering blitz in Ulster, to rouse 'the poor and ignorant — of which the Orangemen chiefly consist' against Home Rule. Few of the Tory campaigners had anything to do with, or any knowledge of, Irish affairs. At one stage, no less than 70 senior Tories were actively campaigning in Belfast and its environs.

The political circus included Bonar Law, MP, leader of His Majesty's Opposition, Head of the Conservative Party and later British Prime Minister; F E Smith, MP, later Lord Birkenhead and Lord Chancellor of England; Walter Long, MP, later Lord Long and Secretary of State for the Colonies; Austen Chamberlain, MP, later British Foreign Secretary; Mr Duke, MP, later Chief Secretary for Ireland in the British Cabinet; and Mr Joynson-Hicks, MP, later British Home Secretary. The Lords included Willoughby de Burke, Londonderry, Claud Hamilton, Allington, Millner and Robert Cecil. There were two former British Prime Ministers, two former Chancellors and a host of former Secretaries — for War, Foreign Affairs, the Colonies, Local Government Board and Post-Master General. There were even included in the party an ex-Governor General of India and of Canada, an ex-First Lord of the Admiralty and a retired Commander-in-Chief of the Mediterranean Fleet.

These sober Tories were no street-corner mob orators; they were all senior, experienced people, past and prospective office-holders, men of wealth and influence. What was the unfortunate Orangeman to think when he heard such men pronounce that Home Rule was a threat to his job, his way of life and his civil and religious liberties? The British politicians knew that these threats were untrue, but many of their listeners believed them and were frightened by what they heard. What were the Orangemen to make of statements made by the most senior members of the Conservative Party, such as Bonar Law's statement to the House of Commons on 18 June 1912: 'If Ulster does resist by force, there are stronger influences than Parliamentary majorities.' [12]

Other Tory politicians, speaking outside Parliament, uttered equally inflammatory statements, such as that of the MP, F E Smith, at a public meeting in Liverpool: 'There is no length to which Ulster would not be entitled to go, however desperate and unconstitutional.'[12] And again, at Nottingham, Smith pronounced: 'They [the Orangemen] will have the full support, not only of the Unionists of Ireland but of the whole of the Unionist members of the House of Commons in all risks, in all hazards, and in every extremity.'[12]

That the whole threatened Orange 'rebellion' was a fabrication, engineered and master-minded by the leader and most high-ranking members of the Tory Party in England, is unquestionably clear from the course of events that followed. The Orangemen were being strongly urged to sign the covenant against Home Rule and to join the private army, the Ulster

Volunteers, that was being organised to defy the authority of the elected government. This private army was commanded by the English general, Sir George Richardson. Many peers of the realm, generals and admirals were among those who signed a covenant in England. Lord Willoughby de Burke and other Tories set about raising another private army in Britain to proceed to Ulster; Lord Roberts, commander of the British army in the Boer War, was actively helping. An illegal trafficker in arms was sent to Germany in February 1914 to purchase arms with monies supplied by the Tory organisation, with the knowledge and approval of the top members of the Party in London. While this illegal importation of arms was being arranged, Bonar Law, leader of the Tories, and Lord Millner were conspiring with General Sir Henry Wilson, Director of Military Operations at the War Office (and later Chief of the Imperial General Staff) to ensure that the projected gun-running would succeed. It was also planned that officers of the British army stationed at the Curragh would refuse to move if ordered north and that, as a final blow against the Liberal Government, the House of Lords would refuse to pass the Annual Army Bill, which would mean that there would be no army in existence after 30 April 1914.

The outcome of this high-level Tory manoeuvre was twofold. During March of 1914, 57 out of 70 officers in the Curragh said, in reply to a hypothetical question, that they would prefer to accept dismissal rather than move north *if ordered*. This was not a mutiny, since no order was ever given. Quoting from Ensor's *History of England*, Nora Robertson (whose father, Lieutenant-General Lawrence Parsons, was a serving officer at the time) writes: 'If it be mutiny to conspire to paralyse from within the disciplined action of an army, unquestionably, there was such a conspiracy, although the actual officers at the Curragh were not its authors ... The political engineers behind the scenes have been overlooked.'[13]

Then, on 24 April 1914, 35,000 rifles and 2,500,000 rounds of ammunition were successfully landed in Larne, Co. Antrim, without interference from the authorities. General Wilson was able to record in his diary that the Government's preparations for naval intervention to prevent the landing were 'frustrated by our action in the army'.[14]

GOVERNMENT SURRENDER TO TORY SUBVERSION

So far as the Liberal Government was concerned, the jig was up. On 12 May 1914, Lloyd George, the Chancellor of the Exchequer, announced that before the Home Rule Bill came into operation, an amending Bill excluding part of Ulster from its provisions would be introduced. Partition was born. It marked the end of John Redmond's efforts to secure a tiny measure of freedom for all Ireland by peaceful means and it signalled the start of efforts to secure freedom by other means. Pearse had forewarned of this possibility in 1912, two years earlier.

The scuttling of the Home Rule Bill marked a definite victory for the Tories. It showed that this political party would stop at nothing, even the subversion of the armed forces, to achieve its ends. It showed what lasting damage the Tories were prepared to do to Ireland, if by such action they succeeded, as Churchill had warned, in toppling the Liberal Government and getting to power themselves. The Tories' proclaimed concern for the Orangemen was motivated solely by self-interest. That they were prepared to ditch them as quickly as to use them on their ladder to power is evident from their double-dealing as far back as 1910. After the indecisive General Election in January of that year, the Tories (represented by Bonar Law, Birkenhead and Chamberlain) went into conference with the Liberals (represented by Lloyd George and Churchill) with a view to forming a coalition government, which would have Home Rule for Ireland as part of its programme. Birkenhead — who had played the part of a most rabid anti-Home Ruler only months before in the pre-election campaign — was now enthusiastic about abandoning the Orange cause and allowing Home Rule to go through in order to get into power. After the conference, he wrote to his Tory colleague, Chamberlain, 'Home Rule is a dead quarrel for which neither the country nor the party cares a damn, outside of Ulster and Liverpool.'[15] Reflecting on the duplicity of his party, Chamberlain wrote, 'What a world we live in and how the public would stare if they could look into our minds and letter bags.'[16]

Seven years later Edward Carson, who thought he was running the show in Ulster, had to admit openly that he, too, was duped by the Tories in their use of the Irish question to get into office. In the course of his speech to the House of Lords on 14 December 1921, he said:[17]

> 'I was in earnest. I was not playing politics. I believed all this. What a fool I was. I was only a puppet and so was Ulster, and so was Ireland in the political game that was to get the Conservative Party into power.'

Carson did not want a partitioned Ireland: he simply did not want Home Rule for any part of Ireland, for the basic reason that the ascendancy did not want it. Nor did the Liberals want to partition Ireland, but in order to outwit the Tory plot to get them out of office, they were prepared to do so. Similarly with the Tories: they were not concerned with the partition of Ireland; they simply saw Home Rule as a means to an end — their end, gaining power.

Despite the impression sometimes given in discussions today that Home Rule was a big issue among the people in 1912-14, it is clear from those who lived through those days, and who played an active part in subsequent events, that so far as the ordinary people were concerned, the entire parliamentary debate on the matter meant little. A quotation from the 1953 statement of Seán Moylan, TD, fully supports this view:[7]

> 'Irish history was not taught in the schools of my youth nor were there many books available to me ... I was a grown man before an opportunity was given me of studying my country's past. But my youthful ears were filled with stories of the Fenians. I followed the processions of 6th March and of 23rd November. I listened to the speeches on those nights. I saw the attitude of the RIC to the crowds. I looked in awe and respect on old toilworn men marching, because I knew that they, unarmed and untrained, had faced the rifles of the police in '67, that they had gone to jail, that they had suffered ...
>
> 'To a boy who had lived with and listened to Fenians, current politics had no appeal; for several years I was in the doldrums. It was not until a branch of the Gaelic League was started that I found myself again in a congenial atmosphere. Here was something real ... I had heard of Sinn Féin but knew nothing of it ... Perhaps I had lived too long with old men, beaten men, and had absorbed their philosophy, and so when 1913 came I found it difficult to realise that either the Irish or the Ulster Volunteers were in earnest. Yet I joined the Volunteers and was not impressed. In my district the

great majority of the members looked upon the movement as an adjunct of the Irish Party ...

'My association with the Kilmallock Volunteers was short-lived. My apprenticeship finished, I left Kilmallock in April 1914, to start business for myself in Newmarket. Here in June 1914, a Volunteer Company was formed. It was composed of over two hundred men. The great majority of the Volunteers in this 1914 Company had no conception of or concern for soldiering. They were a gay irresponsible crowd of young men attracted for the moment by the drilling, marching and shouted orders. That they were first-class raw material for military purposes was proved afterwards by those who joined in large numbers the IRA in the early days of 1920. Their nightly drills in the weeks before the outbreak of war [August 1914] were honoured by the presence of the Unionists ...

'Sometime that year after Mr Redmond's Woodenbridge speech [September 1914], a Volunteer organiser ... arrived from Dublin and stayed a few months. He worked hard but he had the difficult task of convincing a people who, like myself, had never dreamt of fight, of the need, reality or use of a Volunteer organisation, and his success was not great. People talk nowadays of the conflicting orders of 1916 and the might-have-beens. Had the orders agreed, been clear and explicit, there would have been here and there throughout the country an attempt at fighting, but little more, for there was not a country-wide organisation, very little arms and no general will to fight. Roger Casement, for example, was taken by two RIC men in Kerry. And so through 1914 and 1915 the few Volunteers in Newmarket met secretly and drilled half-heartedly. Living in an isolated district, their only contact with the world was through the daily newspapers and these were filled with the war news and contained neither information nor comment on the Volunteer Movement.

'Then came our mobilisation orders for Easter 1916. For the first time we met Companies from adjoining areas ... In the evening of Easter Sunday we were ordered to return to our homes and we were not again called upon ...

'1916 proved that, the first breath-taking shock past, Irishmen's allegiance was still to their own land; that they were proud of the men who made manifest that allegiance ... The spell of national inanition was broken. Ireland would never again be quiescent under foreign rule.'

To a person from a non-Fenian background, the picture was much the same. In his book *Guerrilla Days in Ireland*, Tom Barry records that when he joined the British army in 1915, at the age of 17, he knew nothing about Irish history or Redmond or Home Rule; the rebellion of 1916 was the turning point in his life. [18]

'What was this Republic of which I now heard for the first time? Who were these leaders the British had executed after taking them prisoners, Tom Clarke, Padraic Pearse, James Connolly and all the others, none of whose names I had ever heard? What did it all mean?

'In June 1915, in my seventeenth year, I had decided to see what this Great War was like. I cannot plead I went on the advice of John Redmond or any other politician, that if we fought for the British we would secure Home Rule for Ireland, nor can I say I understood what Home Rule meant. I was not influenced by the lurid appeal to fight to save Belgium or small nations. I knew nothing about nations, large or small. I went to the war for no other reason than that I wanted to see what war was like, to get a gun, to see new countries and to feel a grown man. Above all I went because I knew no Irish history and had no national consciousness. I had never been told of Wolfe Tone or Robert Emmet, though I did know all about the Kings of England and when they had come to the British Throne. I had never heard of the victory over the Sassanach at Benburb, but I could tell the dates of Waterloo and Trafalgar. I did not know of the spread of Christianity throughout Europe by Irish missionaries and scholars, but did I not know of the blessings of civilisation which Clive and the East India Company had brought to dark and heathen India? Thus through the blood sacrifices of the men of 1916, had one Irish youth of eighteen been awakened to Irish Nationality. Let it also be recorded that those sacrifices were equally necessary to awaken the minds of ninety per cent of the Irish people.

'The Great War dragged on. Nineteen-seventeen saw a return from the borders of Asiatic Russia to Egypt, Palestine, Italy, France, and in 1919 to England. Back to

Ireland after nearly four years' absence, I reached Cork in February 1919. In West Cork I read avidly the stories of past Irish history: Eoghan Ruadh, Patrick Sarsfield, John Mitchel, Wolfe Tone, Robert Emmet and the other Irish patriots who strove to end the British Conquest. I read the history of the corpses of the Famine, of the killings of Irishmen without mercy, the burnings, lootings, and the repeated attempts at the complete destruction of a weaker people. In all history there had never been so tragic a fate as that which Ireland had suffered at the hands of the English for those seven centuries. I also read the daily papers, weekly papers, periodicals and every available Republican sheet. Past numbers told the story of 1916, of the ruthless suppression of the Rising, of the executed, the dead, the jailed. Those of 1917 shadowed the gloom of the year after military defeat, while the 1918 issues mirrored rising morale, the coming together of the nation to defeat the conscription of Irishmen to fight for Britain, and the overwhelming victory at the polls for the Republicans who had pledged themselves to set up a Parliament and Government of an independent Irish Republic.'

'WE THE PEOPLE'

In the period between 1916 and 1918, the Irish people at last realised that as far as the British authorities were concerned, Ireland was a conquered country, to be ruled jointly by the British army, the RIC and the ascendancy classes. The freedom which the Irish people regarded as their birthright would not be conceded by the British. Thus, as the American colonists had done in 1775, the Irish would have to use every means available, including military force, to obtain their independence.

At the General Election in December 1918 — the first since 1910 — Sinn Féin, the party sponsoring the establishment of an Irish Republic as proclaimed in 1916, set out its policy, clearly and unambiguously, in its election manifesto: [19]

'Sinn Féin aims at securing the establishment of the Republic:
(1) By withdrawing the Irish Representation from the British Parliament, and by denying the right and opposing the will of the British Government or any other foreign government to legislate for Ireland.
(2) By making use of any and every means available to

render impotent the power of England to hold Ireland in subjection by military force or otherwise.'

The results of the 1918 election were decisive. Out of a total of 105 seats, Sinn Féin won 73 (70%). The Unionists won 26 (24.5%) and the Irish Parliamentary Party, led by Redmond, was practically wiped out, getting only 6 seats (5.5%). (Redmond and his colleagues had spent themselves fruitlessly negotiating with and supporting the British Liberals for years.)

Out of the nine counties that comprised then as now the province of Ulster, the Unionists polled a majority in only four — Antrim, and in parts of Derry, Down and Armagh. They were in a minority in counties Tyrone and Fermanagh, as well as in South Down, South Armagh and Derry city. In the remaining three Ulster counties (Donegal, Cavan and Monaghan), no Unionist was returned. Out of a total of 1,526,910 votes registered, the Unionists (Official and independent combined) received 315,394, or about one-fifth, of the votes.[20]

The people of all Ireland had spoken. If democracy meant anything to the British, this was the time to get out. However, contrary to the wishes of the overwhelming majority of the Irish people (70%), the country was partitioned less than two years later, in 1920. A segment comprising six of the nine counties of Ulster — 17 per cent of the total area of Ireland — was compulsorily retained by the British Crown and set up as a separate 'statelet', incorrectly named 'Northern Ireland'.

By so doing, Britain had partitioned not only Ireland but one of the most ancient, pre-Christian, political sub-divisions of the country — Ulaidh or Ulla — with a distinctive history dating back thousands of years.

SEVEN

British Army: Instrument of Terror

PART I: WAR OF INDEPENDENCE 1919-21

'Law and order have given place to a bloody and brutal anarchy, in which the armed agents of the Crown violate every law in aimless and vindictive and insolent savagery. England has departed further from her own standards, and further from the standards even of any nation in the world, not excepting the Turk and Zulu, than has ever been known in history before.'
— GENERAL HUBERT GOUGH, March 1921

Writing at the time of the Long Kesh hunger strike in 1980 about British policy in Ireland, Most Reverend Dr John Austin Baker, Anglican Bishop of Salisbury, leading Church of England theologian and Chaplain to the House of Commons, said:[1]

'No British Government ought ever to forget that this perilous moment, like many before it, is the outworking of a history for which our country is primarily responsible. England seized Ireland for its own military benefit. It planted Protestant settlers there to make it strategically secure. It humiliated and penalised the native Irish and their Catholic religion; and then, when it could no longer hold on to the whole island it kept back part to be a home for the settlers' descendants, a non-viable solution from which Protestants have suffered as much as anyone.

'Our injustice created the situation; and by constantly repeating that we will maintain it so long as the majority wish it, we actively inhibit Protestant and Catholic from working out a new future together. This is the root of the violence, and the reason why the protesters think of themselves as political offenders.'

This is a fair summary of what Lecky, Yeats, Robertson, Bowen and dozens of other writers, historians and commentators — English, Irish and Anglo-Irish — have said about the same subject over the years. Dr Baker has correctly pointed out that England seized Ireland for its own military benefit. This meant the taking of such military measures as were deemed necessary to effect and consolidate that benefit. Although the measures have changed from time to time, the overall aim has remained unchanged — to crush all resistance to conquest and to subjugate the native population to English rule by terror tactics.

In the early days of the Conquest, the measures were generally as described by the Irish chieftain Donald O'Neill in his *Remonstrance* to Pope John XXII in 1317 (*see Chapter 1*). Here, he complained of murder (with total religious and political immunity) by every conceivable guile and perfidy; assassination while feasting or asleep; poisoning of food and wine; the sword, famine, distress and prison. In the days of Elizabeth I and Cromwell, the measures were as recited by Holinshed, Usher, Spenser and others (*see Chapter 2*) — murder by the sword, starvation following artificially induced famine, scorched earth and so on. By these methods, according to a high English official, people were wiped out at a rate of over 30,000 in six months by starvation and an unknown number by hanging and the sword in Munster alone. In the rebellion of 1798, methods included murder by pitch cap, flogging, musket and artillery fire, and burning in barns.

Throughout the centuries, therefore, murder by the State has been recognised as a perfectly legitimate weapon of subjugation. Today, capital punishment has been abolished in Britain and in Northern Ireland. Legal or judicial murder is not accordingly permitted, but unofficial murder by specially trained marksmen, acting under the pretence that their own lives may be at risk, is not only permitted but actually organised by the State as a means of getting over the legal bar on capital punishment.

All uniformed soldiers are, of course, trained killers. 'We will kill all enemy in that bucket' is but the start of basic tactical training for every recruit.[2] The aim is to reduce killing to a routine skill so as to fit the soldier to kill without thinking. But for counter-insurgency operations, as taught by people like General Kitson, and for other jobs for which normal military organisation and training may not be sufficient, an elite corps known as the Special Air Services (SAS) was organised within the British army in 1942. Members of the SAS receive highly specialised training and operate outside the provisions of the Geneva Convention in regard to military conduct, wearing of uniforms and treatment of prisoners.

A full record of the terror tactics used in Ireland since the start of the Conquest would fill volumes and would be entirely beyond the scope of this account. A brief record, however, of some of the incidents during the 1919-21 period will give an idea of how the British army was used at that time as an instrument of terror.

The result of the 1918 General Election in Ireland sanctioned the establishment of the Irish Republic, as proclaimed in 1916, by a majority of 70 per cent. The British Government, however, under Lloyd George, was not prepared to recognise such a result and the full might of the British army and the RIC was employed to prevent the First Dáil (set up on 21 January 1919) from functioning. By June of that year, English and foreign newspapers reported that the quays of Dublin were 'jammed with tanks, armoured cars, guns, motor lorries and thousands of troops, as if the port was a base of a formidable expeditionary force'.[3]

On 10 September 1919, the British Government declared the Dáil — the legally elected Irish parliament — to be 'a dangerous association'. It was suppressed. For the next 21 months, the forces of the Crown conducted a relentless reign of terror, designed to intimidate, provoke and eventually break the resistance of the people. By early 1920, the British army was enacting the policy suggested by Birkenhead (then Lord Chancellor) in December 1919 — to use such terrorism as would crush the resurgent nation, break Sinn Féin and teach the Irish people that subjection to England was their inevitable destiny.[4]

PROVOCATIVE ACTION

The reign of terror was duly initiated. At first the Irish response was on a small scale. The military activities of the Irish Volunteers was dependent on arms and these were scarce or non-existent in many areas. They had in the main to be obtained through capture from army and RIC patrols, or from raids on police and military barracks.

Certain members of the British Cabinet and the Lord Lieutenant, Lord French, seemed anxious to provoke another rising (in the way Pitt had provoked Emmet in 1803), which would flush out the Volunteers and Sinn Féin supporters, and provide a pretext for their wholesale execution. (This tactic had been used successfully in Amritsar when some 1600 of Gandhi's followers were massacred at a prohibited political demonstration.) The sequence of events that unfolded throughout 1920 strongly supports this view.

On 19 March 1920, Tomás MacCurtain, Lord Mayor of Cork and Officer Commanding the Cork No. 1 Brigade, was murdered at the door of his bedroom in the presence of his wife by hooded men with blackened faces and turned-up collars. Half an hour later, his house was raided and searched by the British army. The coroner's jury found that the Lord Mayor was 'wilfully murdered under circumstances of most callous brutality; that the murder was organised and carried out by the Royal Constabulary, officially directed by the British Government'.[5] According to Macardle, the jury returned a verdict of 'wilful murder against Lloyd George, Lord French and Ian MacPherson, as well as against three inspectors of the RIC and some unknown member of the force'. Despite this remarkable verdict, no one was ever brought to justice for the crime.

At the end of March 1920, General Macready was appointed Commander-in-Chief of the forces in Ireland and was 'given practically a free hand by the Cabinet to suppress rebellion by whatever means may be requisite'.[6] A new force was organised to do the dirty work to which, it was alleged, the regular British army was not accustomed. The Black and Tans constituted this new force and they started work on 25 March 1920. Some six weeks later, another force, the Auxiliaries, was organised to help. Sir Hamar Greenwood was appointed Chief Secretary for Ireland in April and General Tudor became Police Adviser on 22 May.

The stage was now set to make Ireland 'an appropriate hell' for the rebels.[7] The British Government made it quite clear that any measure which the army considered necessary to put down rebellion would be condoned. Selective assassination, shooting on sight, torture of prisoners, issuing of false reports, burning of towns and industrial installations — all these tactics were acceptable and no officer of the Crown would be taken to task over any act he might commit, no matter how heinous. On 3 June 1920, Walter Long, First Lord of the Admiralty, said in the Commons, 'There is not a shadow of foundation for the suggestion that the Irish police are not allowed to shoot.'[8] He went on to say that he was glad that the police had not only shot, but had shot with extremely good effect, and only hoped they would do it again.

On 17 June 1920, Colonel Smyth, as Divisional Police Commissioner for Munster, accompanied by General Tudor, visited Listowel RIC station. In his address to the men, Smyth said:[9]

> 'Now men, Sinn Féin has had all the sport up to the present and we are going to have the sport from now on ... Police and military will patrol the country at least five nights a week ... When civilians are seen approaching, shout "Hands up". Should the order be not immediately obeyed, shoot, and shoot with effect. If the persons approaching carry their hands in their pockets, or are in any way suspicious-looking, shoot them down.
>
> You may make mistakes occasionally and innocent people may be shot, but that cannot be helped, and you are bound to get the right parties some time. The more you shoot, the better I will like you, and I assure you no policeman will get into trouble for shooting any man.'

The Listowel police rebelled then and there against these instructions, leaving Colonel Smyth and General Tudor with no option but to withdraw from the confrontation.

A month later, similar instructions were given to the police in Killarney by the Divisional Officer from Cork. In addition, the men were told that in future no policeman would be subjected to inquiry before a jury in cases of having 'shot with effect'.[10] Five men rejected the orders.

Police elsewhere, however, were more amenable; combined police and military patrols were conducted all over the country for the next twelve months. On 22 June 1920, Denis Henry, the British Attorney-General for Ireland, said in the Commons that the British troops in Ireland had been instructed to behave as if on a battlefield.[11] Within two months, regulations made under the British Administration in Ireland Act 1920 were promulgated which embodied all the suggestions made to the RIC in the course of recent visits by the top brass. The army and the other forces of law and order were now relieved of almost all legal restraints. Pursuant to Article 14(1) and (2) of the Act, any citizen connected in the most remote degree with any proclaimed organisation became automatically liable to penalties. This, of course, covered the vast majority of the population, who had given and still gave their loyalty to Dáil Éireann.

Other articles of the regulations were equally prohibitive. Article 3(6), for example, empowered the military to incarcerate any Irishman or woman without charge or trial for an indefinite time. Articles 3(1-5) and 12 empowered the military to try any person by secret court martial, while Article 4(5) empowered them to try prisoners of war and to sentence them on the charge of 'murder' to be hanged. Article 19(1) empowered the Lord Lieutenant to stop grants to local councils that did not support the Crown, and Article 16(1) empowered him to suppress coroners' inquests and to substitute military inquiries. (On 3 September 1920, coroners' inquests were, in fact, abolished in ten counties and replaced by secret military courts of inquiry. Within the following three weeks, 18 murders of unarmed persons were traced to the forces of the Crown.)

General Macready admitted to French journalists in September 1920 that it might be necessary to shoot half a hundred individuals in Ireland — 'We have most of their names', he confided, 'and the day may come when we shall be able to make a definite clearance of them.'[12] Over the next six months, he put his programme of selective assassination into operation. In October alone, some 17 prominent Sinn Féiners were murdered in circumstances which confirmed Michael Collins' suspicions that 'shooting by roster' had been officially sanctioned.[13] Collins had overwhelming evidence that the English secret service in Ireland was not a secret service at all, but a gang of murderers — subsequently described by General Crozier, Commandant of the Auxiliaries themselves, as General Wilson's 'first *sub-rosa* murder gang'.[14]

A CATALOGUE OF BRUTALITY
Throughout 1920-21, the Irish people were portrayed by British propaganda as 'a race of congenital murderers, outside the pale of humanity, to whom the ordinary rules of civilized warfare could not be applied'.[15] The Irish Republican Army (IRA) were

described as 'a gang of criminals under whose terrorism the people tremble' and whose military operations were represented as 'wanton atrocities'. When the British troops realised the full extent of the licence to murder given to them, Sir Hamar Greenwood made sure that their appetite for the job was kept at fever pitch through the pages of his *Weekly Summary*. In this publication, Sinn Féin was described as 'crime incarnate', for whose propagators 'the rope and the bullet are all too good'.[16] The issue of 4 February 1921 described de Valera as belonging to 'a race of treacherous murderers', a man 'with a fancy for ditch murders ... If the fellow had a thousand lives, they would be less than dung.'

Thus inflamed and encouraged by their superiors, the British army and the police regarded the hunting of Sinn Féiners as a sort of open-air sport and the inflicting of indignities on all members of the civilian population — young and old, male and female — as an essential feature of the reign of terror. They tore through the streets of the towns and along country roads in armoured cars and lorries, shooting from the back of these moving vehicles at innocent passers-by. The indiscriminate murder of unarmed civilians continued throughout 1920 and into 1921 at the rate of about one a day. For April 1921 alone, the figure was thirty. A few examples of such outrages will suffice:

- The firing in April 1920 into a crowd of people singing around a bonfire at Miltown Malbay, Co Clare, which left 3 dead and 9 wounded. A military inquiry was held, but the Attorney-General said in the Commons on 6 May, 'It is not proposed to publish the evidence.'[17]
- The firing into a crowd of spectators and players at a Gaelic football match in Dublin's Croke Park on Sunday, 21 November 1920, killing 14 and wounding about 60.
- The murder of a 73-year-old man, Canon Magner, parish priest of Dunmanway, Co Cork, and Timothy Crowley on 15 December 1920. The priest had received a letter on 10 November threatening him with penalties unless he tolled the chapel bell on Armistice Day. It was signed the 'Black and Tans'. He took no notice of the 'order'. A month later, while standing on the public roadway talking to Timothy Crowley, Auxiliaries from Macroom Castle drove up in a lorry, dismounted and started abusing Crowley. Suddenly the officer in charge shot Crowley. When Canon Magner rebuked him, he turned

and shot him, too. None of the other soldiers intervened; some of them emptied the pockets of the victims and dragged the bodies behind a fence. No one was ever charged.
- The murder of Father Michael Griffin, an Irish-language enthusiast and friend of the Volunteers, whose body was found in a Galway bog on 21 November 1920 with a bullet wound in his head.

In addition to these 'daylight' murders, there were also 'secret' murders of selected prominent individuals, such as:

- Tomás MacCurtain, Lord Mayor of Cork, murdered on 20 March 1920.
- John Lynch of Kilmallock, murdered in his bed in the Royal Exchange Hotel on 22 September 1920. Lynch was not a Volunteer and never carried a weapon. He was a well known and popular man, up in Dublin to hand over £23,000 subscribed locally to the National Loan.
- Michael O'Callaghan, ex-Lord Mayor of Limerick, murdered at the foot of the stairs in his own home (which was entered during curfew hours) by Crown forces in the early hours of 7 March 1921.
- George Clancy, then Lord Mayor of Limerick, murdered in his home at about 1.30am on the same night as O'Callaghan *(above)*.

There is also the long list of those executed under the arbitrary powers conferred on the military by legislation. These 'judicial executions' include:

- Kevin Barry: executed by hanging on 1 November 1920, after trial by a military court martial and torture for his part in an ambush in which 6 soldiers were killed.
- Con Murphy: executed by shooting on 1 February 1921, after sentence by court martial for being in possession of a revolver and 7 rounds of ammunition. His brother was arrested for failing to inform against him. The *Weekly Summary* reported the execution under the heading 'Potential Murderer Shot' (a phrase which has been widely used since to justify the summary execution of suspects, such as the three IRA killed in Gibraltar on 6 March 1988).
- John Allen of Tipperary: executed by shooting in Cork on 28 February 1921, after sentence by court martial for possession of a revolver and some ammunition. His case was referred to the High Court on the question of the

legality of the powers of the military courts. The High Court ruled 'that a state of War actually existed and continued to exist in Ireland'.[18] In accordance with international usage and rulings of the Hague Convention, Allen should therefore have been held as a prisoner of war; in fact, he was executed, along with five other prisoners.

- Six republican prisoners: hanged in Dublin on 14 March 1921.
- Thomas Traynor: hanged in Dublin on 25 April 1921.
- Four Volunteers (Patrick Sullivan, Patrick Roynane, Thomas Mulcahy and Maurice Moore): executed by shooting in Cork on 28 April 1921.
- Patrick Casey: executed in Cork on 2 May 1921.
- Dan O'Brien: executed by shooting in Cork on 16 May 1921.

A particularly repulsive aspect of the whole programme of repression was the torturing behind closed doors of prisoners captured in combat or taken into custody following raids on private homes. A few instances will suffice:

- On 27 July 1920, Patrick Harte and Tom Hales were tortured while being held prisoners in Bandon Military Barrack. Their nails were crushed one by one, not by Black and Tans but by British army officers from Irish families. Tom Hales withstood the punishment, but Harte went mad and was consigned to an asylum.
- A statement made by Patrick Traynor, who was a prisoner for about six weeks before execution, records, 'In all I was interrogated by British Intelligence officers on thirty-three occasions. During each interrogation, I was treated by these Intelligence officers with the utmost cruelty. My fingers were bent back until they nearly tipped the back of my hands. My arms were twisted, a red-hot poker was held to my eyes, and threats to destroy my sight were made. I was kicked and threatened with shooting. On several occasions I was taken to a dark passage under the canteen, which leads to the cells, and was badly beaten.'[19]
- In an affidavit read to the House of Commons by J H Thomas, MP, Kevin Barry had stated, 'The same officer ... ordered the sergeant to put me face down on the floor and twist my arms. I was pushed down to the floor, after my handcuffs were removed by the sergeant who went

for the bayonet. When I lay on the floor, the sergeant knelt on the small of my back, the other two placed one foot each on my back and left shoulder, and the man who knelt on me twisted my right arm, held it by the wrist with one hand, while he held my hair with the other to pull back my head. My arm was twisted from the elbow-joint. This continued to the best of my judgement for five minutes. It was very painful ...'[20]

- On 9 December 1920, Ernie O'Malley was taken prisoner in Co Kilkenny. Macardle records, 'His revolver was found on him. The local Auxiliaries bound him with ropes, questioned him and sentenced him to be shot at dawn. When he refused to answer questions, his boots were taken off and men wearing boots stamped on his feet, breaking his toes. They jabbed his sides with bayonets and threatened to bayonet him to death. Finally he was taken to Dublin Castle and questioned in the Intelligence Room there. One officer beat him with his fists, another half throttled him. One of them then took an iron poker from the fire, red hot, and held it in front of his eyes until his eyelashes were burnt, swearing they would make him talk. He was again beaten and half throttled until he was unable to stand. They then put him against a wall, showed him a revolver, and told him they would give him three minutes. They fired, but there was no bullet in the revolver. O'Malley gave no information and was sent to Kilmainham prison in such a condition that comrades who saw him there did not know who he was. He later escaped from there.'[21]

In the early hours of Sunday, 21 November 1920, Dick McKee, Commandant of the Dublin Brigade, Peadar Clancy, Vice Commandant, and Captain Seán Fitzpatrick (in whose house they were staying) were taken into custody. They were brought to Dublin Castle, headquarters of British Intelligence in Ireland, for interrogation. The planned execution of 14 British spies living in Dublin at that time was carried out by members of the Dublin Brigade some hours after their arrest. Later on Sunday, McKee and Clancy were tortured in an endeavour to extract information about the operation; then they were shot. (Fitzpatrick luckily escaped identification and was transferred along with other prisoners to Beggar's Bush Barracks.)

A report issued to the press on Monday, 22 November, and published in the daily newspapers the following day stated that

McKee and Clancy, along with another Volunteer (Conor Clune from Clare), were shot while trying to escape. One of Collins' agents at Dublin Castle, Detective MacNamara, gave a very different report about what took place inside the Castle that Sunday. He told his story to Charlie Dalton, who records it in his book *With the Dublin Brigade*:[22]

'Before I [Dalton] parted from him [MacNamara], I asked him to tell me about the butchery that had taken place in the Castle on the night of the 21st. In that gloomy spot, standing beside him, I could see only the outline of Mac's face.

"You mean Dick McKee, Peadar Clancy, and Clune?" he said, his voice growing sad.

"I do."

"Well, I heard that they had been brought in prisoners on Saturday night, and I had little hope for them then, and when I heard the alarm sounded in the Castle on the Sunday morning after the shooting, I knew it was all up with them. Such scenes! I shall never forget them. Cabs, taxis, and hacks were rushing up all day filled with spies, touts, and their wives, all in a panic, seeking safety."

"But what about Dick?"

"The guard room where they had put him and the others is just inside the gate, and the Auxiliaries' canteen adjoins the guard room. I went into the canteen to see if I could hear any word of their moving the prisoners, so that I could send word to Michael Collins to arrange a rescue. In the bar the Auxiliaries were all drunk and thirsting for vengeance. Captain X — was there too. I had several drinks with them, but there was not a word about transferring the prisoners, and I had to listen to them cursing them with every foul name. I knew there was no hope, and I felt dreadful, just waiting for what was to come."

"Well, Mac," I said, "they gave them a terrible death, I believe."

"They did. Poor Dick was beyond recognition. I saw the battered corpses being taken away to King George V Hospital. They flung them into a van. I was nearly mad, and I had to act my part somehow. I had to look on while Captain X — pulled back the canvas screen to satisfy his hate with a last look. He flashed his torch on to poor Dick's ghastly face, swearing at him as if the dead ears could still catch an echo of his words, and at the same time hitting the body with his revolver."'

In a statement written in July 1922, after he got out of jail, Seán Fitzpatrick corroborates MacNamara's account of how these men were tortured while in the custody of the Crown:[23]

'I was put into an open motor lorry with side seats with a guard of five or six Tans under section officer Tiney. I was driven from Beggar's Bush Barracks to King George Vth Hospital and brought out to the dead house. I then knew what I was in for ... Tiney lifted the sheet off the face of my dear friend, poor McKee, and said to me, "Do you know him?" I said, "You have his name on the slip of paper pinned on the sheet." Poor McKee's face was battered up a lot. He had big marks all around his face. Some marks looked as if pieces of flesh were knocked out of them. He had a bayonet thrust in his side and his fingers were all cut where he gripped the bayonet. I was then brought to the next slab. Tiney lifted the sheet and showed me the face of P. Clancy. He asked me, "Who is that?" I said, "You have his name on the slip of paper on the sheet." P. Clancy's face looked as if it had got a good beating. His forehead was marked over the eye also. It stuck out well over his face and it looked as if it was burnt. His face was all yellow ... I was then brought to the other slab at the door. They lifted the sheet off Conor Clune and asked me, "Do you know him?" I said, "No." They had his name on a slip of paper pinned on the sheet. Poor Clune was all black. As I was going out they were bringing another man into the dead house in a sheet. They asked me, "Do you know him?" I said. "No." Tiney said to me, "Come on, Sydney, your turn next."

WHOLESALE DESTRUCTION
In conjunction with their campaign of murder, the armed forces of the Crown also pursued a policy of sacking towns and destroying property. No town escaped attack at least once during the 1920-21 period; many were sacked more than once:

Tuam, Limerick, Thurles, Bantry, Kilcommon and Swords among others. Sometimes the sackings took place as reprisals for Volunteer activities in the area, sometimes simply to teach the civilian population the Birkenhead lesson, that 'subjection to England was their inevitable destiny'.[4] Thus, for example, Fermoy was sacked on 8 September 1919 by about 200 British regular troops in retaliation for an ambush on a military party the day before, in which rifles were captured by the local Volunteers.

Mallow was sacked on 29 September 1920 as a reprisal for the successful attack on Mallow military barracks the day before and the capture of 50 rifles, 2 machine guns and, in the words of the officer in command Liam Lynch, 'ammunition to burn'. Some hours after the attack, lorry-loads of soldiers from Buttevant and Fermoy arrived in Mallow, equipped with sprays and incendiary grenades. The local regiment (17th Lancers), who called themselves 'The Death or Glories' and numbered about 40 or 50 men, joined them. Under the command of their officers, 'they burnt the creamery, town hall and ten houses. A Volunteer fire brigade had confined the flames, although they had been fired upon repeatedly. The police from the barracks and the few Tans there gave shelter to some women and children who had fled from their homes; an expectant mother and a woman who had spent the night in a graveyard died of exposure.'[24]

Balbriggan, in north Co Dublin, was sacked on 20 September 1920 as a reprisal for the death of a Black and Tan who was shot in a local public house earlier in the night. Twenty-five houses were destroyed and a small hosiery factory was burnt to the ground. Two young men who had nothing to do with the Volunteers were bayoneted to death in the street.

Lahinch, Ennistymon and Miltown Malbay, all in Co Clare, suffered reprisals on 22 September 1920. The Circuit Court judge for the county, Mr M McDonnell Bodkin, reported to Sir Hamar Greenwood, Chief Secretary for Ireland.[25] The judge told how each of the small towns was 'invaded and shot up' on the same night 'by a large body of the armed forces of the government. Rifle shots were fired apparently at random and a very large number of houses and shops were broken into, set on fire, and their contents looted or destroyed.' Civilians, too, were deliberately killed by the troops: a young married man named

Conole was seized in Lahinch and 'despite the pleadings of his wife, he was taken away a short distance and shot. His charred remains were found next morning in his own house which had been burnt.' The judge also reported that, in Miltown Malbay, an old man named Lynch, aged 75, had been 'shot dead by a soldier in uniform, distant about ten yards', and witnessed and proved by the man's wife who was standing beside him at their own doorway at the time.

Cork city was burnt and looted by military and Tans on 11 December 1920 as a reprisal for a local ambush. Most of the shops and buildings on one side of Patrick Street were totally destroyed by fire, while many other buildings in the city were looted and damaged; many of the public buildings, including the City Hall, were burnt to the ground. Two brothers named Delaney were murdered in their beds. Sir Hamar Greenwood told the House of Commons subsequently that 'there was no evidence that the fires were started by the Crown forces.'[26] At the time, however, strict curfew was in force and the streets were given up to military patrols. Greenwood also 'explained' to the House that the fire which burnt the City Hall 'spread' from Patrick Street — which would have meant that it travelled a quarter of a mile, jumped over several intervening streets without setting the buildings alight and then crossed the River Lee. Many eyewitnesses gave sworn testimony to the effect that soldiers looted business premises in company with Auxiliaries and the Black and Tans, and that they fired on civilians and firemen attempting to put out the fires; they even fought with each other, presumably while under the influence of looted alcohol. In an attempt to exonerate the regular soldiers, General Macready stated that the burning was carried out by the Auxiliaries. Either way, Greenwood's 'explanation' was patently untrue.

The lesser known incidents of the reign of terror are numerous. They particularly affected workers in key areas such as railways, the Post Office and other public utilities. These, the British regarded as their special enemies. On one occasion, senior British officers were shot at in Mallow and on that night after curfew, the Auxiliaries marched into Mallow Junction, killed three railwaymen and wounded several others. The usual procedure on such occasions was to line up the men after beating and tell them to run for it; as they ran, they were picked off.[27]

The total number of unarmed civilians shot in public streets and along country roads from the backs of careering lorries and armoured cars or murdered in their homes and in open places, will never be known exactly, but it certainly ran into several hundreds. Nobody was ever brought to justice because the authorities had solemnly promised that no one would get into trouble for such crimes.

'A BLOODY AND BRUTAL ANARCHY'

By the end of 1920, many people in England had had enough and raised their voices against the barbarities being perpetrated in their name in Ireland. On 29 December 1920, the British Labour Commission had completed an investigation, the result of which was 'a record, laboriously authenticated and documented of destruction, arson, looting, cruelty, outrage and murder perpetrated by the forces of the Crown'.[28] It also recorded how the Auxiliaries and Black and Tans were 'compelling the whole Irish people — men, women and children — to live in an atmosphere of sheer terrorism'. By March 1921, General Hubert Gough, Officer Commanding the Cavalry Regiment at the Curragh in 1914 and the Fifth Army in France during the 1914-18 war, felt compelled to write:[29]

> 'Law and order have given place to a bloody and brutal anarchy, in which the armed agents of the Crown violate every law in aimless and vindictive and insolent savagery. England has departed further from her own standards, and further from the standards even of any nation in the world, not excepting the Turk and Zulu, than has ever been known in history before.'

Brigadier-General F P Crozier, Commandant of the Auxiliaries from 3 August 1920 until his resignation on 18 February 1921, placed the blame for the terror firmly on the Government. He wrote:[30]

> 'In 1920 and 1921 the whole Cabinet should have been marched to the Tower in company with the chief of the Imperial Staff and there shot, *pour encourager les autres* on account of what they permitted to be done in the King's name and by the authority of his uniform in Ireland.'

On the republican side, Seán Moylan, Officer Commanding the Cork II and Cork IV Brigade of the IRA in 1921, wrote in 1953:[31]

'Those who have written of the history of the period lay much stress on the indiscipline and sadism of the Black and Tans, under which general term the RIC were often included, and compared it with the magnificent discipline and forbearance of the regular British troops. Other than combat contact and as prisoners in my hands, I have not known or had experience of Black and Tans, and while there is overwhelming evidence of evil sadistic conduct by many of the members of this body, I have no personal knowledge of any brutal or criminal conduct on their part within the limits of my brigade area. Nor have I or mine suffered in any way at the hands of the RIC.

'Every act of terrorism and murder of which I have known was carried out by the so-called disciplined regular troops of the British Army.'

SEVEN

British Army: Instrument of Terror

PART II: REVOLT IN NORTHERN IRELAND
1969 TO DATE

> *'An arrest operation carried out in Battalion strength in circumstances in which the troops were likely to come under fire involved hazard to civilians in the area which Commander 8 Brigade may have under-estimated.'*
>
> — LORD WIDGERY
> Widgery Tribunal, Conclusion No. 5

The indiscriminate murder of civilians, assassination of selected people and the general terror tactics of the British army used during 1919-21 have been continued in Northern Ireland since 1969. They are not the tactics of any army operating in its own country. They are the tactics of an army of occupation in a foreign country where the conquered people refuse to accept the authority of the conqueror.

One of the outstanding episodes in this latest phase of the British army's bloody record in Ireland is the killing of 13 unarmed civilians and the wounding of 14 in Derry on Sunday, 30 January 1972. It was to be Ireland's Amritsar of the current campaign.

Following the introduction of internment in August 1971, all marches, parades and processions had been banned in Northern Ireland. Several anti-internment marches had nevertheless been held and more were being organised. One was scheduled to go from the Creggan via the Bogside to the Guildhall Square in Derry on 30 January 1972. Being illegal, all such marches attracted attention. They represented a challenge to British authority. The Derry march represented a particular challenge since it was being organised within, and was proposing to emerge from, what was then a 'no-go' area for the police, or Royal Ulster Constabulary (RUC). It was accordingly decided at the highest political level that the march should be used to mount a military operation to destroy the gunmen in the area and so teach the Derry rebels a bloody lesson they would never forget. This decision was contrary to the advice of Chief Superintendent Lagan, head of the RUC in Derry.

Major-General Robert Ford, Commander of Land Forces in Northern Ireland, confirmed to the Widgery Tribunal[1] (which investigated the massacre that followed from that decision) that the whole operation was considered for a fortnight or more before and that there was no last-minute change of plan. The operation was, in other words, carefully worked out in advance; there was no question of the troops doing otherwise on the day of the march than what had been pre-planned.

Lord Balniel, Deputy to the Secretary for Defence, indicated to the House of Commons on 1 February 1972 (and Geoffrey Johnston Smith, Minister for the Army, confirmed in a television interview at a later date) that the final decision to stop the march was taken in London on Monday, 24 January by the Cabinet Sub-Committee on Northern Ireland. This committee included Lord Carrington, then Secretary for Defence, and other ministers. It was a matter for General Ford and the Joint Security Committee in Northern Ireland to prepare the detailed plan for the implementation of the decision.

The Joint Security Committee met the following day (Tuesday, 25 January), but by then the preparation of the military plan seemed to be well in hand. The previous evening, immediately after the high-level political decision had been taken in London, it appears that Brigadier General Kitson, Commander of the 39th Brigade, had summoned Lieutenant-Colonel Derek Wilford, Officer Commanding the 1st Battalion of the Parachute Regiment, to his headquarters in Lisburn. Wilford was instructed to prepare for service in Derry on Sunday, 30 January. Kitson was acting on the orders of General Ford, who had obviously decided to detach this highly trained specialist regiment from the 39th Brigade and put it under the command of the Derry Brigade Commander, Brigadier Andrew MacLellan, for Sunday's job.

Over the next two days, the detailed plan was worked out. On Wednesday afternoon (26 January) Brigadier MacLellan discussed it with his superior, General Ford; on Friday, MacLellan discussed it with his subordinates, Wilford of the Parachute Regiment and others who would be involved.

THE PLAN
Though stated afterwards that the operation was designed merely to stop the march and to arrest stone-throwers ('hooligans'), the choice of troops (the Parachute Regiment) and the manner in which they were directed indicate that one of the major aims was to flush out and destroy the IRA gunmen who had been dominating the Creggan/Bogside area for too long. The map on p. 103 shows the layout of the area. To achieve this objective:

- The march would be stopped by a military barricade, water cannon, etc. across William Street (A on map), on the city side of the Rosville Street junction.
- James Street (B) would also be blocked and would be used as an assembly area for the Parachute troops.
- The only route left open to the marchers would be along Rosville Street towards Free Derry Corner (C), some 300 yards away.
- As the crowd moved along Rosville Street, they could be pursued by the troops from James Street opposite. Part of the company would take up pre-determined positions in the car park on the left (D), behind the Rosville Flats. The remainder of the company would take up positions on the opposite side of Rosville Street, in the Kells Walk area (E), from which they could dominate the people's barricade in the middle of the street (F).
- At the first sign of harassment from stone-throwers and other trouble-makers, the troops in the car park (D) would open fire in an endeavour to flush out the gunmen.
- Fire could then be continued by the troops in position on the Kells Walk side of Rosville Street (E) in the direction of the barricade placed across the street, where it was expected the gunmen would be most likely to take cover.

At about 2.30pm on Sunday afternoon, 30 January 1972, the marchers started to assemble in the Creggan. About an hour later, they had arrived at the William Street/Rosville Street junction, where they found the way blocked by the military. There was only one route open to the march — along Rosville

Street. As anticipated, it proceeded slowly along this route in the direction of Free Derry Corner, where it now intended to hold its meeting. The army had thus accomplished the first part of its mission: it had stopped the march from entering the city centre. It had now to proceed with the other parts of the plan — to arrest the hooligans and to destroy the gunmen, or suspected gunmen, in the march or in the surrounding buildings.

... AND ITS EXECUTION

Accordingly, at about 4.10pm, ten armoured personnel carriers (APCs) accelerated out of the James Street assembly area on the tail of the crowd. They took up pre-determined positions in the car park behind the Rosville Flats in what seemed to be a carefully rehearsed plan. One APC initially parked in the wrong place, but the driver quickly realised his mistake and rectified it.

This part of the Company was under the command of the Mortar Platoon Lieutenant, who was the first out of his APC in the car park. Residents in the flats overlooking the car park reported that firing started within two minutes of the vehicles pulling in and that the first shots were fired by the army. The lieutenant in charge later admitted to the Widgery Tribunal that he had fired two aimed warning shots into a wall of the car park in the vicinity of a threatening crowd, but that he had heard no shots prior to his own firing. He also admitted to the Tribunal that he had lied when claiming on television that he had seen a gunman before he fired.[2] His shots would appear to have been intended to draw the fire of any gunmen in the area in accordance with the army's plan, and as a signal to his colleagues that the operation had started.

There was panic among the few hundred bystanders on the waste ground near the car park when they saw what was happening. They fled towards Free Derry Corner, accompanied by some stragglers who had delayed at the William Street barricade. Pressmen and members of the crowd reported that, in their flight, they heard shots resembling fire from army self-loading rifles coming from the direction of the APC behind them, but that they neither heard nor saw any petrol- or nail-bombers. When the dust had settled, the first casualty of the day — JACK DUDDY, aged 17 — lay dying. He had been shot 'on suspicion' of being 'a potential terrorist' while running out of the car park.

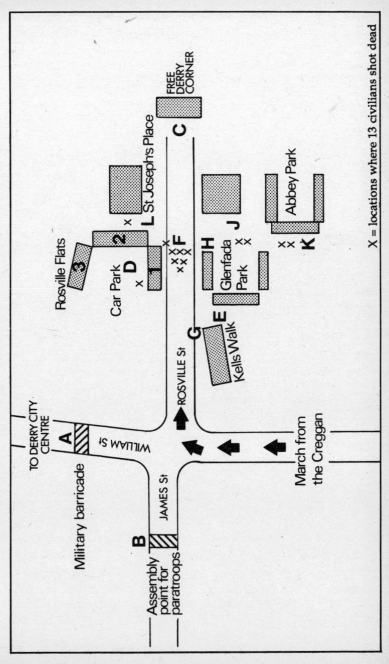

So far, this part of the army's plan — to flush out the gunmen — had not been a success. No gunmen had appeared for the paratroops to engage. Nevertheless, the operation was to proceed as planned; the remainder of the Support Company (some 36 men) went into action from their pre-determined positions in the Kells Walk area of Rosville Street.

Witnesses to the events reported that the troops opened up instantly with a fusillade of fire at some six or seven youths moving around carelessly in the area of the barricade set in the middle of the street. This structure was a ramshackle affair of stones and scrap metal; it offered no protection whatever either from view or from the fire of high-velocity, precision rifles directed towards it by the paratroops. None of these youths was armed; they were, in effect, 'sitting ducks' for the men of the Parachute Regiment to fire upon. In a matter of minutes, six youths were dead or dying, shot in more or less the following order:

2. MICHAEL KELLY: Aged 17. Apprentice electrician. Shot in the abdomen while standing at the barricade.
3. WILLIE NASH: Aged 19. Docker. Shot at the barricade by a bullet through the lung, heart and abdomen.
4. JOHN YOUNG: Aged 17. Shop assistant. Shot at the barricade by a bullet through his left cheek which travelled downwards and tore through his back.
5. MICHAEL McDAID: Aged 20. Barman. Shot at the barricade by a bullet which entered his left cheek just in front of the ear.
6. HUGH GILMOUR: Aged 17. Shot at the barricade by a bullet which entered through the left elbow and exited through the right chest.
7. KEVIN McELHINNEY: Aged 17. Shot as he crawled from the barricade to seek cover in the doorway of the Rosville Flats by a bullet which had fragmented badly.

When no more targets presented themselves at the barricade, the army's shooting subsided, temporarily. Some 20 terrified members of the crowd who had taken cover behind a nearby gable (H on map, p. 103) tried to escape from the slaughter. They started to run down Glenfada Park (J) and the adjoining cobbled precinct, Abbey Park (K). But their retreat was blocked by fresh fire from the same troops, still deployed in the Kells Walk area. The result of this firing was four more dead, shot while trying to escape:

8   JAMES JOSEPH WRAY: Aged 22. Shot twice in the small of the back at Glenfada Park.
9   WILLIAM MCKINNEY: Aged 26. Compositor in the *Derry Journal* newspaper. Shot through the right side at Glenfada Park.
10 GERALD MCKINNEY: Aged 35. Shot through the front at Abbey Park.
11 GERALD DONAGHY: Aged 17. Shot through the front at Abbey Park.

Lord Widgery admitted that the shots which killed these unarmed people were fired without justification and that the firing 'bordered on' the reckless. He concluded that the four dead, and the group of which they formed part, were running from death, rather than acting aggressively, when they were gunned down.

Eleven unarmed civilians had by now been shot dead on this bloody Sunday in Derry. Two more were yet to die before the massacre was ended.

12 PATRICK DOHERTY: Aged 30. Plumber's mate. Shot at St Joseph's Place (L on map) from the direction of Glenfada Park while crawling out to help one of the wounded. A bullet entered his right buttock and travelled virtually parallel with his spine, causing massive internal damage before tearing out through the left chest.
13 BERNARD MCGUIGAN: Aged 41. Painter. Shot in the vicinity of the entrance to Block 1 of Rosville Flats, also from the direction of Glenfada Park, while going to the aid of one of the wounded. McGuigan was carrying a white flag in one hand; the other was empty. The bullet that killed him — the thirteenth victim of the day — entered the left side of his head and emerged through the right eye, shattering his skull and scattering his brains on the pavement.

The second part of the army's mission had now been completed. When the dead and wounded were counted, it was found that 13 unarmed civilians (7 of them of school-going age) had been shot dead and 14 had been wounded, all in the space of about 20 minutes. None of them was what Colonel Smyth and Lloyd George described in 1920 as 'the right men'.[3] But that was not the army's fault; 'the right men' had not presented themselves. Nevertheless, the plan had been executed to the letter. The troops had gone in and shot 'suspects' and 'potential gunmen'; they had even shot boys that might grow up to be 'the right men'. It was the singular misfortune of these Derry youths, and the other victims, that they had chosen to exercise their basic human right to protest (against internment without trial) in a public parade or that they had gone to the assistance of a wounded person.

There is no evidence that the British army had run amok or overstepped its instructions on this occasion. Widgery stated in his report (Conclusion No. 11) that 'there was no general breakdown in discipline.'[1] General Ford had specially selected the Parachute Regiment for the task — a group of experienced, seasoned men, regular British army, highly trained and equipped. Most of the paratroops were either marksmen or first-class shots, proficient in hitting short-exposure and moving targets.

Those who witnessed the massacre confirm that it was carried out coldly, efficiently and in a pre-planned manner. Firing was from well-chosen positions, mostly within 100 yards of the targets. Troops shot with considerable discrimination and accuracy. Each shot seemed well aimed, using telescopic sights in certain cases. Widgery was able to establish that the 27 killed and wounded were shot with the minimum expenditure of ammunition.

The initial positioning of the paratroops in James Street in preparation for the attack and the manner in which they were equipped, deployed and directed by the unit commander during the action (from his forward command post, G on map, overlooking the Rosville Street barricade and beside Glenfada Park) would make one suspect that this operation was planned to kill, not to arrest, 'suspects'. The operation was under the control of the Officer Commanding throughout and he could, if he so wished, have called a halt to the shooting at any stage. However, the shooting continued to the very end of the operation at any target that presented itself — even to the final victim, Bernard McGuigan, with his white flag on an obvious errand of mercy.

For his services to the Crown, Lieutenant-Colonel Derek Wilford of the Parachute Regiment was, in the opinion of his superior, rightly recommended for, and awarded, the Order of the British Empire (OBE) in October of that year.

While the Derry massacre of 13 unarmed civilians in 1972 is probably the single, most notable incident in the current campaign of terror in Northern Ireland, there are many other, lesser known — indeed, almost forgotten — killings of innocent civilians by the British army. A brief reference to a few of these, out of an estimated total of some hundreds, shows that there has been no change in the age-old tactics by which the Crown maintains its control in Ireland. For example:

- On 3 July 1971, 4 civilians were killed in the Falls Road of Belfast (3 shot dead and 1 run over) by some 2000 British soldiers searching for arms. None of the dead was connected with the IRA.
- On 7 July 1971, Seamus Cusack, an unemployed welder, aged 28, was killed in Derry by a single shot from a marksman in the Anglians while trying to rescue a child from the line of army fire. Cusack did not belong to any political organisation.
- On the same day, Desmond Beattie, unemployed and aged 19, was shot in Derry, also by an Anglian marksman. He died instantly.

In the first three months after the introduction of internment on 10 August 1971, 57 civilians were killed, including:

- Father Hugh Mullan, aged 38, curate of St John's Parish church, Falls Road, shot while giving the last rites to a dying man.
- Mrs Sarah Worthington, aged 50, of the Ardoyne area, a mother of 9 and a widow, shot near her home.
- Francis McGuinness, aged 18, from Anderstown, shot by the army at Finaghy Road.
- Noel Phillips from Ballymurphy, shot outside the Henry Taggart Memorial Hall.
- Daniel Taggart from New Barnsley, shot outside the army post at the Henry Taggart Memorial Hall.
- Leo McGuigan, aged 15, shot in the head in the Ardoyne area.

The vast majority of these random shootings were, as in the 1920-21 period, of innocent, unarmed people who had nothing to do with politics. Mrs Thompson was shot for rattling her dust-bin lid, a recognised warning signal in nationalist areas for British troops engaged in house-to-house searches. A deaf mute was shot in Strabane for 'unusual behaviour'; Harry Thompson was shot while stopped at traffic lights.

The latest victim in this category of indiscriminate killings was that of Aidan McAnespie, shot dead from a British army observation tower at Aughnacloy on 21 February 1988. McAnespie was on his way to play a Gaelic football match on that fateful Sunday evening. Although not a member of any organisation, save his trade union and the GAA, he had been continually harassed by the security forces. He was regularly stopped, threatened with death and abused at the border checkpoint which he had to pass each day to get to his work in Monaghan Poultry Products. He was repeatedly searched and held for long periods at the army base. After he passed the checkpoint on the day of his death, he would have been visible for at least two minutes to the soldier in the tower who shot him — a soft target for a heavy machine gun in a fixed position with or without telescopic sights. This soldier has since been exonerated and another bloody warning has been given to young Irish nationalists who do not show proper respect for the British army of occupation.

SEVEN

British Army: Instrument of Terror
PART III: GIBRALTAR 1988

Res ipsa loquitor, as the lawyers say — 'the thing speaks for itself.' When two unarmed men and an unarmed woman are shot dead from behind, and shot while lying wounded on the ground, in a public street, in broad daylight, at pointblank range, by armed members of a regular regiment of the British army in civilian attire, the action must be called what it is — deliberate, cold-blooded, premeditated, extra-judicial murder by agents of the Crown. To say otherwise would be to ignore the facts concerning the public execution by shooting of three acknowledged members of the Belfast IRA — Daniel McCann, Mairéad Farrell and Seán Savage — in Gibraltar at about 3.45pm on Sunday, 6 March 1988.

In the official version of the executions given in the House of Commons on the day after the shooting (Monday, 7 March), the Foreign Secretary, Sir Geoffrey Howe, admitted that the three were unarmed when shot. He also stated that contrary to the official reports put out on Sunday night and repeated on Monday morning, there were no explosives in the white Renault car which one of the IRA unit was seen parking in the centre of Gibraltar before 1pm on Sunday. Their 'suspicious movements', however, posed an 'immediate risk' to other lives and warranted shooting them dead.

The Foreign Secretary went on to explain that this unit of the IRA had been under close surveillance by the Spanish police for some months. The British had evidence of a planned attack on a guard-mounting ceremony in Gibraltar on Tuesday, 8 March. The Gibraltar police had been alerted, he said, and had asked for military assistance. He told the House that shortly before 1pm on Sunday, one of the three had brought a Renault car into Gibraltar and parked it in a narrow street around the corner from the Governor's residence, near a primary school, a home for old people and the spot where the troops participating in the ceremony would assemble the following Tuesday. One and a half hours later (about 2.30pm), the driver of this car was joined by the other two, who came into Gibraltar on foot. 'Their presence and actions near the car', he added, 'gave rise to strong suspicion that it contained a bomb, which appeared to be corroborated by a rapid technical examination of the car.' All three then started to walk back towards the border. They were 'challenged by the security forces' in the vicinity of the Shell garage and, according to Sir Geoffrey, 'made movements which led the military personnel operating in support of the Gibraltar police to conclude that their own lives and those of others were at stake and in the light of this response, they shot them dead.'

Despite the 'strong suspicion' that the Renault car contained a bomb 'which appeared to be corroborated by a rapid technical examination' and the fact that it was parked in a populated area near Bishop Fitzgerald's school and a home for old people, Sir Geoffrey did not explain why no attempt was made after the IRA rendezvous to issue a bomb alert or to keep the public away by cordoning off the area or to evacuate residents who were alleged to be at 'immediate risk'.

Nor did the Foreign Secretary explain what 'movements' the wounded IRA members could make which warranted repeated shooting at them as they lay dying on the roadway.

CORONER'S INQUEST
Six months after the shootings, a coroner's inquest opened in Gibraltar, on 6 September 1988, to establish the cause of death. Evidence was heard for nineteen days and then the verdict was announced, on 30 September — lawful killing of all three IRA members.

In what follows, references to the evidence given at the inquest are mainly from reports published in the *Irish Times*, 7 to 30 September 1988. On the opening day of the inquest, the lawyer for the British Government and for the Governor and Chief of Police for Gibraltar, Mr John Laws, told the court that certificates had been prepared and placed before the court indicating those areas on which evidence should not be given and which would be closed to inquiry. One from the Home Office vouchsafed the need to protect sources of intelligence-gathering, by not giving certain dates and times. The Secretary for Defence, too, vouchsafed the need to protect details and requirements of operations and equipment. The inquest was thus debarred from inquiring into the vital question, among others, of who decided to despatch troops of the SAS regiment from England, allegedly to arrest the IRA unit in Gibraltar, when there was a battalion of experienced troops (the Royal Anglians) already stationed there.

CROWN PATHOLOGIST'S EVIDENCE

Giving evidence on 8 September, the Crown Pathologist, Professor Alan Watson of Glasgow University, told the court that he had been requested to carry out a post-mortem examination of the three bodies. He had done so on the evening of 7 March 1988 to determine the cause of death.

Professor Watson said that Mairéad Farrell had died from internal haemorraging, caused by three bullets which entered her back, passed through her chest and exited her front, severely damaging her heart and liver. There were also, he added, five wounds to her face, head and neck, which had been produced by two bullets. In reply to questions, he said:

- the bullets to her body had gone in the back and out the front;
- the angle at which the bullets entered her back was upward and because of her small stature (only 5'1") the gunman would have had to be bending well down or she would have had to have been lying on the ground on her face;
- she could have been lying down when some of the shots were fired;
- the close grouping of the holes to her body would indicate that she was not moving about when shot since the type of weapon used (a Browning 9mm revolver) could not produce such a grouping on a moving target [because the trigger and bolt have to be pulled for each shot];
- the closeness of the holes also indicate that she had been shot from a distance of between two and six feet;
- she could have been seized by the person shooting, who was only some feet away.

In his report on the second victim, Professor Watson said that Daniel McCann died from two gunshot wounds to the back and two to the head, causing multiple fractures and extensive brain damage. In reply to questions, he said:

- the first shot was probably to the face or the chest;
- the second shot was probably to the top of the head while he was lying down;
- all four bullets that hit the victim were lethal;
- the victim's heart was intact as was his skeleton, excepting the skull, since the entry holes to the back had passed between the ribs and had come out in the front of his body.

On the subject of the third victim, Professor Watson said that Seán Savage had been shot 16 times and had died from a number of wounds to the head, chest and limbs. A contributory factor in his death was gunshot wounds to the lungs. Entry holes showed that he had been shot five times in the back, fives times in the head, five times in the front and once in the hand. There were multiple fractures to the skull, including considerable loss of tissue. His arm had been broken, as had his leg. He had sustained a total of 27 wounds in what, the Crown Pathologist testified, could be described as 'a frenzied attack'.

Professor Watson went on to read a long list of the wounds sustained by Savage. This took more than 15 minutes of the court's time. In reply to questions, he said:

- Savage had been brought down from the back and then hit in the face, or he was facing the gunman when hit and then fell;
- bullets had been fired into his head while he lay on the ground;
- having been shot five times in the back, the victim would be incapable of movement and unable to draw a gun;
- if someone was hit in the head, they died at once.

In corroborating evidence given on the same day as Professor Watson, Derek Pounder, Professor of Forensic Medicine at the University of Dundee, said that he had seen the ballistics and pre-autopsy reports, photographs, clothes and documents, but not the bodies. He agreed with Professor Watson that:

- Farrell was shot three times in the back from about three feet;
- she could have been shot while lying down;
- McCann was shot as described by Professor Watson;
- Savage was shot while he lay on the ground;
- the wound to the top of his left shoulder appeared to be an exit wound, which would have come from inside the

chest when he was hit while lying on the ground;
- the angle of entry of bullet wounds towards the upper part of his torso showed that Savage was shot by someone standing near his feet.

SAS MODUS OPERANDI

The killings described by the Crown Pathologist and by Professor Pounder were carried out by soldiers from a regular unit of the British army — the SAS — dressed in civilian attire. They gave evidence at the inquest from behind a screen which veiled them from the public view. They were identified as Soldiers A, B, C and D.

These soldiers were sent out on the public street in Gibraltar on 6 March 1988 allegedly to arrest the three IRA volunteers. On their own evidence, they were within arresting distance of all three at the same time — about 3.45pm. Soldiers A and B were directly behind McCann and Farrell respectively at the Shell petrol station on Winston Churchill Avenue. Soldiers C and D were behind Savage, less than 100 yards away towards the town centre.

Instead of arresting them, however, the soldiers opened fire instantly and without warning, and shot them in the back, in the head and on the ground until they were dead. They did so on the pretext that each member of the unit (McCann, Farrell and Savage) separately made a movement, either to draw a gun or to press a button on a detonating instrument, which would require a tuning aerial to operate if of the kind produced in court, which the soldiers must have known could not be concealed on their persons.

Soldier A said, in evidence on 13 September, 'I was *just going to* shout a warning and *at the same time* I was drawing my pistol. Events overtook the warning.' Soldier B said, also on 13 September, 'Fire from Soldier A was *instantaneous* with the shout from Soldier A. It was all in a split second.' (Italics are author's emphasis.)

Soldier C said, on 15 September, 'A gun was made to kill.' He fired as fast as he could — six shots in four or five seconds. Soldier D, testifying on the same day as C, said, 'They didn't have to give a warning if they considered the risk great enough.' He fired the first shot at Savage. In reply to questions, he said that he fired to kill because that was the way he was trained. He also said that it did not indicate anything to him that four SAS soldiers were sent out to arrest three IRA members and instead had opened fire on them all in a matter of split seconds and had kept on firing until they were sure they were all dead.

Soldier E, the tactical commander, testified on 13 September that once firing started, the intention was to kill all three members of the IRA.

The Gibraltar operation was a clear 'shoot to kill without warning' job, efficiently executed by regular troops of the British army while in civilian attire. Each of the soldiers involved had a long service in the SAS, ranging from six to twelve years. They were highly trained in the use of hand guns at close quarters and, on their own evidence, went into action carrying a total of 132 rounds of 9mm ammunition — 11 magazines with 12 rounds in each. On the evidence of an officer in the Gibraltar police, testifying on 7 September, after the shootings Soldier A handed in a magazine and 7 rounds; Soldier B, 5 rounds; Soldier C, a magazine and 6 rounds; and Soldier D, a magazine and 3 rounds — making a total of 3 magazines and 21 rounds returned. On this reckoning, between 75 and 111 rounds (depending on the number of rounds in the returned magazines) were expended in a killing operation that pretended to be an arrest mission.

'CONSPIRACY TO MURDER'

The SAS is a specialised regiment of the British army, organised and trained specifically for combat duties behind enemy lines in times of war. Capture and liquidation of enemy headquarters, communications and vital installations are typical missions. For the successful accomplishment of such tasks, members of the regiment are trained to act quickly and ruthlessly, at close quarters and, as was made clear at the Gibraltar inquest, to kill without warning, to leave no wounded and to take no prisoners.

Because of these fundamental principles of their training, members of the SAS are rarely called upon to aid the civil power in Britain, except in special situations where, for example, armed police are unable to make an arrest (as was the case in the siege of the Iranian Embassy in London in 1980). When they are eventually called in, their job is not to arrest the opposition, but to apply their specialised training to liquidate it. As further proof of their methods of operation, it was established at the inquest into the five Arabs killed in the Iranian Embassy siege that two of the dead were actually 'executed' after they had surrendered.[1] The sixth got away only because he had successfully hidden himself among the hostages.

Members of this regiment are, however, regularly deployed in Northern Ireland against the IRA to achieve ends which cannot be achieved by normal arrest-and-trial procedures, now that the death penalty has been abolished in Northern Ireland.

Obviously troops from this specialist regiment were not despatched from England to Gibraltar simply to arrest three members of the IRA. There was a regular infantry battalion of the British army (the Royal Anglians), with long service in Northern Ireland, already stationed in Gibraltar, together with several supporting units. These troops were available to assist the local police in any arrest operation planned. It is clear from the evidence given at the inquest that the SAS were not supporting the Gibraltar police on 6 March 1988, but rather the reverse. Sufficient extra police were held on duty that Sunday afternoon to fetch the SAS team to their target and to ferry them away again immediately after the shootings.

The whole evidence suggests, beyond reasonable doubt, that the SAS were sent there for the express purpose of killing the IRA unit and were thus the essential element in what the counsel for the next of kin, Paddy McGrory, called in his concluding speech at the inquest 'a conspiracy to murder'.

The 'explanations' for the killings given by the Foreign Secretary to the House of Commons on 7 March 1988 and by the SAS soldiers at the coroner's inquest in September 1988 do not stand up to analysis. Nobody who genuinely wants to get at the truth about this matter could accept the extraordinary coincidence that each of the three IRA members would separately make movements to draw non-existent guns or to press buttons on non-existent detonating instruments. Neither could anyone accept that these four highly trained soldiers, equipped as they were with the elements of total surprise, offensive disposition and back-up from other security personnel, were not 100 per cent certain that they could overpower and arrest the IRA volunteers if that was their objective. Above all, it is not credible that Seán Savage drove a white Renault car through the Spanish/Gibraltar frontier post at around noon on 6 March *without being noticed*.

At a press briefing on 9 March 1988, the Spanish State Security Department of the Ministry of the Interior gave reporters details of the Spanish police investigations into the suspected IRA members, which began in November 1987.[2] The Spanish police had alerted British Intelligence. On 15 November 1987, McCann and Savage, travelling as Reilly and Coyne, were spotted in Madrid airport arriving from Malaga. In February 1988, a woman was noticed travelling to Gibraltar every Tuesday. On Friday, 4 March, McCann, Savage and Farrell were detected arriving in Malaga and checking into a hotel in Torremolinos. The Spanish Ministry said they were in constant contact with British Intelligence in London, to whom they fed this information.

At a further briefing on 21 March, Agustin Valladolid, then chief spokesman for the Spanish State Security, stated (according to a report in *The Observer* on 25 September) that on Sunday, 6 March, Savage's white Renault car was under Spanish surveillance all the way down the coast to its arrival in Gibraltar. Four or five police cars 'leap-frogged' each other on the road while trailing the victims to avoid arousing suspicion. A helicopter spotted the car during part of the route. Police agents were in constant contact with their headquarters by radio. Agents were placed at fixed observation points along the road. The British in Gibraltar received 'minute-by-minute details' of the Renault's movements directly from the Spanish police and were aware of the car's arrival at the border. Valladolid also stated that during the Spanish surveillance operation, two members of the British Security Service had worked with the police in Malaga.

To get into the Gibraltar colony on Sunday, 6 March, Savage had to stop his white Renault car, in accordance with standard procedure; he had to get out, report to the immigration centre and present his passport and car papers for examination. During all that time, he would have been under surveillance by the Gibraltar security officials, as was everyone else entering the colony. Savage was well known to the officials by sight and by his passport name of 'Coyne'; they also knew from the Spanish 'minute-by-minute' police reports precisely when he had arrived at the Gibraltar frontier post.

The senior military officer in charge of the operation (Soldier F), giving evidence on 9 September, said that his unit knew

Savage, McCann and Farrell; it was told that the IRA would run a lethal car bomb into Gibraltar some time over the weekend for detonation on Tuesday, 8 March. Despite this information, given at the midnight briefing on 5-6 March, it was alleged at the inquest that the victims crossed the Gibraltar frontier 'unnoticed'. This is difficult to understand since their progress was relayed regularly to the Operations Room. It is therefore hard to see how Savage, in his conspicuous white Renault car which could be carrying the lethal bomb they were all supposed to be watching for, could pass 'unnoticed' through the frontier post.

The much more likely theory is that not only was the car 'noticed' by the surveillance people, but that Savage was identified, his car inspected and found to contain no explosives. Dead men tell no tales: unless the officer who did the inspection speaks out nobody will ever know the truth. Nor will it be possible to prove what took place at the frontier post. More than likely, Soldier G or some explosives expert was sent to examine the car while it was held at the frontier and, having established that it did not contain a bomb, reported accordingly to Soldier F, who in his wisdom decided to allow Savage to drive further into the trap and to park his car as a bait to lure the other IRA members. A single arrest and an empty car would certainly have been a premature move by him, given the intelligence information which MI5 had made available at midnight — that a lethal bomb could be anticipated.

The only reasonable explanation for the failure of the police to issue a bomb alert and to clear the area in the vicinity of Ince's Hall after Savage had parked his car there around 12.30pm on 6 March was that they knew for certain, following inspection at the frontier, that the car contained nothing. The pretence that it did contain a bomb had, however, to be maintained because that alone was to provide the pretext for killing, rather than arresting, whatever members of the IRA might turn up.

THE POLITICAL DECISION

The fate of the Gibraltar Three had probably been sealed in mid-February 1988 at the highest political level. 'Top-secret information', referred to by the Foreign Secretary in the Commons on 7 March, had been built up following several months of close surveillance by the Spanish and other police forces. This information told of the movements and alleged intentions of an IRA unit located in the southern Spain/Gibraltar area. Sources had uncovered the IRA's plans for an attack on the security forces in Gibraltar. Undoubtedly this information had reached the ministerial committee supervising the Intelligence Services, the Cabinet Sub-Committee which deals with security aspects of Northern Ireland, the Defence Secretary George Younger, the Foreign Secretary Sir Geoffrey Howe and the Prime Minister herself, Mrs Margaret Thatcher. The intelligence was good and the response could be anticipated. It was a job for the SAS.

Troops from the SAS regiment were to be sent to Gibraltar to locate and liquidate this IRA unit in the cleanest and least embarrassing way possible to the British Government. Once it had entered the Crown Colony to carry out its mission, the IRA unit was not to be allowed to get back to Spain again alive. It appears that the SAS members detailed for the job started to assemble in Gibraltar late in February; by 1 March, the full team of some 9 men and 2 women had been brought together there.

As things turned out, the SAS did anything but a clean job. Their predecessors in 1920, the Black and Tans, would probably have murdered their victims quietly in their beds (as John Lynch was murdered in the Royal Exchange Hotel at 2am on 22 September 1920) or kidnapped them and left their bodies with bullets through their heads in some unfrequented spot (as they did with Father Griffin in November 1920). But the 1988 killers appear to have found themselves forced to kill openly and crudely, in the public gaze on a bright Sunday afternoon, persons whom they could have murdered privately, secretly and without witnesses. They did, however, get 'the right men' in accordance with overriding instructions.

It then became a matter for Prime Minister Thatcher and her ministers to pick up the pieces and make the best of their embarrassment. This got underway immediately. With centuries of practice in explaining away imperial misdeeds of all sorts, the

British Establishment lost no time in producing a foolproof story to cover all aspects of the matter. Buckets of official whitewash were quickly applied to hide the truth and no investigation would be allowed which might uncover the evidence that the 'green light' for the summary execution, rather than the arrest, of three unarmed members of the IRA came from the very top.

This type of ministerially inspired execution is by no means unusual in the long story of British brutality in Ireland. Even in this century Tomás MacCurtain, George Clancy, Canon Magner and dozens of others have suffered the same fate. Organisations, such as Amnesty International, concerned with civil liberties, human rights and freedom struggles in many parts of the world today probably know little or nothing about Britain's brutal record in Ireland. They are horrified when they find that the British army, with political sanction, consider themselves free to gun down, on sight and without warning, unarmed members of the IRA. As one of Britain's leading mass-circulation newspapers, *The Sun*, proclaimed on 9 September 1988 — 'Dogs of war deserve to die like dogs. That is why it was right that those three IRA terrorists should be put down.'

PROPER PROCEDURE

Those concerned with the upholding of the rule of law would, however, do well to compare the handling of the O'Hare affair in Ireland in November 1987 with the behaviour of the British in Gibraltar in March 1988. In infinitely more dangerous circumstances, Dessie O'Hare (an acknowledged ruthless and determined killer who had vowed never to be taken alive) was challenged by an unarmed garda officer on 27 November 1987 at Minister's Cross, Urlingford, Co Kilkenny. On that occasion, O'Hare fired his gun and tried to crash through a roadblock in his BMW car, which was then stopped and ditched by fire from a platoon of ordinary soldiers in position some distance away. O'Hare was wounded in the exchange of fire. Disabled, but still armed, he was again confronted by the police and arrested; he was taken to hospital, operated upon and brought before the courts as soon as he was well enough. He was charged with kidnapping dentist John O'Grady on 14 October 1987, of holding him for 22 days and of mutilating him by cutting off some of his fingers. Convicted of the offences, O'Hare is currently serving a prison sentence of 40 years.

A few weeks earlier, on 5 November, Detective Garda Martin O'Connor and a couple of his colleagues, without any military back-up, surprised and confronted the other members of O'Hare's gang (all armed) at a house in Dublin's West Cabra. The police succeeded in wrenching O'Grady from the gang. Garda O'Connor was shot and seriously wounded in the stomach during the exchange of fire.

Despite the known ruthlessness and danger to the lives of the gardaí which O'Hare's gang presented, all its members were eventually confronted by ordinary policemen, arrested and brought before the courts in accordance with proper procedure. O'Hare and his colleague Hogan (who fired at Garda O'Connor) were each sentenced to 40 years imprisonment; the other three were given sentences of 20, 15 and 7 years respectively.[3] The rule of law was upheld: not the rule of the jungle displayed by the British army and British politicians at Gibraltar.

'EXTRA-JUDICIAL EXECUTIONS'

In a letter to Prime Minister Thatcher in April 1988, Amnesty International called the Gibraltar shootings which followed from the decision to send in the SAS 'extra-judicial executions'.[4] The only comment that Britain's Prime Minister could make was to call the letter 'utterly disgraceful'. The Chairman of the Conservative Northern Ireland Committee, Sir John Biggs Davison, called it 'prejudiced impertinence'.

Enoch Powell, former MP for South Down, did not, however, appear to be quite so confident. In a letter to the London *Independent*, he said that it was 'possible' that the fatal shooting of the three IRA members in Gibraltar was 'deliberate, cold-blooded, premeditated murder'.[5]

The Prime Minister's reaction towards Amnesty in the House of Commons may be explained by the fact that she herself was probably the prime mover (as in the *Belgrano* affair) in the Gibraltar executions.

As stated earlier in this chapter, murder by the Crown has ever been recognised as a legitimate weapon of subjugation in Ireland. The British army is the primary instrument by which that subjugation is maintained, through the regular perpetration of murders and the use of terror tactics designed to 'make life hell for rebels' and to keep the populace in continuous fear.

In their evidence at the Gibraltar inquest, the officers of the

SAS (Soldiers E and F) sought to portray the troops in their regiment as just ordinary soldiers in the British army. If shooting unarmed people without warning and shooting wounded people on the ground when they could be arrested represents the standard conduct of troops in the British army, then one can readily accept the statement of Seán Moylan, TD, when he wrote in 1953 that 'every act of terrorism and murder of which I have known was carried out by the so-called disciplined regular troops of the British army.'[6]

While it is true that some of the British massacres in Ireland (such as the one at Croke Park on Bloody Sunday in 1920) were carried out by local commanders acting on their own initiative, the massacres at Derry in 1972 and at Gibraltar in 1988 have the distinction of being the outcome of decisions taken by ministers of the Crown.

The organisation of army personnel into a *'sub-rosa* murder gang' in 1920 by General Sir Henry Wilson, Chief of the Imperial General Staff, also had the approval of Crown ministers — Prime Minister Lloyd George and Chief Secretary for Ireland Sir Hamar Greenwood. It was this fact, among others, that caused Brigadier General F P Crozier, Commandant of the Auxiliaries, to resign his post in February 1921. It was also one of the factors that led to General Hubert Gough's outburst in March 1921, that 'England has departed further from the standards even of any nation in the world, not excepting the Turk and Zulu, than has ever been known in history before.'

Gibraltar 1988 demonstrates that nothing has changed. Irish rebels must, as always, be crushed to the dust by the so-called disciplined troops of the British army.

EIGHT
So What?

> ' ... *Physically speaking, we cannot separate.*
> *We cannot remove our respective sections*
> *from each other, nor build*
> *an impassable wall between them.*
> *A husband and wife may be divorced,*
> *and go out of the presence and*
> *beyond the reach of each other;*
> *but the different parts of our country*
> *cannot but remain face to face, and*
> *intercourse, either amicable or hostile,*
> *must continue between them ...*
> *This country, with its institutions, belongs to*
> *the people who inhabit it.*'
> — ABRAHAM LINCOLN
> *First Inaugural Address,* 4 March 1861,
> to his Fellow-Citizens of the United States

If one accepts the fundamental principle enshrined in charters of liberty around the world, that freedom is the birthright of every nation, all genuine believers in freedom and liberty must now ask, 'What about Ireland?'

In 1920, a small segment of this country (incorrectly named 'Northern Ireland') was cut off from the national territory (*see Chapter 6*). This separate statelet, comprising 17 per cent of the total area, was set up contrary to the wishes of the overwhelming majority of the Irish people, as expressed in the 1918 General Election. No Irish representative wanted the statelet and no Irish representative voted for it. Because of this subversion of normal democratic procedure, it is now obvious to everyone what should have been obvious then — that this artificial entity is ungovernable, save with the day-to-day support of British military force.

SO WHAT? 123

That the British Tories had an ulterior party motive in the events of 1910-20, which led to the creation of the statelet, is abundantly clear from the speeches and letters of their leader, Bonar Law, and from other prominent members of the party, such as Birkenhead, Chamberlain and Long. Their perceptive opponent, Winston Churchill, saw the political chicanery of the Tory policy; he spelt out their motives in his speech at Bradford on 14 March 1914 (*see Chapter 6*). But once the statelet was created, other reasons were soon found for maintaining it. These reasons, since accepted by the other political parties in England, are all derived from the argument advanced by Pitt for the forcible annexation of Ireland under the Act of Union 1800 — that is, imperial necessity. The case is categorically stated in the confidential minutes of the British Cabinet in 1949, No. 49(4) (released 30 years later, in 1979).[1]

> 'So far as can be foreseen, it will **never** be to Great Britain's advantage that Northern Ireland should form part of a territory outside His Majesty's jurisdiction. Indeed, it seems unlikely that Great Britain would **ever** be able to agree to this, **even if** the people of Northern Ireland desired it.' [Bold type is author's emphasis.]

This 'never ... ever ... even if' statement is that of Attlee's 1949 Labour Cabinet, but the sentiments are those of Pitt. It was Pitt's view in 1800 that if the United Irishmen (which were then made up mainly of Presbyterians, Catholics and a small number of radicals of the Established Church) had been able to get help from France during the rebellion of 1798 (as Wolfe Tone had been promised), the available British forces would not have been able to hold Ireland. It was probably an exaggerated fear. Not being part of the landmass of Europe, Napoleon's interest in Ireland (and the Spanish interest in an earlier period) was probably limited to the effect that rebellion there could have in diverting British forces away from other theatres of colonial war in which Britain and the continental powers were regularly engaged — Canada, the Americas and other places.

An invasion of England by France using Ireland as a base never appeared likely. Ireland itself was no economic asset to anybody, except the garrison which was already in possession of the land. To force the union of England and Ireland in order to protect England from France seems to make little sense; to force a union in order to protect the garrison and put it in a superior controlling position over an increasingly unreliable and expanding population does, however, make excellent colonial sense.

The thinking behind Cabinet Minute 49(4) (*above*) appears to be based on the time-worn military advice, that one must always protect one's flank and rear, and that if a foreign power, hostile to Britain, sought to establish itself in any part of Ireland from which it could attack England, then England would have to oppose it in order to protect itself. For that reason, so the argument runs, it is unlikely that Great Britain will ever agree to surrender its present foothold in Northern Ireland, even if the people so desire it.

It is significant that there is nothing in the Anglo-Irish Agreement 1985 that would suggest any change in this thinking. The reference to a 'united Ireland' in Article 1(c) of that treaty does not imply any commitment to an *independent* united Ireland *outside* His/Her Majesty's jurisdiction. Therefore, it can only mean a commitment to a *subordinate* united Ireland *within* that jurisdiction. This was the position envisaged by the British under the 1912 Home Rule Act. It is the direct opposite to the Irish claim for an independent united Ireland outside British jurisdiction. This claim was endorsed by the majority of the Irish people in the General Election of 1918, by the Constitution of 1937 and by the unanimous declaration of Dáil Éireann adopted on 10 May 1949 (*see p. 125*).

In his victory broadcast on 13 May 1945, marking the end of World War II in Europe, Winston Churchill gave general expression to the basic British view that Britain's needs were superior to other people's rights, which is the essence of Cabinet Minute 49(4) (*above*). On that occasion, Churchill said that although 'the approaches' to Britain 'which the southern Irish ports and air-fields could so easily have guarded were closed by the hostile aircraft and U-boats ... His Majesty's Government never laid a violent hand upon them [Southern Ireland], though at times it would have been quite easy and quite natural ...'[2]

Provoked into replying by this and other carping references to Ireland in Mr Churchill's speech, the then Taoiseach, Eamon de Valera, in a broadcast from Radio Éireann on 17 May 1945, said:[3]

UNANIMOUS DECLARATION OF DÁIL ÉIREANN
ADOPTED ON THE JOINT PROPOSITION OF:
An Taoiseach: John A. Costello
and
Leader of the Opposition
Eamon de Valera
on 10th May 1949

"Dáil Éireann,

"SOLEMNLY RE-ASSERTING the indefeasible right of the Irish Nation to the unity and integrity of the national territory,

"RE-AFFIRMING the sovereign right of the people of Ireland to choose its own form of Government and, through its democratic institutions, to decide all questions of national policy, free from outside interference,

"REPUDIATING the claim of the British Parliament to enact legislation affecting Ireland's territorial integrity in violation of those rights, and

"PLEDGING the determination of the Irish people to continue the struggle against the unjust and unnatural partition of our country until it is brought to a successful conclusion;

"PLACES ON RECORD its indignant protest against the introduction in the British Parliament of legislation purporting to endorse and continue the existing Partition of Ireland, and

"CALLS UPON the British Government and people to end the present occupation of our Six North Eastern Counties, and thereby enable the unity of Ireland to be restored and the age-long differences between the two nations brought to an end."

> On the same date Dáil Éireann directed that the above Declaration be transmitted to the Governments and the Parliaments of all countries with whom Ireland had diplomatic relations.

The foregoing Resolution of Dáil Éireann represents the only Declaration of Policy in regard to Partition adopted by Dáil Éireann since the Constitution of Ireland was enacted by the People on 1st July 1937.

'Mr Churchill makes it clear that in certain circumstances he would have violated our neutrality and that he would justify his action by Britain's necessity. It seems strange to me that Mr Churchill does not see that this, if accepted, would mean that Britain's necessity would become a moral code, and that when this necessity became sufficiently great, other people's rights were not to count.

'Surely Mr Churchill must see that if this contention be admitted in our regard, a like justification can be framed for similar acts of aggression elsewhere, and no small nation adjoining a great power could ever hope to be permitted to go its own way in peace ...

'That Mr Churchill should be irritated when our neutrality stood in the way of what he thought he vitally needed, I understand, but that he or any thinking person in Britain or elsewhere should fail to see the reason for our neutrality I find it hard to conceive ...

'In later years I have had a vision of a nobler and better ending, better for both our people and for the future of mankind ... I regret that it is not to this nobler purpose that Mr Churchill is lending his hand rather than, by the abuse of a people who have done him no wrong, trying to find in a crisis, like the present, excuse for continuing the injustice of the mutilation of our country.'

But the vision which de Valera held for the ending of British injustice in Ireland was quickly dispelled. Within a few months, Churchill was out of office and in February 1948 de Valera, too, was in opposition. The potentially explosive situation which lay at the root of partition was ignored by succeeding British governments. The inevitable eruption occurred 20 years later — in August 1969 — again under a Labour government (Wilson's).

Contrary to what present-day propagandists would like people to believe, the eruption was not created by the IRA. There was no IRA active at the time. The upheaval was an entirely popular revolt by the people who had had enough of injustice. The reaction of Wilson's Government was to send in the British army to put down the revolt (just as the Israelis are doing today in the West Bank). It was as a reaction against the use of force by the British army that the IRA was revived and remains active to this day.

Apart from the immorality of the annexation of Ireland by Britain under the 1800 Act of Union (of which Gladstone once declared, 'there is no blacker or fouler transaction in the history of man'[4]) Britain still chooses to ignore the fact that, since the establishment of freedom over part of the country in 1921, Ireland has consistently pursued a policy of non-alignment with all foreign powers. Being a small island she poses no threat to Britain or to any other country. If invasion was attempted, it would be resisted. Neither does Britain appear to recognise the fact that no country hostile to it would even think of attempting to establish itself in this country because of obvious unacceptable costs to itself, such as:

- certainty of most determined resistance within Ireland;
- possibility of intervention by other neighbouring powers who would consider such an event to be a threat to their security;
- possibility of retaliation against positions elsewhere in the world vital to the attacker's interests.

In today's world of nuclear weapons and intercontinental delivery systems, Britain's 'never ... ever ... even if' ideas (*see p. 123*) on defence seem more irrelevant than ever. Everyone now accepts that conflict between the nuclear superpowers (to one of which Britain is allied) has long since reached a stalemate position. Maintaining hold on a small piece of neighbouring territory for purposes of 'defence' in these circumstances (described by Churchill as the 'universality of potential destruction') is surely meaningless in a military context.

Such is the official basis of the British claim on Northern Ireland. The claim of the Irish people, on the other hand, is that Northern Ireland, like every other part of Ireland, belongs to the Irish people as a whole. It is a claim which is unequivocally set down in Article 2 of the Irish Constitution:

> 'The national territory consists of the whole island of Ireland, its islands and the territorial seas.'

This is no more than an accurate statement of historical and geographical fact. It has been so since human habitation was first established on the island and will always be so while the island of Ireland exists, simply because it is true, irrespective of who occupies it. The Irish people lay claim to no territory that has not been part of Ireland for thousands of years.

Geographically, the island is a clearly defined landmass of 32,000 square miles, uninterrupted by any significant natural barriers and separated from Britain by a sea barrier roughly the same width as that between Britain and France at its closest point.

It is universally recognised that Ireland is one of the most clearly defined national territories in the world. Even the English politicians responsible for partition were fully aware of this fact. Speaking in 1912, Prime Minister Asquith said: [5]

> 'Ireland is a nation, not two nations but one nation. There are few cases in history, and as a student of history in a humble way I myself know none, of nationality at once so distinct, so persistent and so assimilative as the Irish.'

Churchill, Lloyd George, Ramsay MacDonald and even Carson himself saw Ireland as a single entity and repeatedly said so.

In the light, therefore, of the way in which Ireland was partitioned in 1920 (under threat of mutiny in the army and other pressures organised by the Tory Party and contrary to the democratically expressed wishes of the Irish people) and in view of the weakness of the military argument underlying Cabinet Minute 49(4), together with the strength of Ireland's inalienable claim to full control over its own national territory, it has to be asked why Britain persists in using its military force to remain in occupation of Northern Ireland.

It cannot, at this stage, be said that Britain is staying to protect its garrison. The Northern 'loyalists' are far from being the reliable garrison that existed throughout all Ireland in Fitzgibbon's day. In any case, the Tories were quite prepared to abandon them in 1910 to get into power and would undoubtedly do so again if it suited them. There does not appear to be any General Wilson around now to fight their cause on the inside. Neither does Britain's stay appear to be dictated by economic considerations (when all of these are on the debit side).

There is general belief, however, that Britain is staying either because of American pressure that Northern Ireland is strategically important to the Western Alliance (despite the apparent fallacy of that argument) or because of the risk of violence spilling over on to mainland Britain in the event of a sudden withdrawal. Whatever the reason, it is the opinion of many that the option of least disadvantage to Britain at the moment is to do nothing but stay put, and let the Northern

Ireland sore fester on within the current 'acceptable level of violence.'

Given the ability of the British to follow this course more or less indefinitely because of their superior military strength, it has then to be asked why the Provisional IRA, with much inferior military strength, seem to be fully determined to continue more or less indefinitely also with their efforts to get the British government to remove their army from Ireland as the first essential step to internal peace, and as the prelude to a lasting peace between the two countries. It is a question which stands at the root of all armed resistance against foreign rule everywhere. People who value their freedom and who have had to answer that question in the past all come up with more or less the same answer. In his Statement of 1953, Seán Moylan, TD, expressed his feeling about it while awaiting trial in May 1921:[6]

> 'I knew the determination of my comrades outside and I believed the IRA would be annihilated before surrendering ... I did not believe that the IRA were going to win. I knew their weakness numerically ... I knew the power of Britain and, if I had any conception at that time about the activities with which I had been connected, it was that they formed part of an age-long war of attrition which could not be immediately successful, but which some time, near or distant, would eventuate an Irish liberty. I felt that there would never again be acquiescence to British rule in Ireland.'

Speaking in the House of Lords on 18 November 1777, after the declaration of American independence, William Pitt, Earl of Chatham, stated, 'If I were an American as I am an Englishman, while a foreign troop was landed in my country, I never would lay down my arms — never, never, never.' Nearer to our own day, the speech delivered by Churchill to the Commons on 4 June 1940 gives a similar reaction to a similar challenge: 'We shall defend our island, whatever the cost may be. We shall fight on the beaches. We shall fight on the landing grounds. We shall fight in the fields and in the streets. We shall fight on the hills. We shall never surrender.'

The answer today from active republicans in Northern Ireland, and from that large section of the people which supports armed opposition to the British army and other Crown forces, is dictated by the fact that their country has been partitioned by

Britain against the wishes of the majority of the Irish people and that, as a result, they have been trapped under unjust and hostile British rule. They have seen themselves treated as 'croppies' and second-class citizens in their own country for generations, and they have decided to accept no more of it. They claim their inalienable right to full freedom as Irishmen, free of foreign interference, the same as Englishmen in England, Frenchmen in France or Americans in the USA. They accordingly regard themselves as on a par with the Maquis, the Polish underground, Tito's guerrilla fighters, the Mujahedin, the embattled farmers at Lexington and Concord who 'fired the shot heard round the world', the ANC and the national liberation fronts in a dozen other states, all fighting for freedom from foreign domination.

To the charges of being murderers and perpetrators of terrible atrocities against innocent civilians (such as Enniskillen, Harrods and others), the IRA will answer that all wars are indescribably obscene. If the public could only visualise the mountains of mutilated and burnt bodies piled in mass graves following the massacres of millions of civilians at Dresden, Hiroshima, Nagasaki, Vietnam and elsewhere in recent wars, they would quickly realise that the obscenities of the big powers are infinitely more widespread, more calculated and more terror-oriented than the atrocities committed by the guerrilla fighters in Ireland, endeavouring to eject an army of occupation.

When senior British politicians, such as Lloyd George, Sir Hamar Greenwood and others, said that the IRA of 1920-21 were just a gang of murderers and criminals under whose terrorism the people trembled, General Crozier did not agree. He said, the IRA 'were not a "murder gang" in the correct meaning of that term, but revolutionaries whose ancestors had been simmering for centuries, and who had at last become aware of the fact that in times of cut-throat upheaval "necessity knows no law."'[7] Crozier's comment is still broadly true today.

What Collins had to say to Crozier about atrocities is also of relevance: 'I never had any false ideas about the way we treated you or you treated us. England embarked on an underground war of assassination as she did in Spain a hundred and twenty years before, and I replied with the same weapon. England's shock troops were assassinators. Mine were ambushers, but at times we, too, assassinated. We had no jails and we had therefore to kill all spies, informers, and double-crossers.'[8]

Those who rant about the futility of the use of force to achieve political ends and say that agitation should be 'within the law' (ie British law) seem to forget the dictum of Von Clauswitz that war is but a continuation of politics by other means; that the presence of Britain in Ireland over the centuries rests on the continued use of force; that partition itself was born out of the threat of force and the open support for it by the Tory party; that the claim that Northern Ireland is part of the United Kingdom is currently upheld by full-scale British military and police force; that the use of force by the Provisional IRA was initiated only after peaceful agitation for half a century was shown to be entirely ineffective and it became clear to those who wanted freedom from British rule in their own country that it would never be won otherwise than through force.

As somebody once said, 'Moral force unhappily is not all powerful. In many cases, it must inevitably end in open conflict. It is proved untrue by the whole history of the struggle for liberty.'

Up to now, the reaction of British governments to the Northern revolt has been consistent with the view implied in Cabinet Minute 49(4) — that Northern Ireland is still required as a British military base. Between 1800 and 1921, the British had the same view about the whole of Ireland. Accordingly, no undermining of British authority can be permitted and military force must be employed to stamp out all revolt. If this involves shooting to kill without warning (such as the death in the hayshed of Michael Justin Tighe or of three unarmed IRA volunteers at Gibraltar), or the indiscriminate killing of thirteen civilians at Derry on Bloody Sunday, or the torture and killing of prisoners while in internment, that is nothing new. Ireland has been through it all before in 1920-21 and on several occasions throughout the previous centuries.

In the end, things may move quickly. But, at this stage, it must be said that there is no sign that Britain proposes to vacate its Northern Ireland base. And so, what must undoubtedly be the longest war of attrition in history (in progress now 817 years since King Henry II landed in Waterford on 17 October 1171 with his 4000 troops and his Papal title in his pocket) seems set to continue indefinitely.

Naturally, British politicians committed to this futile policy will continue to churn out the fiction that Northern Ireland is the same as Finchley or Yorkshire, although neither Her Majesty their Queen, nor any member of her family nor the Prime Minister can walk abroad in their Irish Kingdom without substantial military protection.

The fact is, of course, that the annexation of Ireland by Britain under the Act of Union in 1800 and the Partition of Ireland in 1920 against the wishes of the majority of the Irish people are both without any moral foundation. Britain has no more moral right to be in Northern Ireland currently than it had to be in India or Cyprus or Aden or Egypt or Rhodesia in the past. All history shows that there can be no end to violence in the area until Britain quits.

The only hope for the future is that some day, somehow, common sense will prevail and that a majority of the English people will tell their politicians that anything without a moral foundation must in the end crumble; that the part of Ireland cut off under the Partition Act of 1920 is no more part of the United Kingdom than the British sector in Berlin; and that the sooner the present fiction is ended the better for all those who have to bear the cost and for Britain's reputation throughout the world.

SELECT BIBLIOGRAPHY

Barry, Tom (1949) *Guerrilla Days in Ireland*. Irish Press Ltd, Dublin. Reprinted Anvil Books 1981.
Béaslaí, Piaras (1926) *Michael Collins and the Making of a New Ireland*. Volumes 1 and 2. Phoenix Publishing Co, Dublin.
Bowen, Elizabeth (1942) *Bowen's Court*. Longmans, Green & Co, London.
Colum, Mary (1947) *Life and the Dream*. Macmillan, London.
Crossman, Richard H.S. (1975-77) *Diaries of a Cabinet Minister*. Volumes 1-3. Hamish Hamilton, London.
Crozier, F.P. (1932) *Ireland for Ever*. Jonathan Cape, London.
Curtis, Edmund (1936) *A History of Ireland*. Methuen & Co, London.
Dalton, Charles (1929) *With the Dublin Brigade, 1917-21*. Peter Davies Ltd, London.
Davitt, Michael (1904) *The Fall of Feudalism in Ireland, or The Story of the Land League Revolution*. Harper & Brother, London and New York.
Dubois, Paul (1908) *Contemporary Ireland*. Introduction by T.M. Kettle, MP. Maunsel & Co, Dublin, and Baker & Taylor, New York.
Fitzgerald, Brian (1952) *The Anglo-Irish: Three Representative Types — Cork, Ormonde, Swift — 1602-1745*. Staples Press, London and New York.
Gallagher, Frank (1957) *The Indivisible Island: The History of the Partition of Ireland*. Victor Gollancz, London.
Giraldus Cambrensis. *Historial works containing 'The Topography and the History of the Conquest of Ireland'*. Translated by Thomas Forester. George Bell & Sons, 1881.
Gwynn, Stephen (1924) *History of Ireland*. Macmillan, London, and Talbot Press, Dublin.
Henley, Pauline (1928) *Spenser in Ireland*. Longmans, Green & Co, London, and Cork University Press.
Hickey, D.J. and Doherty, J.E. (1980) *A Dictionary of Irish History since 1800*. Gill and Macmillan, Dublin.
Hogan, David (1953) *The Four Glorious Years*. Irish Press Ltd, Dublin.

Irish Historical Documents 1172-1922 (1945) Edited by Edmund Curtis and R.B. McDowell. Methuen & Co, London.

Landreth, Helen (1949) *The Pursuit of Robert Emmet*. Richview Press, Dublin.

Lecky, W.E.H. (1892) *A History of Ireland in the 18th Century*. Volumes I-V. Longmans, Green & Co, London.

Lyons, F.S.L. (1971) *Ireland since the Famine*. Weidenfeld and Nicolson, London.

Macardle, Dorothy (1937) *The Irish Republic. A documented chronicle of the Anglo-Irish Conflict and the Partitioning of Ireland with a detailed account of the period 1916-23*. Preface by Eamon de Valera. Victor Gollancz, London.

Madden, Richard R. (1923) *The United Irishmen: Their Lives and Times*. Martin Lester Ltd, Dublin.

Mitchel, John. *The History of Ireland*. Volumes 1 and 2. R & T Washbourne Ltd, London. Published *c*. 1869.

Moylan, Seán. Unpublished Statement, dated 6 May 1953.

O'Malley, Ernie (1936) *On Another Man's Wound*. Rich & Cowan, London.

Robertson, Nora (1960) *Crowned Harp*. Allen Figgis & Co, Dublin.

Tone, Theobald Wolfe (1826) *Life of Theobald Wolfe Tone*. Volumes 1 and 2. Published in Washington; printed by Gales and Seaton.

Young, Arthur (1780) *A Tour of Ireland made by Arthur Young in the years 1776, 1777 and 1778, and brought down to the end of 1779*. London. Edited by A.W. Hutton, 2 volumes, 1892. Reprinted Shannon 1970.

Webster, Hutton (1919) *Medieval and Modern History*. D.C. Heath & Co, Boston.

Widgery Tribunal, Report into the loss of life in Derry on 30 January 1972. HMSO, London, April 1972.

CHAPTER NOTES AND REFERENCES

Full references for authors and titles of works are given in the Bibliography (pp.133-4).

INTRODUCTION
1. Final paragraph of the American Declaration of Independence on 4 July 1776 by the Representatives of the United States in Congress assembled.
2. *Sunday Tribune*, 20 Dec. 1987. Interview by Deirdre Purcell of Ken Livingstone, former head of the Greater London Council and Labour MP for Brent.
3. *The Times* (London), 18 Jan. 1988. Editorial on Seán MacBride, SC, was headed 'His infamous career'. *The Times* refused to publish a letter from this author pointing out the inaccuracies and bias in their editorial; the response was 'Seán MacBride's career was covered in completely neutral fashion, both in our news report and in the obituary.'

The *Sunday Tribune* of 24 Jan. 1988 reported that the *Sunday Telegraph* published an obituary on Seán MacBride under the headline 'Death of an evil man'. The *Sunday Tribune* of 10 July 1988 reported that the obituary on MacBride in the *Sunday Telegraph* was the subject of a complaint to the British Press Council by Dublin writer Ulick O'Connor and by William O'Donnell of London. They pointed out the failure of the newspaper to publish letters submitted by them critical of the obituary. Their complaint was rejected by the Press Council.
4. Crossman; **5.** Landreth, p. 379; **6.** Lecky, Vol I, p. 104; **7.** Dubois, pp. 34, 351; **8.** ibid. p. 352. Also, Lecky, Vol. V, p. 80; **9.** Hickey and Doherty; **10.** Lecky, Vol. III, p. 171 and Vol. V, p. 372; **11.** Macardle, p. 74. Evidence of Sir Anthony McDonnell, Under-Secretary for Ireland (1902-8) before the Primrose Committee; **12.** Lyons, p. 45.

CHAPTER 1
1. Ir. Hist. Docs., p. 17. Giraldus Cambrensis quotes the original Latin text of the *Bull Laudabiliter* in Book II of his *Expugnatio Hibernica*. The Bull was granted, probably in 1155, during the pontificate of Adrian IV (1154-59), the only English pope. Henry II, however, did not act upon it until October 1171, when he invaded Ireland. **2.** Webster, p. 154; **3.** ibid. p. 157; **4.** Ir. Hist. Docs., pp. 19-22; **5.** Giraldus Cambrensis, p. 20; **6.** Henley, pp. 164, 165, 178, 188; **7.** Ir. Hist. Docs., pp. 38-46.

CHAPTER 2
1. Lecky, Vol. I, p. 14; 2. ibid. pp. 5-6; 3. ibid. p. 13; 4. ibid. p. 6. Also, Henley, pp. 36-7; 5. Lecky, Vol. I, p. 6; 6. ibid. pp. 7, 8; 7. ibid. p. 7; 8. ibid. p. 8; 9. Unpublished Geraldine Documents (1881). Edited by Rev. Samuel Hayman and others. Section on 'The Whyte Knight', p. 68; 10. ibid. p. 84; 11. Lecky, Vol. I, p 7; 12. ibid. pp. 8-9; 13. ibid. p. 18; 14. ibid. pp. 22-3; 15. ibid. p. 23; 16. Curtis, p. 222; 17. Lecky, Vol. I, pp. 27, 28; 18. ibid. p. 42; 19. ibid. p. 82; 20. ibid. p. 40; 21. ibid. pp. 83-84; 22. ibid. p. 84; 23. ibid. p. 85; 24. ibid. pp. 85-6; 25. ibid. p. 86; 26. ibid. p. 87; 27. ibid. pp. 87-8; 28. ibid. p. 88; 29. ibid. pp. 88-9; 30. ibid. p. 89; 31. ibid. p. 100; 32. ibid. pp. 101-3; 33. ibid. p. 103; 34. ibid. p. 102; 35. ibid. p. 104; 36. Curtis, p. 253; 37. ibid. p. 254; 38. Fitzgerald, p. 250; 39. Young; 40. Lecky, Vol I, p. 135; 41. Robertson, pp. 14, 16-17; 42. Bowen, pp. 248, 453; 43. Henley, pp. 179-81.

CHAPTER 3
1. Mitchel, Vol. I, p. 18; 2. ibid. p. 32; 3. Lecky, Vol. I, p. 144; 4. ibid. p. 145; 5. ibid. p. 147; 6. ibid. p. 146; 7. ibid. p. 148; 8. ibid. p. 151 *et seq*; 9. Mitchel, Vol. I, p. 39; 10. Lecky, Vol. I, pp. 157, 158, 159; 11. *Irish Times*, 9 Dec. 1978. Report of speech made by Mr Enoch Powell, Unionist MP for South Down, at AGM of the Mourne Divisional Unionist Association in Newcastle, Co Down; 12. Lecky, Vol. I, p. 152; 13. ibid. p. 148; 14. ibid. p. 166; 15. ibid. pp. 169-70.

CHAPTER 4
1. Population figures from Dubois, p. 352; Curtis, p. 395; Lyons, p. 62; 2. Landreth, p. 379; 3. Madden, Vol. I, p. 181; 4. ibid. p. 182; 5. ibid. p. 187; 6. Tone, Vol. I, p. 55; 7. ibid. pp. 51-2; 8. Lecky, Vol. III, p. 16; 9. Mitchel, Vol. II, p. 39.

The military force in Ireland during and immediately after the insurrection of 1798 was:
From Parliamentary returns:

The Regulars	32,281
The Militia	26,634
The Yeomanry	51,274
The English Militia	24,201
Artillery	1,500
Commissariat	1,700
Total	137,590

10. Lecky, Vol. II, pp. 4-5; 11. Lecky, Vol III, p. 171; 12. ibid, pp. 171, 173-4; 13. ibid. pp. 369-70, 371; 14. Lecky, Vol. V, p. 325 *et seq*; 15. ibid. p. 330 *et seq*; 16. ibid. p. 372; 17. Lecky, Vol. II, pp. 418-19.

CHAPTER 5
1. Lecky, Vol. V, p. 372; **2.** Dubois, p. 222; **3.** ibid. p. 220; **4.** ibid. p. 229; **5.** *Irish Times*, 14 Nov. 1903; **6.** Davitt, p. 525; **7.** Dubois, p. 185; **8.** Curtis, p. 365; **9.** Macardle, p. 74; **10.** Mitchel, Vol. II, pp. 200-1. Also, Gwynn, p. 460; **11.** Lyons, p. 45; **12.** Dubois, p. 353; **13.** Mitchel, Vol II, p. 222; **14.** Davitt, p. 47; **15.** ibid. p. 50; **16.** ibid. p. 64; **17.** ibid. pp. 50-1; **18.** ibid. p. 51; **19.** *Irish Times*, 13 Oct. 1887. 'Verdict of the Jury into the shootings at Mitchelstown'; **20.** Declaration of Independence, 4 July 1776, by the Representatives of the United States in Congress assembled; **21.** *Freeman's Journal*, 10 March 1867; **22.** Dubois, p. 57.

CHAPTER 6
1. Colum, p. 65; **2.** Dubois, p. 372; **3.** *Evening Mail*, 4 April 1900; **4.** ibid. 5 April 1900; **5.** *Irish Times*, 14 Nov. 1903; **6.** *Daily Express* report published in the *Regimental Record of the 2nd Battalion*, by C F Romer and A E Mainwaring, pp. 229-35; **7.** Unpublished Statement by Seán Moylan, TD, dated 6 May 1953; **8.** Macardle, pp. 81-2; **9.** Gallagher, p. 75; **10.** ibid. p. 81; **11.** ibid. p. 84; **12.** ibid. p. 83; **13.** Robertson, p. 107; **14.** Gallagher, p. 99; **15.** ibid. p. 86; **16.** ibid. p. 87; **17.** ibid. p. 84; **18.** Barry, pp. 2-3; **19.** Macardle, p. 263; **20.** ibid. p. 266.

CHAPTER 7, PART I
1. Pamphlet entitled *Ireland's Right to Sovereignty, Independence and Unity is inalienable and indefensible*. Published by the late Seán MacBride, SC, about 1983; **2.** This is a phrase that came into use during World War II when troops were being trained in the barrack square in the basic procedures for moving small numbers under the protection of covering fire. 'That bucket' simulated a machine-gun post or similar opposition and was used as a training aid simply because it was readily available; **3.** *Freeman's Journal*, 10 June 1919. Also Macardle, p. 299; **4.** Macardle, p. 321; **5.** ibid. p. 334; **6.** *Morning Post*, 3 April 1920. Also Macardle, p. 340; **7.** Macardle, p. 379, quoting *Weekly Summary*, circulated to the police from August 1920 onwards; **8.** Macardle, p. 346; **9.** ibid. p. 360 *et seq*; **10.** ibid. p. 362; **11.** ibid. p. 354; **12.** ibid. p. 381; **13.** ibid. p. 397; **14.** Crozier, p. 165; **15.** Macardle, pp. 329, 379, quoting *Weekly Summary*; **16.** Macardle, p. 427; **17.** ibid. p. 345; **18.** ibid. p. 424; **19.** Béaslaí, Vol. 2, pp. 62-3; **20.** Macardle, p. 393; **21.** ibid. p. 394; **22.** Dalton, pp. 113, 115; **23.** Unpublished diary of Captain Seán Fitzpatrick; **24.** O'Malley, p. 195; **25.** Crozier, pp. 276-7; **26.** Béaslaí, Vol. 2, p. 104; **27.** Hogan, p. 201; **28.** Macardle, p. 419; **29.** ibid. p. 432; **30.** Crozier, p. 205; **31.** Unpublished Statement by Seán Moylan, TD, dated 6 May 1953.

CHAPTER 7, PART II
1. Widgery Tribunal; 2. 'Insight Report', *Sunday Times*, 23 April 1972; 3. Macardle, p. 362.

CHAPTER 7, PART III
1. *Sunday Press*, 13 March 1988; 2. *Irish Times*, 10 March 1988; 3. *Sunday Tribune*, 17 April 1988; 4. *Irish Times*, 12 April 1988; 5. ibid. Report on a letter from Enoch Powell published in the London *Independent*, headed 'Killings could have been murder — Powell'; 6. Unpublished Statement by Seán Moylan, TD, dated 6 May 1953.

CHAPTER 8
1. Cabinet Papers 49(4). Public Records Office, London. Released 31 Dec. 1979; 2. *Irish Press*, 14 May 1945; 3. *Irish Press*, 18 May 1945; 4. Dubois, p. 51; 5. *Irish Times*, 30 July 1912. Also, Gallagher, p. 91; 6. Unpublished Statement by Seán Moylan, TD, dated 6 May 1953; 7. Crozier, p. 203; 8. ibid. p. 220.

BIOGRAPHICAL AND EXPLANATORY NOTES

ABJURATION, OATH OF: An oath asserting the son of James II had 'no right or title whatsoever' to the Crown. Swearer thereby pledged to perpetual loyalty to the Protestant line. In 1709, the Irish Parliament enacted that all registered priests would have to take the Oath: also that any two Irish magistrates could require any Irish layman to take it. Penalty for refusal was life imprisonment and confiscation of all property. *See also* PRAEMUNIRE.

AGAR-ROBERTES PROPOSAL: Proposal made by Liberal MP, Agar-Robertes, during the second reading of the 1912 Home Rule Bill, that counties Derry, Down, Antrim and Armagh be excluded from Home Rule. Opposed by Liberal Government; accepted by leader of the Ulster Unionists, Edward Carson, and Tory leader, Bonar Law.

ANNALS OF THE FOUR MASTERS; A history of Ireland from the earliest times to 1616. Compiled in the Franciscan monastery of Donegal between 1632 and 1636 by Michael O'Clery, Conary O'Clery (his brother) the copyist, Cucogry O'Clery (his cousin) head of the sept, and Ferfesa O'Mulconry from Roscommon. Michael O'Clery, the author (*c.* 1575-1643), was a lay brother in the Franciscan order; the other three were laymen.

ASQUITH, HERBERT HENRY: 1852-1928. Born Yorkshire. 1st Earl of Oxford and Asquith; entered Parliament 1886. Prime Minister (Liberal) 1908-16. Introduced Bill in 1912 proposing Home Rule for All Ireland. In the face of a hypothetical mutiny by a small number of army officers at the Curragh and political pressure from Conservative Party, he agreed to the exclusion of part of the province of Ulster from the Bill, thereby initiating the Partition of Ireland.

BALDWIN, STANLEY: 1867-1947. 1st Earl Baldwin of Bewdley. Prime Minister (Conservative) 1923-29 and 1935-37. In power in 1925 when the assurances given by Lloyd George, in relation to Article 12 of the Anglo-Irish Treaty of 1921, were abandoned. *See also* BOUNDARY COMMISSION.

BALFOUR, ARTHUR: 1848-1930. 1st Earl of Balfour. Chief Secretary for Ireland 1887-91. Prime Minister (Conservative) 1902-05. Coined notorious instruction to RIC, 'Don't hesitate to shoot', during the Plan of Campaign in 1887, which led to the massacre of three men in Mitchelstown in September and many subsequent deaths.

BARRY, KEVIN: 1902-20. Born Dublin. A medical student in UCD and member of the Volunteers. Captured after an attack on a British army bread-van at Upper Church Street (20 Sept. 1920) and sentenced to death. Tortured while awaiting death. Hanged at Mountjoy on 1 Nov. 1920, aged 18.

BARRY, TOM: 1897-1980. Enlisted in British army in June 1915; served in Mesopotamia until end of World War I. Returned to Ireland in 1919; joined IRA in West Cork; organised, trained and led one of the most successful flying columns in the War of Independence. Commanded important ambushes, including Toureen (22 Oct. 1920), Kilmichael (28 Nov. 1920) and Crossbarry (19 March 1921). Opposed Anglo-Irish Treaty of 1921. Remained in Army Council of IRA until late 1930s.

BIRKENHEAD, 1st EARL OF: F E Smith, 1872-1930. Elected to Parliament 1906. Served in Ulster Volunteer Force as ADC to Carson. Solicitor-General in 1915 and later Attorney-General. Led the prosecution of Roger Casement. Lord Chancellor 1915-22. Member of British Delegation that negotiated Anglo-Irish Treaty of 1921.

BLUESHIRTS: A short-lived political organisation (1932-35) that evolved from an association of retired army officers, called the Army Comrades Association (ACA). Founded in Feb. 1932 by Commandant Edmund (Ned) Cronin; so called because members took to wearing blue shirts in April 1933; in July, the name was changed to 'National Guard'. General Eoin O'Duffy, former Commissioner of Garda Síochána, became leader. Strongly opposed to de Valera and Fianna Fáil; supported the pro-Treaty Cumann na nGaedheal party in 1932-33 election. Amalgamated with Cumann na nGaedheal and the National Centre Party in Sept. 1933 to form a new party — United Ireland Party, or Fine Gael, which still exists.

BOUNDARY COMMISSION: A commission provided for under Article 12 of Anglo-Irish Treaty of 1921 to determine boundaries between 'Northern Ireland' and the rest of Ireland in accordance with the wishes of the inhabitants. In order to secure their agreement to the Treaty, the Irish delegates were assured that the boundaries laid down in the Partition of Ireland Act 1920 would be redrawn by the Commission, so as to exclude from the new statelet of Northern Ireland large areas with nationalist majorities (ie Tyrone, Fermanagh and parts of Armagh, Down and Derry).

Speeches by the British delegates in the Commons and Lords (Lloyd George, 14 Dec. 1921; Chamberlain, 16 Dec. 1921; Birkenhead, 9 Dec. 1925; Churchill, 16 Feb. 1922; Worthington Evans, 17 Feb. 1922) confirm that without this clear assurance the Treaty would never have been signed by the Irish delegates. This assurance was subsequently repudiated by the British government and under an agreement dated 3 Dec. 1925 the border remained as fixed by the Act of 1920.

BOWEN, ELIZABETH: 1899-1973. Descended from Colonel Henry Bowen, officer in Cromwell's army, who was granted a great holding in north-east Cork. Elizabeth was a distinguished writer, her works including *Bowen's Court*, an account of the Bowen family in Ireland.

BOYLE, RICHARD: 1566-1643. Came to Ireland penniless in 1588. Created 1st Earl of Cork (The Great Earl) in 1620. Bought Raleigh's vast estates for £1000; acquired the Earl of Desmond's old College of Youghal. Built Bandon and several other towns. Founded many industries and became a powerful magnate.

BURGHLEY, LORD: 1520-98. Sir William Cecil, Lord Treasurer and Secretary of State under Elizabeth I.

BURKE, EDMUND: 1729-97. Orator and statesman. Born Dublin. Entered Parliament 1766. Works include *On the Sublime and Beautiful* and *Reflections on the Revolution in France*.

CAMBRENSIS, GIRALDUS: Gerald of Wales or Gerald de Barri. Born Pembrokeshire, c. 1140. Of his 17 books all in Latin, he wrote two relating to Ireland: *The History and Topography of Ireland* and *Expugnatio Hibernica*. In 1183, paid his first visit to Ireland, where his family were prominent in the Conquest. Came a second time in 1185 as tutor to Prince John.

CAREW, SIR GEORGE: 1558-1629. Came to Ireland in 1575. President of Munster 1600. Reputed author of *Pacata Hibernia*, a history of the Munster wars (1599-1602), published under the name of his son, Sir Thomas Stafford.

CARSON, SIR EDWARD: 1854-1935. Born Dublin. Irish Solicitor-General 1892; held same post in England 1900-06. Represented Queensbury in trial of Oscar Wilde *v* Marquis of Queensbury. Represented Dublin University as a Unionist MP 1892-1918. Elected leader of Ulster Unionist Party in 1910. Member of British Cabinet during World War I. Resigned leadership of UUP to become Lord of Appeal in London 1921. Totally opposed to Home Rule.

CASEMENT, SIR ROGER: 1864-1916. Born Dublin, son of Protestants from Co Antrim. Entered British consular service 1892. Knighted for his work in exposing ill-treatment of natives in Belgian Congo and Putamayo region of South America. Joined Volunteers in 1913 and became a member of Provisional Committee. Went to Berlin in 1914 to negotiate for arms; disappointed at German decision to send only 20,000 guns; returned to Ireland. Landed at Banna Strand in Kerry from a German U-boat at dawn on Good Friday 1916. Captured by two RIC men, sent to Dublin and later to London where convicted of high treason. Hanged at Pentonville on 3 Aug. 1916. His remains repatriated in 1965 and re-interred in Glasnevin Cemetery, Dublin.

CASTLEREAGH, VISCOUNT: Robert Stewart, 1769-1822. Born Co Down. Created 2nd Marquess of Londonderry. Initially a Liberal, Castlereagh sympathised with ideas of United Irishmen. Supported Catholic Relief Act 1793. Later became a strong Conservative; as Keeper of the Privy Seal, he dispensed bribes, patronage, sinecures and titles on an unprecedented scale, thereby securing the passage of Act of Union between Britain and Ireland in 1800. Appointed Secretary for Foreign Affairs in 1812. During 1820-22, suffered severe depression and finally took his own life.

CEANNT, EAMONN: 1881-1916. Born Ballymore, Co Galway, where his father was member of RIC. Joined Sinn Féin 1908; joined Irish Republican Brotherhood (IRB) 1913 and became member of Supreme Council 1915. Founder member of Volunteers. Commanded South Dublin Union during Easter Rising of 1916. One of the seven signatories to Proclamation of Independence. Executed on 7 May 1916.

CHAMBERLAIN, ARTHUR NEVILLE: 1869-1940. Prime Minister (Conservative) 1937-40. Negotiated Anglo-Irish Agreement of 1938, which brought the Economic War between Britain and Ireland to an end. Gave back the Treaty Ports, retained by British since 1921. Resigned in May 1940 after German breakthrough of Maginot line and collapse of western defence.

CHILDERS, ROBERT ERSKINE: 1870-1922. Born in England; English father and Irish mother (Anna Barton). Reared at Glendalough, Co Wicklow, at home of his cousin, Robert Barton. Served in Boer War and in World War I. Ferried arms for Volunteers in July 1914 in his yacht, *Asgard*. Elected to Dáil as member for Kildare/Wicklow. Opposed Anglo-Irish Treaty of 1921. Captured in Nov. 1922 in possession of revolver; executed on 27 Nov. 1922. Author of *Riddle of the Sands* and many other works.

CHURCHILL, SIR WINSTON: 1874-1965. Eldest son of Lord Randolph Churchill. Entered politics as a Conservative 1900-05; sat as a Liberal 1906-08; Conservative Liberal 1908-22; and Conservative 1924-65. Supported Home Rule for Ireland. Given a hostile reception in Belfast in 1912. One of the British signatories to the Anglo-Irish Treaty of 1921. Opposed the return to Ireland in 1938 of the Treaty Ports (dockyard at Berehaven, Queenstown/Cobh and Lough Swilly). Succeeded Chamberlain as Prime Minister in May 1940.

CLANCY, GEORGE: 1879-1921. Born Grange, Co Limerick. Formed branch of Gaelic League at UCD. Persuaded Thomas Kettle, Francis Sheehy-Skeffington, James Joyce and Tomás MacCurtain to take up Irish language. Taught Irish at Clongowes Wood. Elected Mayor of Limerick in January 1921. Shot dead two months later at his home by British security forces.

CLARKE, THOMAS: 1858-1916. Born Isle of Wight where his father was serving in British army. Emigrated to USA where he joined Clan na Gael. Returned to England on a dynamiting mission; arrested in 1883 and sentenced to life imprisonment. Released 1898 and went to USA. Returned to Dublin in 1907. Elected to Supreme Council of IRB. First Signatory to the Proclamation of Independence 1916. Executed 3 May 1916.

COLBERT, CON: 1896-1916. Born near Newcastle West, Co Limerick. An early member of Fianna Éireann. Fought at Marrowbone Lane during 1916 Rising. Executed 8 May 1916.

COLLINS, MICHAEL: 1890-1922. Born Clonakilty, Co Cork. Went to London in 1906 to work as a Post Office clerk. Joined IRB 1915; became President of Supreme Council. Fought in GPO 1916. A member of Provisional Executive of Irish Volunteers. Elected to First Dáil. Minister for Home Affairs, subsequently for Finance 1919-22. Organised effective IRA counter-intelligence to British intelligence system operating from Dublin Castle. One of the signatories to Anglo-Irish Treaty in 1921. Made a controversial pact with de Valera before June 1922 Election; subsequently repudiated. Under pressure from Westminster, he attacked Republican forces in the Four Courts on 28 June 1922, thus precipitating the Civil War. Killed in ambush at Beal na mBlath on 22 Aug. 1922. Author of *The Path to Freedom*.

CONNAUGHT RANGERS: A regiment in British army, raised in Galway in 1793 for service initially in Flanders, but subsequently in West Indies, India, Egypt and elsewhere. Soldiers from this unit mutinied in India on 28-30 June 1920 on hearing of atrocities being committed by British army in Ireland. Fourteen of the 75 protestors were sentenced to death; 13 of the sentences were commuted, one (James Daly) was executed on 1 Nov. 1920.

CONNOLLY, JAMES: 1868-1916. Born Edinburgh. Joined British army as a youth and served some time in Ireland. Deserted at 21. Emigrated to USA 1903. Returned to Dublin 1910 and following year became Belfast organiser for Irish Transport and General Workers Union. Assisted Jim Larkin in defence of Dublin workers against 1913 Lockout. Active organiser of Irish Citizen Army which he led into GPO in Easter 1916; fought alongside Pearse and Irish Volunteers. Involved in drafting Proclamation of Independence. Severely wounded in fighting. Executed by shooting while propped in a chair at Kilmainham Jail on 9 May 1916. Author of *Labour in Irish History*; *Labour, Nationality and Religion* and *Reconquest of Ireland*, among others.

CORN LAWS REPEAL (1846): Repeal of existing British duties on foreign corn and other agricultural products had long been demanded by manufacturing and trading interests in England; repeal was opposed by the landlords who profited from the higher rents which protection yielded. Sir Robert Peel repealed these laws in 1846 and thus opened the English market to cheap corn from America and elsewhere. Peel also proposed to abolish duty on foreign beef, mutton and bacon. Henceforth, agricultural produce was to be admitted duty-free to English market. Although this repeal made provisions for the English consumer cheaper, it impoverished the Irish producers and the result was more land clearances, evictions and unemployment.

CORNWALLIS, CHARLES: 1738-1805. 1st Marquis and 2nd Earl. Fought against 'the rebels' in American War of Independence. Forced to surrender to Washington at Yorktown on 19 Oct. 1781. Sent to Ireland as Commander-in-Chief and Lord Lieutenant to suppress 1798 rebellion of United Irishmen. Accepted surrender of General Humbert's French forces in Sept. 1798. Strong supporter of Union between Great Britain and Ireland.

CROKE, THOMAS WILLIAM: 1824-1902. Born Ballyclough, Co Cork. His mother, Elizabeth Plummer, was a Protestant. Catholic Archbishop of Cashel 1875-1902. Supporter of constitutional nationalism; initially, he backed the Land League and Parnell, but later condemned the 'No Rent' manifesto. Opposed Parnell's leadership of Irish Parliamentary Party after the O'Shea divorce case in 1890. First patron of Gaelic Athletic Association (GAA).

CROZIER, BRIGADIER GENERAL FRANK PERCY: 1879-1937. Served in Boer War and World War I. In command of 119th Infantry Brigade in Nov. 1916. Appointed Commandant of Auxiliaries in 1920. Became centre of controversy over his efforts to discipline them; he dismissed two members for undisciplined behaviour, contrary to the order of General Tudor who immediately reinstated them. Crozier resigned in protest in Feb.1921. A vehement critic of General Sir Henry Wilson who, Crozier said, was 'responsible for the first *sub-rosa* murder gang' run by the military early in 1920. Author of *Ireland for Ever, The men I killed* and other works.

CULLEN, CARDINAL PAUL: 1803-78. Born Ballitore, Co Kildare. Catholic Archbishop of Dublin 1852-78. Appointed Cardinal 1866. Opposed every popular national movement, even the moderate Independent Irish Party which merely sought the three Fs (*see* TENANT LEAGUE) for exploited tenant farmers in Ireland. More concerned with strengthening Church's temporal power than with terrible conditions of poor in post-Famine Ireland. Ordered his clergy to abstain from politics, except where specific Catholic interests were involved. Promoted an Irish Brigade to defend the Papacy against Garibaldi in 1859. Denounced Fenians and refused to allow body of Young Irelander, Terence Bellew McManus, into the Pro-Cathedral or any church in Dublin in 1860.

BIOGRAPHICAL AND EXPLANATORY NOTES 145

CUSACK, MICHAEL: 1847-1907. Born Co Clare. Taught at Blackrock College and Clongowes Wood. Co-founder with Maurice Davin of Gaelic Athletic Association (GAA) for the preservation and cultivation of national pastimes (mainly football, hurling and handball).

DALY, EDWARD: 1891-1916. Born Limerick. Commanded Four Courts during Easter Rising 1916. Executed on 4 May 1916.

DAVIES, SIR JOHN: 1569-1626. Attorney-General for Ireland in early 1600s. Master-minded execution of the land-confiscation scheme and subsequent plantation of Ulster. Enforced the Common Law of England throughout Ireland, replacing ancient Brehon Code and Irish system of land tenure. Decisions by him and other judges abolished Irish law of chieftainship, tanistry and equal sharing of family estate among heirs. Author of *Discovery of the True Causes why Ireland was never entirely subdued to the English Crown*, published in 1612.

DAVIS, THOMAS OSBORNE: 1818-45. Born Mallow, Co Cork. Both parents Protestants: father, a surgeon in British army; mother, Mary Atkins, of Cromwellian stock. Educated TCD; called to the Bar, never practised. Co-founder with John Blake Dillon and Charles Gavan Duffy of *The Nation* newspaper in 1842. Member of Young Ireland Party and supporter of Repeal Association. Wrote extensively in prose and verse; author of *The West's Asleep, A Nation Once Again, Clare's Dragoons* and many other poems. Died aged 27.

DAVITT, MICHAEL: 1846-1906. Born Straide, Co Mayo. Family evicted from small holding in 1850. Went to Lancashire to work as child-labourer in cotton mill; lost an arm in factory accident in 1856. Joined IRB; involved in raid on Chester Castle in 1867. Chief army purchaser for Fenians until 1870, when he was captured and imprisoned for 15 years. Involved in foundation of the Land League, persuaded Parnell to join them. Imprisoned on several occasions during Land War. Elected MP for various constituencies. Left Parliament in protest against Boer War and went to South Africa to support Boer cause. Author of *The Fall of Feudalism in Ireland* and other works.

DE VALERA, EAMON: 1882-1975. Born New York. Irish mother (Catherine Coll) and Basque father (Vivian de Valera). Reared Bruree, Co Limerick. Commanded Boland's Mill during Easter Rising 1916. Sentence of death commuted to life imprisonment. President of Sinn Féin 1917-21. Arrested in 1918; escaped from Lincoln Jail the following year. Visited USA to advance the cause of Irish Republic. Rejected Anglo-Irish Treaty of 1921 along with 57 other deputies of Dáil Éireann (64 approved). Founded Fianna Fáil Party on 16 May 1926, primarily to achieve the re-unification of Ireland. Entered Dáil on 12 August 1927 and formed his first Government after General Election of 1932. President of League of Nations 1938-39. Adopted policy of neutrality in World War II and rejected pressures from both Britain and USA to grant military facilities. President of Ireland 1959-73.

DEVON COMMISSION (1843-47): Appointed by Prime Minister Peel under chairmanship of Lord Devon to investigate landlordism, land usage and workers' conditions in Ireland. Commission concluded, *inter alia*, that there were too many small holdings and that consolidation of small farms was essential; that at least 200,000 holdings would have to go and that some one million people, thus rendered homeless, would have to be removed, some of them to settle on wastelands which they could improve, the rest to go to Britain's colonies under state-assisted emigration scheme. The Great Famine of 1845-49 rendered the Devon Commission's conclusions of mere academic interest.

DEVOY, JOHN: 1842-1928. Born Johnstown, Co Kildare. Joined Fenians while a teenager; subsequently enlisted in French Foreign Legion to get military experience. Became organiser for IRB in 1862. Along with John Boyle O'Reilly and Patrick 'Pagan' O'Leary, Devoy recruited some 15,000 Irish soldiers serving with British army into the Fenians. Arrested in 1866, sentenced to 15 years, released 1871 on condition he left Britain until the end of his sentence. Spent remainder of his life mainly in USA, assisting Irish Republican movement from there.

DRUMMOND, THOMAS: 1797-1840. Born Scotland. Under-Secretary for Ireland 1835-40. Established Irish Constabulary in 1836 (prefixed 'Royal' after Fenian Rising of 1867). Set up the Poor Law and Workhouse System in 1838. Merged the hated tithes into fixed rents under the Tithe Act 1838. Coined the famous phrase, 'Property has its duties as well as its rights.' *See also* RIC.

EDUCATION ACT 1831: Act passed under Chief Secretary E G Stanley, 14th Earl of Derby. It established a system of non-denominational British-oriented primary education aimed at making every Irish pupil a 'happy English child'. Teaching of Irish history, language and songs precluded from syllabus. Revised only in 1924.

EMMET, ROBERT: 1778-1803. Born Dublin. Joined United Irishmen in 1796. Expelled from TCD in 1798 because of his connection with them. After '98 Rebellion, he left for Paris to make preparations for a further rebellion. Led a premature rising in Dublin on 23 July 1803. Captured at Harold's Cross on 25 August, tried and, after a celebrated speech from the Dock, condemned to death. Publicly hanged and beheaded at St Catherine's Church, Thomas Street, on 20 Sept. 1803; place of burial unknown.

EVENING MAIL: A Dublin evening newspaper, founded in 1823. Unionist outlook. Ceased publication 1962.

FITZGERALD, LORD EDWARD: 1763-98. Of Protestant parentage, Lord Edward was younger brother of William Robert Fitzgerald, 2nd Duke of Leinster and 21st Earl of Kildare. Served in British army against American 'rebels'. Later joined United Irishmen; one of leaders who planned Rebellion of 1798. Betrayed by infamous Higgins and tracked to a house in Thomas Street, where a violent struggle took place between him and the troops of Major Sirr. Fitzgerald severely wounded. Captured and taken to Newgate Jail on 19 May 1798 (5 days before the Rising). Died on 4 June, probably from blood poisoning.

FITZGIBBON, JOHN: 1749-1802. Earl of Clare. Born Donnybrook, Dublin. Graduated in law from TCD. Father born a Catholic, but converted to Protestantism to pursue a legal career. Both father and son made a fortune at the Bar. In 1778 John represented TCD in Parliament; in 1783, he represented Kilmallock. His diligence in upholding British tradition and interest in Ireland knew no bounds and his rise was rapid, becoming Attorney-General in 1783, Chancellor and Peer in 1789 and Viscount in 1793. Following his leading role in securing recall of Viceroy Fitzwilliam, he was made Earl of Clare in 1795. Opposed Grattan and Volunteers, relief for Catholics, parliamentary reform and Catholic emancipation. Unswerving supporter of Act of Union 1800.

FITZPATRICK, CAPTAIN SEAN: 1885-1942. Intelligence officer in IRA's Dublin Brigade. Arrested on 20 Nov. 1920 along with Dick McKee and Peadar Clancy, who were brutally tortured before their executions. Fitzpatrick not identified at the time, but later charged and jailed for 2 years.

FORTY-SHILLING FREE-HOLDERS: Holders of a lease for life of house or land where the interest of the lessee was deemed to be worth 40/- a year. Such free-holders were granted the right to vote in 1793, irrespective of religion, but Catholics were still debarred from taking a seat in Parliament. As a result of this widening of franchise, many landlords tended to subdivide their estates into smaller holdings to increase number of electoral supporters. Emancipation Act of 1829 allowed Catholics to sit in Parliament, but it raised franchise qualifications from 40/- to £10, thereby reducing electorate from some 230,000 to about 14,000 out of a total population of 7 million.

GOMBEEN MAN: A money-lender or purveyor of other essential goods who charged exhorbitant rates of interest. Resulted in serious exploitation of the poor, in desperate need of money to pay their rent or be evicted.

GONNE MacBRIDE, MAUD: 1866-1953. Born near Aldershot, where father was British army officer. Became involved with Fenianism in her early 20s; met John O'Leary in 1886 and W B Yeats in 1889. Organised support for Boers in 1900-01. Organised protests against Queen Victoria during visit to Dublin in 1900. Founded republican-suffragette organisation, Inghinidhe na hÉireann, in 1900. Married Major John MacBride 1903; went to live in Paris with her young son Seán after breakup of marriage. Returned to Dublin after execution of her husband in 1916. Imprisoned 1918. Opposed Anglo-Irish Treaty of 1921. Imprisoned during Civil War. Author of *A Servant to the Queen*, published in 1938.

GOUGH, GENERAL SIR HUBERT DE LA POER: 1870-1963. Born in London of Anglo-Irish stock (Waterford). Educated Eton and Sandhurst. Commissioned in 16th Lancers 1889. In 1911 returned to Ireland as Brigadier General commanding 3rd Cavalry Brigade at Curragh; involved in the 'Curragh Incident' in 1914. Commanded 5th Army in World War I. Severe critic of Britain's actions in Ireland during 1920-21 period.

GRIFFITH, ARTHUR: 1871-1922. Born Dublin. Member of IRB until 1910. Opposed Home Rule Bill of 1912. Joined Volunteers in 1913. Advocated policy of economic self-sufficiency and protective tariffs to allow new industries to develop in a self-governing Ireland; the name 'Sinn Féin' was adopted for the new political movement which developed after 1916. One of the signatories to the Anglo-Irish Treaty of 1921. Elected President of Dáil Éireann after debate on Treaty. Died in office 12 Aug. 1922.

HEUSTON, SEAN: 1891-1916. Born Dublin. Founder member of Irish Volunteers. Commanded Mendicity Institute in 1916. Executed on 8 May 1916.

HUGHES, DR. JOHN: 1797-1864. Catholic Archbishop of New York. Author of fierce denunciation (20 March 1847) of blasphemy that the Great Famine of 1840s in Ireland was 'the will of God'.

HYDE, DR. DOUGLAS: 1863-1947. Born Sligo. Son of a Protestant rector. Co-founder of Gaelic League 1893. First President of Ireland 1938-45. Published numerous volumes of poetry and prose, in both English and Irish.

IRISH PARLIAMENTARY PARTY: The party of Irish representatives who took their seats in British House of Commons. Grew out of Home Rule League, founded by Isaac Butt in 1873. Led by Parnell from 1880 until 1890. Split into several factions after Parnell's death in 1891. From 1900, John Redmond led a re-united party until it was wiped out in 1918 General Election, gaining only 6 seats.

IRISH REPUBLICAN ARMY (IRA): Members who took the Irish Republican Brotherhood (IRB), or Fenian, oath constituted the first Irish Republican army. The Volunteers who gave their allegiance to the Republic, proclaimed in 1916, also constituted an Irish Republican army, but were generally called the Irish Volunteers. The reorganised Volunteers, built up after 1916 Rising, became known as the IRA, following the setting up of the First Dáil in Jan. 1919 as the proclaimed assembly of the Irish Republic, with its own army, Minister for Defence, police force, etc. The IRA's strength has varied from time to time since 1921 as circumstances have dictated. *See also* IRB, IRISH VOLUNTEERS.

IRISH REPUBLICAN BROTHERHOOD (IRB): Founded in Dublin on 17 March 1858 by James Stephens. The Fenians were founded in New York about the same time by John O'Mahony. Aim of both organisations was the establishment of an Irish Republic. Members were required to take an oath of allegiance to the Republic 'now virtually established' and to obey the orders of superior officers and of the Supreme Council. Members of IRB thus constituted the Irish Republican Army, though they were popularly described as 'The Fenians'. Members infiltrated other nationalist organisations, notably the Irish Volunteers founded in Nov. 1913. A small group from the Secret Military Council of the IRB were also Volunteers — Clarke, Pearse, MacDiarmada, MacDonagh, Ceannt and Plunkett; they planned and brought about the Rising by the Irish Volunteers in 1916. Following the setting up of the First Dáil in Jan. 1919 and the recognition of Volunteers as the Army of the Irish Republic, the IRB declined and was dissolved in 1924. *See also* IRA, IRISH VOLUNTEERS.

IRISH VOLUNTEERS: Formed in 1913 to become the army of the Home Government then envisaged under legislation going through the British Parliament. To ensure control over the organisation, John Redmond, MP, demanded and was given half the seats on the Provisional Committee. Shortly after outbreak of World War I, Redmond urged the Volunteers to join British war effort (Woodenbridge speech, 20 Sept. 1914). A majority, known as the National Volunteers, answered his call; a minority, about 11,000 men, refused and were reorganised in Oct. 1914 under Eoin MacNeill as Chief of Staff. Key posts in the new 'Irish Volunteers' were held by Pearse, Plunkett and MacDonagh. They, along with others from the IRB's Secret Military Council, planned the 1916 Rising by the Irish Volunteers and the Irish Citizen Army, led by James Connolly. *See also* IRA, IRB.

KEOGH, WILLIAM: 1817-78. Born Galway. Politician in Independent Irish Party and supporter of Tenant League. Along with John Sadlier deserted to become member of British administration under Lord Aberdeen. Became Solicitor-General, Attorney-General and a judge. Committed suicide in 1878. *See also* TENANT LEAGUE.

'KING'S SHILLING': Bounty payable by the recruiting sergeant to a recruit upon enlistment in British army. Hence the disparaging phrase, 'taking the shilling'.

LECKY, WILLIAM EDWARD HARTPOLE: 1838-1903. Born near Dublin. Reared in Protestant Unionist tradition. Became celebrated historian and politician. Educated Cheltenham and TCD. With the approval of Queen Victoria, Prime Minister Salisbury offered him post of Regius Professor of History at Oxford in 1892; Lecky declined. Elected to fill vacant seat at Dublin University 1895. Opposed Home Rule. Author of many notable historical works, including *A History of Ireland in the 18th century* and *A History of England in the 18th century*.

LLOYD GEORGE, DAVID: 1863-1945. Born Manchester of Welsh parents. Prime Minister (Liberal) of England 1916-22. Mounted a vicious campaign of terror in Ireland during 1920-21, using Black and Tans, Auxiliaries and up to 100,000 regular British army troops to break morale of people and military arm (IRA) of the Irish Parliament, duly elected in 1918. One of the signatories to Anglo-Irish Treaty of 1921. To secure signatures of Irish delegates, he assured them that the areas with nationalist majorities, cut off from the rest of Ireland under the Partition Act 1920 (ie Tyrone, Fermanagh and parts of Down, Armagh and Derry), would be returned by Boundary Commission provided for under Article 12 of the Treaty. This assurance was later repudiated when the Commission sat. *See also* BOUNDARY COMMISSION.

LOGUE, CARDINAL MICHAEL: 1839-1924. Catholic Archbishop of Armagh and Primate of All Ireland 1887-1924. A conservative. Opposed the policy of force followed by Sinn Féin after General Election of 1918.

LONG, WALTER HUME: 1854-1924. Born Bath. 1st Viscount Long of Wraxall. Chief Secretary for Ireland 1905. Returned as MP for South Co Dublin in 1906. Leader of Unionist Party; succeeded by Sir Edward Carson in 1910.

LUBY, THOMAS CLARKE: 1822-1901. Born Dublin. Educated TCD. Son of a Church of Ireland rector; nephew of Fellow of TCD. Founder member of Irish Republican Brotherhood (IRB) in 1858. Sentenced to 20 years by Judge William Keogh; released in 1871, following agitation by Amnesty Association; went to USA.

LYNCH, LIAM: 1890-1923. Born Anglesborough, Co Limerick. Member of Supreme Council of IRB. Commanded Cork II Brigade of the IRA; appointed Commandant of First Southern Division on its formation in 1921. Opposed Anglo-Irish Treaty. Killed in action near Newcastle, Co Tipperary, on 10 April 1923. Buried in Kilcrumper graveyard outside Fermoy.

MacBRIDE, MAJOR JOHN: 1865-1916. Born Westport, Co Mayo. Joined IRB in 1880s; member of Supreme Council in 1916. Commanded Irish Brigade on side of Boers during Boer War. Married Maud Gonne in 1903; one son, Seán. Fought in Easter Rising 1916 in Jacob's Factory under Thomas MacDonagh. Although not involved in planning of Rising, he was executed on 5 May 1916.

MacBRIDE, SEAN: 1904-88. Born Paris. Son of Maud Gonne and Major John MacBride. Joined Volunteers 1919. One of Collins' aides in London during Anglo-Irish Treaty negotiations, acting as bodyguard, courier, etc. Opposed Treaty. Returned to legal studies after Civil War. Chief of Staff of IRA 1936; resigned after enactment of Constitution in 1937. Called to Bar in 1937 and practised as a lawyer for rest of life. Founded Clann na Poblachta in July 1946. Won 10 seats at General Election of

1948. Joined with other parties to form first Inter-Party Government. Minister for External Affairs when Republic of Ireland Act 1948 passed. Lost seat in 1957. Active campaigner for international human rights: founder member and Chairman of Amnesty International, Secretary-General of International Commission of Jurists and UN Commissioner to Namibia, among other posts. Awarded Nobel Peace Prize in 1976 and Lenin Peace Prize in 1977.

MacCURTAIN, TOMAS: 1884-1920. Born Ballyknockane, Co Cork. Joined IRB 1907. Joined Volunteers on their formation in Cork on 14 Dec. 1913. Commandant of IRA for Co Cork before reorganisation into three separate brigades in Jan. 1919. Elected Lord Mayor of Cork on 30 Jan. 1920. Murdered in his home on 20 March 1920 by members of RIC. Coroner's jury of 17 April 1920 returned verdict of 'wilful murder' against Lloyd George, Lord French, Ian MacPherson, 3 named inspectors of RIC and some unknown members of that force.

MacDIARMADA, SEAN: 1884-1916. Born Co Leitrim. Joined IRB 1906; appointed full-time organiser 1908. Imprisoned in 1915 and after release co-opted to Secret Military Council of IRB, which planned 1916 Rising. Fought in GPO garrison during Easter week. Member of Provisional Government of Irish Republic proclaimed on Easter Monday 1916. Executed on 12 May 1916.

MacDONAGH, THOMAS: 1878-1916. Born Cloughjordan, Co Tipperary. Educated Rockwell College and UCD. Founder member of Irish Volunteers in 1913. Joined IRB Sept. 1915; co-opted to Secret Military Council planning 1916 Rising. Commanded Jacob's Factory during Rising. Executed 3 May 1916. Author of several volumes of poems, plays and a treatise on *Literature in Ireland*.

MacSWINEY, TERENCE: 1879-1920. Born Cork. Commandant of Cork I Brigade and TD for Mid-Cork in First Dáil. Succeeded Tomás MacCurtain as Lord Mayor of Cork on 30 March 1920. Arrested under Defence of Realm Act on 12 August 1920 while presiding at meeting in City Hall. Went on hunger strike; transferred to Brixton Prison where he continued hunger strike for 74 days until his death on 25 Oct. 1920. Author of *Principles of Freedom* and other works.

MAGINN, DR. EDWARD: 1802-49. Catholic Bishop of Derry. Wrote strong letters to Lord Stanley during the Famine condemning indifference of British government and general attitude of clergy toward the plight of the famine-striken millions.

MALLIN, MICHAEL: 1880-1916. Born Dublin. With British army in India. Returned to Ireland and joined Irish Citizen Army, becoming Chief of Staff. Commanded College of Surgeons during Easter Rising of 1916, with Countess Markievicz as his second-in-command. Executed on 9 May 1916.

MARKIEVICZ, COUNTESS CONSTANCE: 1868-1927. Born Lissadell, Co Sligo. Protestant parentage. Married Polish artist, Count Casimir Markievicz. Became involved in radical politics. Founded youth organisation, Fianna Éireann, in 1909; organised soup kitchens in Dublin slums during workers' Lock-out of 1913. Became officer in Irish Citizen Army; second-in-command to Michael Mallin at College of Surgeons in 1916. Sentence of death commuted. First woman to be elected to British House of Commons; refused to take seat. Minister for Labour in First Dáil (Sinn Féin). Opposed Anglo-Irish Treaty of 1921. Died in a public ward in Sir Patrick Dunn's Hospital in 1927.

McCRACKEN, HENRY JOY: 1767-98. Presbyterian and cotton manufacturer. Member of United Irishmen. Led Rebellion of 1798 in Antrim, commanding some 4000 men. Attacked Antrim town on 7 June; captured and executed in Belfast.

McDONNELL, SIR ANTHONY PATRICK: 1844-1925. Under-Secretary for Ireland 1902-08. In his evidence to Primrose Committee (*see entry*), stated that Ireland had been heavily over-taxed since the Union, that the people were becoming enfeebled and their taxable capacity less and less. Said also that in the 60 years between 1851 and 1910, according to Registrar-General's reports, 4,187,000 people had emigrated from Irish ports; submitted that this was a scandal to British administration.

MITCHEL, JOHN: 1815-75. Born Dungiven, Co Derry. Son of Unitarian Minister. Graduated in law from TCD in 1834. Joined Young Ireland movement. Advocated that starving people should withhold their harvest, not pay rent or rates, and resist restraint and eviction. Arrested and charged under new Treason/Felony Act before a packed jury. Sentenced to 14 years transportation to Tasmania. Escaped to USA in June 1853. Returned to Ireland in 1874; elected MP for North Tipperary in 1875, but unseated on grounds that he was a convicted felon who had not completed his sentence. Re-elected at following election. Died while the victory was being celebrated. Author of *Jail Journal*, among others.

MITCHELSTOWN MASSACRE: On 9 Sept. 1887, three unarmed civilians (Lonergan, Shinnick and Casey) were murdered by RIC at a 'Plan of Campaign' meeting (*see entry*) of tenant farmers. They were victims of Chief Secretary Balfour's policy to fight the Plan of Campaign with all the resources at his command and of the notorious instructions to the police, 'Don't hesitate to shoot'.

MOYLAN, BISHOP FRANCIS: 1735-1815. Catholic Bishop of Cork. Strong supporter of Act of Union between Great Britain and Ireland 1800.

MOYLAN, SEAN: 1889-1957. Active IRA officer 1914-24. Commanded Cork II and Cork IV Brigades in 1921. Sinn Féin TD for North Cork in Second Dáil. Opposed Anglo-Irish Treaty of 1921, declaring that it would 're-establish and re-intrench the forces and traditions of the Pale behind the new frontier — the frontier of Northern Ireland' (Official Report of Treaty Debate, p. 145). Fianna Fáil TD 1932-57. Minister for Lands 1943-48, for Education 1951-54 and for Agriculture at the time of his death in Nov. 1957.

MORIARTY, BISHOP DAVID: 1814-77. Catholic Bishop of Kerry. Strong supporter of British interest in Ireland. Opposed Home Rule. Vehemently condemned Fenians in a notorious sermon in Killarney Cathedral on 9 March 1867.

NORBURY, FIRST EARL: John Toler, 1745-1831. Born Co Tipperary. Elected MP for Tralee 1776. Opposed Catholic emancipation and political reform. Appointed Solicitor-General 1789, Attorney-General 1798. Voted for the Union 1800 and received post of Chief Justice as reward. Presided at trial of Robert Emmet in 1803.

O'CONNELL, DANIEL: 1775-1847. Born Carhen, Co Kerry. Called to the Bar 1798. Member of Lawyers Corps of Artillery in 1797. Returned to Kerry during '98 Rebellion. Successfully defended the 'common people' in many famous trials. Agitated for Catholic emancipation during 1820s; eventually granted in 1829, though at the expense of disfranchising the 40/- free-holders (*see entry*). O'Connell entered Parliament as MP for Clare on 4 Feb. 1830. Elected Lord Mayor of Dublin 1841-42. Led movement for Repeal of the Union 1840-43, which petered out after his last 'Monster Meeting' on 8 Oct. 1843 at Clontarf was proscribed. Died at Genoa on 15 May 1847 on his way to Rome.

O'HANRAHAN, MICHAEL: 1877-1916. Born New Ross, Co Wexford. Second-in-command to Thomas MacDonagh at Jacob's Factory during 1916 Rising. Executed on 4 May 1916.

O'LEARY, JOHN: 1830-1907. Born Tipperary. Studied medicine at TCD. Strong nationalist; worked for newspaper *The Irish People*; arrested in 1865 and sentenced to 20 years. After 9 years in English prisons, released on condition that he went into exile for remainder of sentence. Returned to Dublin 1885. President of Supreme Council of IRB 1885-1907. Exercised a strong nationalist influence over W B Yeats, Douglas Hyde, Maud Gonne and others to whom he was a symbol of Young Ireland.

O'LEARY, PATRICK 'PAGAN': Born *c.* 1825, Macroom, Co Cork. Often confused with John O'Leary. Patrick O'Leary worked as recruiting officer for IRB, particularly active among Irish soldiers in British army. Arrested in Athlone in 1867 while administering Fenian oath to a soldier. Sentenced to several years imprisonment. Called

'Pagan' because of his belief that the worst thing that had happened to the Irish was their conversion to Christianity, which taught them to love their enemies. Died in USA.

O'MAHONY, JOHN: 1815-77. Born Kilbeheny, Co Limerick. Graduated in Classics from TCD. Made a distinguished translation of Geoffrey Keating's *History of Ireland* in 1857. Founded the American counterpart of the IRB, known as the Fenians, in 1858. Organised a Fenian Regiment (99th of New York National Guard) in which he held rank of Colonel and which took part in American Civil War 1861-65. Opposed Fenian venture into Canada, advocated by his successor Colonel W E Roberts. Raised some £80,000 for Fenian movement between 1858 and 1864, but himself died in poverty in a New York tenement. Remains returned to Ireland and buried in Glasnevin Cemetry; Catholic Cardinal Cullen of Dublin refused to allow body into Pro-Cathedral for lying-in-state ceremony, which took place in Mechanics Institute.

O'MALLEY, 'ERNIE': 1898-1957. Born Castlebar, Co Mayo. Fought in 1916 Rising. Active IRA officer in War of Independence, acting as roving GHQ organising officer. Captured in Kilkenny on 9 Dec. 1920. Brutally tortured while in custody of the Crown. Imprisoned in Kilmainham; escaped 1921. Author of *On Another Man's Wound* and *The Singing Flame*.

ORR, WILLIAM: 1766-97. A respectable and popular Presbyterian member of United Irishmen in Antrim. Charged in 1797 under Insurrection Act of 1796 with administering United Irishmen's oath in his home to two soldiers, Wheatly and Lindsay. Wheatly admitted in an affidavit after the trial that he had perjured himself; members of the jury also admitted that they were drunk. Orr had not, in fact, administered the oath, but a William McKeever, a delegate from Derry. The affidavit and depositions were placed before Lord Lieutenant, Lord Camden, but to no avail; Orr executed on 14 Oct. 1797, aged 31.

PARNELL, CHARLES STEWART: 1846-91. Born Avondale, Co Wicklow. Son of Anglo-Irish Protestant land-owners. Entered Parliament as MP for Meath in 1875. Became involved with Michael Davitt in Land League from 1879 and leader of Irish Parliamentary Party 1880-90. In 1887, *The Times* of London published a series headed 'Parnellism and Crime', but a Parliamentary Commission established that the letters on which the series was based were forgeries. In Dec. 1889, a member of Parnell's party, Captain O'Shea, filed for a divorce against his wife Catherine (Kitty), citing Parnell as co-respondent. Case tried in Nov. 1890, not contested. The Irish Party split on the issue; 44 members walked out. The Standing Committee of Catholic Hierarchy issued a statement calling on the Irish people to reject Parnell's leadership. He continued to lead a minority party until his premature death on 6 Oct. 1891.

PEARSE, PATRICK HENRY: 1879-1916. Born Dublin. Called to the Bar but did not practise. Founder member of Irish Volunteers. Joined IRB 1913. Became member of its Secret Military Council and helped plan 1916 Rising. As Chairman of Provisional Government of Irish Republic, Pearse read the Proclamation of Independence from the GPO on Easter Monday 1916. Executed on 3 May 1916. Author of several volumes of poems, plays and prose.

PEEL, SIR ROBERT: 1788-1850. Born Lancashire. Chief Secretary for Ireland 1812-18. Prime Minister (Conservative) 1834-35 and 1841-46. In 1814, introduced a new police force to Ireland, the Peace Preservation Force, popularly known as 'peelers' or 'bobbies'. Opposed O'Connell's Repeal Movement and defeated his Repeal Campaign in 1843. Granted an annual endowment of £25,000 to Maynooth College in 1845. Established the Queen's Colleges in Belfast, Cork and Galway; condemned as 'godless colleges' by Catholic hierarchy and O'Connell.

'PETER THE PACKER': Peter O'Brien, 1842-1914. Born Ballynalacken, Co Clare. As Crown Prosecutor during trials of prominent Land Leaguers in 1881-82, he was noted for the practice of 'packing juries' by calling on jurors whom he did not want on the jury to 'stand by'; hence his nickname. Created Solicitor-General 1887-89, Lord Chief Justice 1889, awarded a baronetcy 1891 and raised to Peerage in 1900.

PETTY, SIR WILLIAM: 1623-87. Chief source of statistical information about Ireland after Cromwellian wars. Produced the first scientific mapping of Ireland, the 'Down Survey', which formed basis for Cromwellian Settlement under which Petty reckoned 11 million (English) acres, out of a total of 20 million for the island, were confiscated and planted. Also, according to Petty, in the eleven years between 1641 and 1652, 616,000 Irish people had perished by the sword, by plague or by famine artificially produced, out of a total population of 1,466,000.

PITT, THE YOUNGER, WILLIAM: 1759-1806. Prime Minister (Tory) 1783-1801 and 1804-06. Secured the passage of the Act of Union between Great Britain and Ireland 1800.

PLAN OF CAMPAIGN: Plan devised by members of the Irish Parliamentary Party to meet situations arising from collapse of agricultural prices in mid-1880s. Tenants who were unable to pay their rents were advised to offer rents which they could afford; if refused by the landlord, to pay the sums to the Campaign organisers who would bank them in the name of a committee of trustees and use the funds to assist evicted tenants. The British Government sought the assistance of the Vatican to silence clergymen involved; a Papal Rescript condemning the Plan was issued on 20 April 1888, following a visit to Ireland by Monsignor Ignazio Persico. Vatican intervention was resented and largely ignored. In 1890, the Campaign petered out and was over by 1893. Settlements had been reached with the landlords in many cases.

PLUNKETT, JOSEPH MARY: 1887-1916. Born Dublin. Son of George Nobel, Count Plunkett. Joseph educated privately and at Stonyhurst. Member of IRB and joined Irish Volunteers in 1913. Member of Secret Military Council of IRB that drew up plans for 1916 Rising. Fought in GPO during Rising. Executed on 4 May 1916. Married to Grace Gifford in jail on night before his death. Volume of his poetry published posthumously.

POPE'S BRASS BAND: Facetious title given to a group of about 24 MPs who banded together at Westminster to oppose the Ecclesiastical Titles Act 1851, which forbade Catholic bishops in England from assuming titles assigned to them by the Pope. Group included George Henry Moore and the infamous renegades from the Tenant League, Sadlier and Keogh.

PRAEMUNIRE: A writ (so called from its first two words in Latin, *Praemunire facias* meaning 'warn so and so to appear') charging a sheriff to summon to court a person accused under either of two ancient statutes dating from 1353 and 1393, designed to curb the power of the Pope in certain matters. Under 1353 statute, English subjects were forbidden to prosecute in a papal court a suit which was recognisable in England. Under the 1393 statute, all persons introducing Papal Bulls and sentences of excommunication (thereby acknowledging papal jurisdiction in England) could be imprisoned for life and their property confiscated.

During the reign of Henry VIII, it was argued that persons accused under 1393 statute of praemunire were allowing the Pope to interfere with the King and His Realm, contrary to Henry's new English law. During the period of Penal Laws in Ireland, praemunire was used as a ploy to confiscate lands from Catholic land-owners who would not take the Oath of Abjuration (*see entry*); they were thus, in the eyes of the Crown, deemed to be upholding papal jurisdiction in the King's Realm of Ireland and liable to life imprisonment and confiscation of property.

PRIMROSE COMMITTEE: Set up by British Government under chairmanship of Sir Henry Primrose, to inquire into financial relations of Ireland and Britain for the purpose of financial clauses in 1912 Home Rule Bill. Committee recommended that while an Irish Government should take over local expenditure, no Irish Government should be saddled with the whole of the existing Irish expenditure. Thus, the Committee proposed that immediate charges in respect of old age pensions, estimated at £3 million, should be borne by the Imperial Exchequer.

QUARANTOTTI RESCRIPT: Quarantotti, Vatican Vice-Prefect of Congregation for Propagation of Faith, issued a rescript, or Pope's ruling, in 1814 granting British Government the right to veto appointment of Catholic bishops and archbishops in Ireland to whom it had proper objection as a condition of Catholic emancipation. The

BIOGRAPHICAL AND EXPLANATORY NOTES 157

Rescript was denounced by a majority of bishops and O'Connell; emancipation eventually granted without the condition.

REDMOND, JOHN: 1856-1918. Born Ballytrant, Co Wexford. Led the minority of Irish Parliamentary Party which supported Parnell. Favoured Home Rule Bill of 1912, but rejected Partition. Reluctantly agreed to accept temporary exclusion, which was the thin end of the Partition wedge. Called on Volunteers (himself a member) at Woodenbridge in Sept. 1914 to support British in World War I; majority answered his call, but minority, dominated by IRB, rejected it. Died in March 1918 before his Party was annihilated in that year's General Election, securing only 6 seats.

ROBERTSON, NORA: 1887-1965. On paternal side descended from the Parsons of Elizabethan Munster Settlement; maternal line of the Graves, who came to Ireland in 1650 in Cromwell's time. Family distinguished in many fields. Nora Robertson's book, *Crowned Harp*, is a personal account of the last years of the Crown in Ireland.

ROYAL IRISH CONSTABULARY (RIC): Armed police force for Ireland, formed in 1836 by an Act introduced by Under-Secretary Thomas Drummond. It absorbed all existing police forces, including Sir Robert Peel's 'bobbies' founded in 1814. The prefix 'Royal' was granted after the constabulary had successfully repressed the Fenian uprising in 1867. Rank and file members of RIC were recruited mainly from farming class, mostly Catholics. RIC highly successful in upholding British interest over their own people.

RUSSELL, THOMAS: 1767-1803. Born Bessborough, Co Cork. Son of British army officer. With British army in India in 1782. Served as officer in Belfast in 1790, where he made contact with a radical political club. Accompanied Wolfe Tone to Belfast to found United Irishmen in 1791. Arrested in 1796 for acting as their recruiting agent; held without charge until 1802. Returned to Dublin 1803 to rescue Emmet after his abortive uprising; Russell was betrayed, found guilty of high treason and hanged outside jail gates at Downpatrick.

SADLEIR, JOHN: 1815-56. Born Shrone Hill, Co Tipperary. Politician and businessman. Like William Keogh, pledged to Tenant League but deserted to British administration; became Lord of the Treasury. Later embezzled £1,250,000 from Tipperary Joint Stock Bank which he formed to buy the Kingston Estate at Mitchelstown, Co Cork, under the Encumbered Estates Acts. Committed suicide in 1856, as did Keogh in 1878. *See also* KEOGH, TENANT LEAGUE.

STEPHENS, JAMES: 1824-1901. Born Kilkenny. Founded Irish Republican Brotherhood (IRB), a secret oath-bound society, popularly known as the Fenians, on 17 March 1858. Co-founders included Thomas Clarke Luby, O'Donovan Rossa, John O'Leary and Charles Kickham;

active organisers included John Devoy, William Roantree and Patrick 'Pagan' O'Leary. Built up an extensive organisation, estimated at 85,000 of which some 15,000 were serving in British army. In response to pressure from USA, where John O'Mahony had formed the Fenians, a rising was planned for March 1867; it failed and Stephens escaped arrest, spending time in France and Switzerland before returning to Ireland. *See also* IRB.

TANDY, JAMES NAPPER: 1740-1803. First Secretary of Dublin Branch of United Irishmen. Prominent in Republican politics 1791-93. Escaped to USA in 1793. Returned to Ireland via France in 1798. After Humbert's French troops surrendered at Ballinamuck that year, Napper Tandy left Ireland again; arrested in Hamburg and handed over to British. Tried and convicted of high treason. Life spared on condition he left Ireland for ever. Died in Bordeaux.

TENANT LEAGUE: Founded in 1850 by Charles Gavan Duffy and Frederick Lucas to secure the 'three Fs' — fair rent, fixity of tenure and free sale — for Irish tenant farmers. Fifty representatives, including the infamous Sadlier and Keogh, pledged to oppose any British Government not prepared to grant these rights. Elected MPs in General Election of 1852 and formed Independent Irish Party. Five months later, Sadlier and Keogh broke their pledge and accepted offices in Lord Aberdeen's administration. Their defection led to collapse of the Tenant League and the disappearance of the Independent Party. Work taken up by Land League in 1879.

TONE, THEOBALD WOLFE: 1763-98. Born Dublin. Barrister. Published pamphlet entitled *An argument on behalf of the Catholics in Ireland* under nom de plume 'A Northern Whig', which led to formation of United Irishmen in Belfast on 18 Oct. 1791. Tone went to USA and France, seeking military help for a planned effort to establish Irish Republic, spurred on by Americans' fight against British in 1776. France provided 15,000 troops but force unable to land due to storms; Tone later captured at Lough Swilly, tried in Dublin and sentenced to hang. His request to be shot was refused; took his own life on 19 Nov. 1798.

TROY, ARCHBISHOP JOHN: 1739-1823. Born Porterstown, Co Dublin. Catholic Archbishop of Dublin 1784-1823. Strong supporter of British administration; repeatedly condemned United Irishmen and the Defenders. His concern that Irish clerical students should not go to France, to be influenced by republican democratic ideas, led to foundation of Maynooth College in 1795. Avid supporter of the Act of Union 1800. Presided over meeting of hierarchy in Maynooth in 1799 where a resolution was signed giving British government the right to veto future appointments to hierarchy in return for Catholic emancipation.

BIOGRAPHICAL AND EXPLANATORY NOTES 159

ULTRAMONTANISM: Recognition of the absolute authority of the Pope in matters of faith and morals (literally, 'beyond the mountains', ie the Alps).

USHER, ARCHBISHOP JAMES: 1581-1656. Born Dublin. Anglican Archbishop of Armagh. A noted Royalist. Left Ireland in 1641 owing to the war. Author of works on sacred history, *The Annals* and many other treatises.

WHATELY, DR. RICHARD: 1787-1863. Born London. Anglican Archbishop of Dublin 1831-63. One of 20 commissioners in the first Board of Education set up under the Education Act 1831.

WILSON, GENERAL SIR HENRY: 1864-1922. Born Currygrane, Co Longford. Served in Boer War. Made Brigadier General in 1907. Transferred to War Office 1910. While at Army HQ, maintained close liaison with Tory leader, Bonar Law, and other Tories in plot to subvert Home Rule Bill of 1912 and to oust Liberals from power. Advocated stern repression in Ireland and execution of IRA leaders during War of Independence. Assassinated on 22 June 1922 on steps of his house in Eaton Place, London, by two ex-British army soldiers, Dunne and O'Sullivan. O'Sullivan had lost a leg at Ypres. Both maintained that they were justified by the verdict of their consciences; both were executed on 10 August 1922.

YEATS, WILLIAM BUTLER: 1865-1939. Born Dublin. Strongly influenced by John O'Leary, President of Supreme Council of IRB 1885-1907. Yeats demonstrated his Fenian loyalties on such occasions as Queen Victoria's visit to Ireland in 1900 and in 1916. Awarded Nobel Prize for Literature in 1923.

YOUNG, ARTHUR: 1741-1820. Noted agricultural writer. Travelled in Ireland between 1776 and 1779. His *Tour of Ireland*, published in 1780, gives a detailed account of agricultural conditions in Ireland at the time.

HISTORICAL CHART OF
ENGLISH SOVEREIGNS, POPES, ADMINISTRATIONS AND IMPORTANT EVENTS IN IRELAND — 1171 TO PRESENT

ENGLISH SOVEREIGNS	POPES	IMPORTANT EVENTS
1. Henry II (1154-89)	Adrian IV (Nicholas Breakspear), 1154-59 Alexander III, 1159-81 Lucius III, 1181-85 Urban III, 1185-87 Gregory VIII, 1187 Clement III, 1187-91	1155: *Bull Laudabiliter* issued. 1171: Invasion of Ireland by Henry II. 1171-72: Henry grants Charter to Dublin. 1172: Henry grants Meath to de Lacy.
2. Richard I (1189-99)	Celestine III, 1191-98 Innocent III, 1198-1216	
3. John (1199-1216)	*as above*	1210: King John organises Anglo-Irish government.
4. Henry III (1216-72)	Honorius III, 1216-27 Gregory IX, 1227-41 Celestine IV, 1241 Innocent IV, 1243-54 Alexander IV, 1255-61	1227: All Connaught granted to Richard de Burgh by Henry III.

ENGLISH SOVEREIGNS	POPES	IMPORTANT EVENTS
Henry III continued	Urban IV, 1261-64 Clement IV, 1265-68 *vacancy* Gregory X, 1271-76	
5. Edward I (1272-1307)	Boniface VIII, 1294-1303 Clement V, 1305-14, *who removed to Avignon where the Popes lived until 1377*	1272-1327: Norman Conquest of Irish lands reached its height.
6. Edward II (1307-27)	John XXII, 1316-34	1317: *Remonstrance of the Irish Princes to Pope John XXII.*
7. Edward III (1327-77)	Benedict XII, 1334-42 Clement VI, 1342-52 Innocent VI, 1352-62 Urban V, 1362-70 Gregory XI, 1370-78 1377: *Papal Court returns to Rome.*	1353: First statute of Praemunire.
8. Richard II (1377-99)	Urban VI, 1378-89 Boniface IX, 1389-1404 *Anti-Popes at Avignon:* Clement VII, 1378-94 Benedict XIII, 1394-1417	1393: Second statute of Praemunire.

ENGLISH SOVEREIGNS	POPES	IMPORTANT EVENTS
9. Henry IV (1399-1413)	Innocent VII, 1404-06 Gregory XII, 1406-09 Alexander V, 1409-10 John XXIII, 1410-15	
10. Henry V (1413-22)	Martin V, 1417-31	1422: Proclamation for expulsion of Irishmen from England.
11. Henry VI (1422-61)	Eugenius IV, 1431-47 Nicholas V, 1447-55 Calixtus III, 1455-58 Pius II, 1458-64	1449: First known use of the term 'Pale', to denote area under Dublin control.
12. Edward IV (1461-83) 13. Edward V (1483)	Paul II, 1464-71 Sixtus IV, 1471-84	1468: Earls of Desmond and Kildare and Edward Plunkett attainted at Tiptoft's Parliament in Drogheda. Desmond executed.
14. Richard III (1483-85)	Innocent VIII, 1484-92	1487: First recorded use of firearms in Ireland by troops of Aodh Ruadh Ó Domhnaill.
15. Henry VII (1485-1509)	Alexander VI, 1492-1503 Julius II, 1503-13	1494: Parliament at Drogheda. 'Poynings' law enacted.

ENGLISH SOVEREIGNS	POPES	IMPORTANT EVENTS
16. Henry VIII (1509-47)	Leo X, 1513-21 Adrian VI, 1522-23 Clement VII, 1523-34 Paul III, 1534-49	1541: Henry VIII declared 'King of Ireland' by Act of Irish Parliament.
17. Edward VI (1547-53)	Julius III, 1550-55	1550-57: Plantation of Leix and Offaly.
18. Mary (1553-58)	Marcellus, 1555 Paul IV, 1555-59	1555: Bull of Pope Paul IV making Ireland a Kingdom.
19. Elizabeth I (1558-1603)	Pius IV, 1559-65 Pius V, 1566-72 Gregory XIII, 1572-85 Sixtus V, 1585-90 Gregory XIV, 1590-91 Clement VIII, 1592-1605	1569-73: First Desmond revolt. 1579-83: Second Desmond revolt. 1585: Plantation of Munster. 574,000 acres confiscated.
20. James I (1603-25)	Leo XI, 1605 Paul V, 1605-21 Gregory XV, 1621-23 Urban VIII, 1623-44	1606: Irish custom of gavelkind declared illegal by Royal judges. 1607: Plantation of Ulster. 500,000 acres confiscated. Also Flight of the Earls. 1621: Plantations in Leitrim, Kings Co., Queens Co. and Westmeath.

ENGLISH SOVEREIGNS	POPES	IMPORTANT EVENTS
21. Charles I (1625-49)	Innocent X, 1644-55	1641: Rebellion begins in Ulster.
The Commonwealth and the Protectorate (1649-60)	Alexander VII, 1655-67	1641-52: Population loss due to war, 616,000. 1652-53: Cromwellian confiscation of 11,000,000 acres.
22. Charles II (1660-85)	Clement IX, 1667-70 Clement X, 1670-76 Innocent XI, 1676-89	1681: Execution of Oliver Plunkett.
23. James II (1685-88)	*as above*	
24. William III & Mary II (1689-94)	Alexander VIII, 1689-91 Innocent XII, 1691-1700	1690: Battle of the Boyne. 1691: Treaty of Limerick. 1691-1703: Williamite land confiscations.
25. William III (1694-1702)	Clement XI, 1700-21	1695 to near the end of 18th century: Penal Laws against Catholics.
26. Anne (1702-14)	*as above*	

SOVEREIGNS	POPES	ADMINISTRATIONS	IMPORTANT EVENTS
27. George I (1714-27)	Innocent XIII, 1721-24 Benedict XIII, 1724-30	Stanhope/Townshend (1714-17) Stanhope (1717-21) Walpole (1721-42)	1722: Wood's halfpence. 1724: Swift's *Drapier Letters*.
28. George II (1727-60)	Clement XII, 1730-40 Benedict XIV, 1740-58 Clement XIII, 1758-69	Carteret (1742-44) Pelham (1744-54) Newcastle (1754-56) Devonshire/Pitt (1756-57) Newcastle/Pitt (1757-61)	1731: RDS founded. 1758: 'Wide Street Commissioners' appointed. 1760: Catholic Committee founded.
29. George III (1760-1820)	Clement XIV, 1769-74 Pius VI, 1775-1800 Pius VII, 1800-23	Bute (1761-63) Grenville (1763-65) Rockingham (1765-66) Chatham (1766-68) Grafton (1768-70) North (1770-82) Rockingham (1782) Shelburne (1782-83) Fox/North (1783) Pitt, the Younger (1783-1801) Addington (1801-04) Pitt (1804-06)	1761: Whiteboys in Munster. 1763: Oakboys in Ulster. 1776: American Declaration of Independence. 1789: Revolution in France. 1793: Catholic Relief Act. 1798: Rebellion in Ulster and Leinster. 1801: Union of Great Britain and Ireland. 1803: Rebellion by Robert Emmet. Executed 23 July.

SOVEREIGNS	POPES	ADMINISTRATIONS	IMPORTANT EVENTS
George III continued		Grenville/Fox Coalition (1806-07) Portland (1807-09) Perceval (1809-12) Liverpool (1812-27)	1808: Christian Brothers founded.
30. George IV (1820-30)	Leo XII, 1823-29 Pius VIII, 1829-30	Canning (1827) Goderich (1827-28) Wellington (1828-30)	1829: Catholic Emancipation.
31. William IV (1830-37)	Gregory XVI, 1831-46	Grey (1830-34) Melbourne (1834) Peel (1834-35) Melbourne (1835-41)	1831: National Education Act. 1836: RIC established.
32. Victoria (1837-1901)	Pius IX, 1846-78 Leo XIII, 1878-1903	Peel (1841-46) Russell (1846-52) Derby (1852) Aberdeen (1852-55) Palmerston (1855-58) Derby/Disraeli (1858-59) Palmerston (1859-65) Russell (1865-66) Derby (1866-68) Disraeli (1868)	1838: Poor Law established. Tithe Act passed. 1846-49: The Famine. 1850: Tenant League formed. 1852: Sadleir and Keogh accept office. 1858: IRB founded. 1867: The Fenian Rising.

SOVEREIGNS	POPES	ADMINISTRATIONS	IMPORTANT EVENTS
Victoria continued		Gladstone (1868-74) Disraeli (1874-80) Gladstone (1880-85) Salisbury (1885-86) Gladstone (1886) Salisbury (1886-92) Gladstone (1892-94) Rosebery (1894-95) Salisbury (1895-1902)	1879: Land League founded. 1879-82: The 'Land War'. 1884: GAA founded. 1891: Parnell dies. 1893: Gaelic League founded. 1899: Irish Literary Theatre founded. Sinn Féin founded.
33. Edward VII (1901-10)	Pius X, 1903-14	Balfour (1902-05) Campbell/Bannerman (1905-08)	1904: First performance of Abbey Theatre.
34. George V (1910-36)	Benedict XV, 1914-22 Pius XI, 1922-39	Asquith (1908-16) Coalition (1915-22) Lloyd George (1916-22) Bonar Law (1922-23) Baldwin (1923-24) MacDonald (1924) Baldwin (1924-29) MacDonald (1929-35) Baldwin (1935-37)	1912: Third Home Rule Bill introduced. 1916: Easter Rising. Proclamation of Republic. 1920: Partition of Ireland. 1921: Anglo-Irish Treaty. 1925: Boundary agreement between Irish Free State and Great Britain.
35. Edward VIII (1936) Abdicated.			

SOVEREIGNS	POPES	ADMINISTRATIONS	IMPORTANT EVENTS
36. George VI (1936-52)	Pius XII, 1939-58	Chamberlain (1937-40) Churchill (1940-45) Attlee (1945-51)	1937: New Constitution approved by Irish people. 1938: Anglo-Irish Agreement ends Economic War. 'Treaty Ports' returned. 1939-45: World War II. 1948: Republic of Ireland Act (21 December).
37. Elizabeth II (1952-)	John XXIII, 1958-63 Paul VI, 1963-78 John Paul I, 1978 John Paul II, 1978-	Churchill (1951-55) Eden (1955-57) Macmillan (1957-63) Douglas Hume (1963-64) Wilson (1964-70) Heath (1970-74) Wilson (1974-76) Callaghan (1976-79) Thatcher (1979-)	1969: First Civil Rights march (January). 1972: Bloody Sunday massacre, Derry. 1973: Sunningdale Agreement. 1984: New Ireland Forum Report. 1985: Anglo-Irish Agreement. 1988: Gibraltar killings.

INDEX

Aberdeen, Lord, 149, 158
Abjuration, Oath of (1709), 40-1, 139, 156
Acton, Lord: on end of papal supremacy, 17; on corrupting influence of power, 43
Adrian IV, Pope, 7, 8-9, 44, 62, 135
Adventurers,English, 19, 27, 32, 33, 54, 57
Agar-Robertes proposal, 139
agrarian war, 27, 30
agricultural prices collapse, 57, 61, 144, 155
Allen, John, 90-1
Alexander II, Pope, 11
Alexander III, Pope, 10
Alexander VI, Pope, 11
Allington, Lord, 75
American Civil War, Fenians in, 154
American colonists' revolt against British, 2, 37, 46, 57, 66, 81, 158
Amnesty Association, 150
Amnesty International, 119, 120, 151
Amritsar Massacre (India, 1919), 86, 99
Anglo-Irish Treaty (1921), 139, 140
Anglo-Irish Agreement (1938), 142
Anglo-Irish Agreement (1985), 124
Annals of the Four Masters, 21, 139
Anne, Ferocious Acts of, *see* penal laws
annexation of Ireland by Britain (Act of Union, 1800), 57, 73, 83, 123, 126, 132
appeal, removal of right of, 60
Army Comrades Association, 140
ascendancy, Protestant, 34, 40, 73, 78, 81
Asquith, Herbert Henry, 128, 139
Aston, Sir Arthur, 31
Attlee, Clement, 123
Australia, Irish emigration to, 5, 62
Auxiliaries, 86, 88, 89, 93, 96, 97, 144, 150

Baker, Dr John Austin, 83-4
Baldwin, Stanley, 139
Balfour, Arthur, 59, 61, 66, 139, 152
Balniel, Lord, 100
Barry, Kevin, 90, 91-2, 140
Barry, Tom, 80-1, 140
Becket, Thomas, 11, 12
Belgrano affair, 120
Birkenhead, Lord (F.E. Smith), 74, 75, 77, 85, 95, 123, 140
Black and Tans, 86, 89, 94, 96, 97, 98, 118, 150
Blueshirts, 140
Blood Sunday: (1920), 89, 121 (1972), 1, 99-107, 121
Bodkin, Judge McDonnell, 95-6
Boer War, 70, 76, 142, 144, 145, 147, 150, 159
Borlase, 27
Boundary Commission, 140, 150
Bowen, Elizabeth, 34-5, 84, 141
Bowes, Lord Chancellor, 36, 38
Boyle, Richard, 35, 141
Boyne, Battle of, 33
Brehon Laws, 14, 16, 145
British Administration in Ireland Act (1920), 87-8
British army in Ireland:
atrocities committed by, 20-3, 27-32, 86-7, 88-98
recruitment, 58-9, 149
recruitment into Fenians/IRB, 146, 153, 158
strength of, 32, 50, 58, 136, 150
terror tactics of, 85-121
British Army Bill (1914), 76
British Cabinet Minute 49(4), 123-4, 131
British Empire, 52, 54, 58, 67, 70, 71, 106
British Establishment, 2, 3, 119
British tradition in Ireland, 13, 43, 51-2, 71, 147, 153
Bruce, Edward, 17

Bull Laudabiliter, 7, 8-9, 62, 135
Burghley, Lord, 22, 141
Burke, Edmund, 37, 39, 42, 44
Butler, Simon, 47
Butt, Isaac, 148
Byron, Lord, 56, 73

Cambrensis, Giraldus, 13, 15, 135, 141
Canada, Irish emigration to, 5, 62
Carew, Sir George, 19, 20, 21-2, 25, 28, 141
Carrington, Lord, 100
Carson, Sir Edward, 77-8, 128, 139, 140, 141, 150
Carte, 27, 28, 29, 30, 31
Carteret, Lord, 43
Casement, Roger, 6, 79, 140, 141
Castlehaven, Lord, 29
Castlereagh, Viscount, 45, 142
Catholics: and Act of Supremacy, 25, 36
    deprivation of civil rights, 36, 38-44, 46, 48, 58, 66, 83
    English fears about, 49, 50, 52, 123
    land-owning class, 28-9, 31, 33, 36
Catholic Committee, 46
Catholic emancipation, 48, 54, 153, 156, 158
    Act of (1829), 56, 62, 147
    see also disfranchisement
Catholic hierarchy: British veto of appointments to, 156-7, 158
    on Famine, 63-5, 151
    on Fenians, 62, 67, 153
    on nationalism, 62, 65, 69, 144
    on property, 63
    on Parnell, 154
    on Union, 53-4, 62
Catholic Relief Act (1793), 49, 51, 142
Catholics, 'respectable', 53
Caulfield, Bishop (Wexford), 53
Ceannt, Eamonn, 142, 149
Cecil, Lord Robert, 75

Cecil, Sir William, *see* Burghley, Lord
Census Commissioners, 4
Chamberlain, Arthur Neville, 77, 142
Chamberlain, Austen, 74, 123
Charles I, King, 31
Charles II, King, 33
Charles, Crown Prince, 41
Childers, Robert Erskine, 6, 142
Churchill, Randolph, 73, 142
Churchill, Winston, 142
    on defending Britain, 126, 129
    on Irish unity, 68, 128
    on nuclear war, 127
    on Tory chicanery (1912), 74, 77, 123
    victory speech (May 1945), 124
Cistercian Order, 17
civilians, indiscriminate killing of, 89-90, 95-7, 102-8
civil rights, 38, 46, 65, 106, 119
Civil War, Irish, 143, 147
Clancy, George, 90, 119, 142
Clancy, Peadar, 92-4, 147
Clanricarde, Lord, 29
Clarendon's *History*, 30
Clarke, Thomas, 80, 143, 149
class divide, 4, 14-15, 42, 45-6
'clearance schemes',
    see evictions; land
Clotworthy, Sir John, 27
Clune, Conor, 93-4
Coercion Acts, 65
Colbert, Con, 143
Cole, Sir William, 30
Collins, Michael, 88, 93, 130, 143, 150
colony in Ireland, English, 13, 15, 51, 57
Colum, Mary, 68
'common enemy', 42-3
'common people', 4, 18, 24, 25, 32, 35, 44, 53, 55, 59, 65, 67, 73
Common Prayer, Book of, 25
condemnation of British policy in Ireland, 20, 29, 30, 43-4, 61, 81, 97-8, 121, 151, 152
confiscations, *see* land
Connaught, province of, 32, 50

INDEX 171

Connaught, Duke of, 59, 70
Connaught Rangers, 143
Connolly, James, 80, 143, 149
Connolly, Lady Louisa, 52
conqueror's law, 3, 57
'conquered people', 37, 56, 68, 99
conquistadores, 13
Conservatives, *see* Tories
'conspiracy to murder', 114, 115
Constitution, Irish (1937), 124, 125, 127
Coote, Sir Charles, 20, 28
Cork: murder of mayors, 86, 90, 151
  sacking of city, 96
Corn Laws (1846), 57, 143-4
Cornwallis, Lord, 53, 144
coroner's inquests: Gibraltar (1988), 110-17, 121
  MacCurtain (1920), 86
  Mitchelstown (1887), 66
  suppression of, 88
covenant against Home Rule (1912), 75-6
Croke, Archbishop Dr Thomas, 67, 144
Croke Park Massacre, *see* Bloody Sunday (1920)
Cromwell, Oliver, 20, 31-2, 34
Cromwellian Act of Settlement (1652), 32-3
Crossman, Dick, 2
Crowley, Timothy, 89-90
Crozier, Brigadier General, 88, 97, 121, 130, 144
  on British terror tactics (1920-21), 97
  on General Wilson's 'sub-rosa murder gang', 88
  on IRA, 130
Cullen, Cardinal Paul, 144, 154
Cumann na nGaedheal, 140
Cumberland, Duke of, 74
Curragh: army camp, 58
  'mutiny', 76, 139, 148
Curry's *History*, 29, 30
Curtis, Edmund, 24, 32, 33
Cusack, Michael, 67, 145

Dáil Éireann:
  Declaration on partition (1949), 124, 125
  First (1919), 85, 88
Dalton, Charlie, 93
Daly, Edward, 145
'dangerous associations', 60, 85
Davies, Sir John, 19, 20, 32, 145
Davin, Maurice, 145
Davis, Thomas Osborne, 5, 145
Davison, Sir John Biggs, 120
Davitt, Michael, 63-4, 145, 154
De Beaumont, Gustave, 61
De Burke, Lord Willoughby, 75, 76
Derry march (1972), *see* Bloody Sunday (1972)
Desmond, Earl of, 19, 21, 22, 34, 141
De Valera, Eamon, 89, 140, 143, 145
  reply to Churchill (May 1945), 124-6
Devon Commission, 61, 146
Devoy, John, 146, 158
Dictatus Papa, 9
Dillon, John Blake, 145
Discoverers, 26
disfranchisement, 56, 62, 147, 153
'domestic enemies', 42
'Dominus Hiberniae/Terrae', 14
Dorset, Duke of, 42
Down Survey, Petty's, 155
Drogheda, siege of, 31-2
Drummond, Thomas, 59, 146, 157
Dublin Castle, 92, 93
Dublin Evening Post, 45
Duffy, Charles Gavan, 145, 158

Earls, Flight of the, 23
Easter Rising (1916), 6, 79-81
  Church's attitude to, 62
  planning of, 149
Ecclesiastical Titles Act (1851), 156
economic policy in Ireland, Britain's 5, 61, 64
education, 39, 68-9, 146
  Education Act (1831), 146, 159
Edward II, King, 17, 18
Election (1918), General, 81-2, 85, 122, 124, 148, 150, 157

electioneering in Belfast (1912), Tory, 74-6, 142
Elizabeth I, Queen, 19, 22, 141
Elizabethan Wars, 19-25, 27
emigration, 5, 61-2, 71, 146, 152
Emmet, Robert, 4, 5, 45, 55, 56, 65, 80, 85, 146, 153, 157
'enemies to God and man', 37, 44
'English child, a happy', 69, 146
Ensor's *History*, 76
Episcopalians, 46
Evening Mail, 146
evictions, 57-8, 59, 61, 155
'extra-judicial executions', 120
Eustace, Sir Maurice, 28

Faerie Queen, The, 35
Famine, The Great, 4, 61-4, 71, 146, 148, 151
farming, mixed, 13-14
Farrell, Mairéad, 109, 111-17
Fenians, 59, 65, 66-7, 68, 69, 71, 78, 145, 148, 149, 154, 157-8
   Church's attitude to, 62, 67, 153
   see also IRB
Ferdinand and Isabella, 12
feudalism, 3, 13-15, 18, 63
Fianna Fáil, 140, 145
Fine Gael, 140
Fitzgerald, Brian, 33-4
Fitzgerald, Lord Edward, 5, 146
Fitzgibbon, John (Lord Chancellor), 49, 50-2, 54, 57, 58, 147
Fitzpatrick, Capt Seán, 92, 94, 147
Fitzwilliam, Lord Lieutenant, 48
Forbes, Lord, 29
Ford, Major-General Robert, 100-1, 106
forty-shilling free-holders, 49, 56, 147, 153
France, 37, 50, 53, 56, 69, 123, 158
Franciscan Order, 139
freedom, principle of, 1, 81, 122, 130
French, Lord, 85, 86
'French Principles', 49
French Revolution, 45, 46, 55
Friar Simon, 17
Froude, 22

GAA, 144, 145
Gaelic Athletic Association, *see* GAA
Gaelic League, 67, 78, 142, 148
garrison, English, 31, 51, 54, 58, 123-4, 128
Geneva Convention, 85
genocide, 19-35
George III, King, 44
Gerald of Wales, *see* Cambrensis, Giraldus
Gilbert, General, 19, 20
Gibraltar Inquest (Sept. 1988), 110-17, 121
Gibraltar killings (March 1988), 90, 109-21
Gifford, Grace, 156
Gladstone, William Ewart, 57, 60, 73, 127
Gonne, Maud, 6, 69, 147, 150, 153
'gombeen' man, 66, 147
Gordon, Duke of, 74
Gough, General Hubert, 83, 97, 121, 148
Greenwood, Sir Hamar, 86, 89, 95, 96, 121, 130
Gregory VII, Pope, 9
Grey, Lord Deputy, 21
Griffin, Father Michael, 90, 118
Griffith, Arthur, 148
guerrilla warfare, 34
gun-running by Tories, 76

Habeas Corpus Act, suspension of, 49
Hague Convention, 91
Hales, Tom, 91
Hamilton, Lord Claud, 75
Harte, Patrick, 91
'hell for rebels', 86
'hell or Connaught, Go to', 32
Henry II, King, 7-15, 25, 44, 62, 135
Henry VIII, King, 3, 25, 156
Henry, Denis (Attorney-General), 87
Heuston, Seán, 148
history, preclusion from schools of Irish, 69, 78, 80, 146

INDEX 173

Hitler, Adolf, 20, 69, 73
Holinshed, 21, 84
Home Rule, 72-8, 142
  Bill (1912), 61, 77, 124, 139, 156, 159
  Irish people's attitude to, 78-81
  Tory subversion of, 72-8, 159
  see also partition of Ireland
Home Rule League, 148
Howe, Sir Geoffrey, 109-10, 118
Hughes, Archbishop Dr John (New York), 64-5, 148
human rights, *see* civil rights
Hyde, Douglas, 6, 67, 148, 153

'imperial necessity', 50, 57, 123
Independence, American Declaration of, 1, 129
Independence, Irish Proclamation of, 155
Independence, Irish War of (1919-21), 83-99, 139, 150, 159
Independent Irish Party, 144, 149, 158
India, 21, 80
Indians, American, 2, 3, 36, 51
Innocent III, Pope, 10, 11
Insurrection Act (1796), 49, 50
internment, Northern Ireland, 99, 106
IRA, 79, 88-9, 101, 109 *et seq,* 126, 129-31, 148
Iranian Embassy siege (London, 1980), 114-15
IRB, 67, 148, 149, 157-8
Irish Citizen Army, 143, 149, 151, 152
Irish Constabulary, 59-60, 146
  see also RIC
Irish Irelanders, 71
Irish Parliamentary Party, 73, 79, 82, 144, 148, 154, 155, 157
Irish people, descriptions of, 2, 7, 8, 10-11, 12, 15, 37, 42-3, 54, 58, 88
Irish People, The, 153
Irish Republican Army, *see* IRA
Irish Republican Brotherhood, *see* IRB

Irish Volunteers, *see* Volunteers
Israelis, 126

James I, King, 26
James II, King, 33, 41, 139
Jefferson, Thomas, 66
John, King, 11
John XXII, Pope, 7, 15, 18
juries, composition of, 66, 155

Keogh, William, 66, 149, 150, 156, 157, 158
Kilcolman Castle, Doneraile, 21, 35
Killarney: Dr Moriarty's speech in Cathedral (1867), 67, 153
  police station (1920), 87
'King and Country', 70, 71
'King's shilling', 59, 149
Kinsella, Thomas, 1
Kitson, Brigadier General, 84, 100
Kulaks of Russia, 15

Labour Commission, British, 97
Lagan, Chief Superintendent (Derry), 100
laissez faire, British policy of, 5
land: clearance schemes, 57-8
  collective ownership of, 14, 19
  confiscations of, 19-20, 23, 27, 32-3, 36, 38, 40-1, 52, 54, 145, 155, 156
  feudal system of, 3, 14-15
  penal laws and, 39-41
  Protestant ownership of, 45, 52
Land League, 59, 144, 145, 154, 155, 158
landlords, 15, 33, 51, 52, 57-9, 61, 63, 65, 146, 155
Langrishe, Sir Hercules, 42
language, preclusion from schools of Irish, 69, 146
Larkin, Jim, 143
Law, Bonar, 74, 75, 76, 77, 123, 139, 159
laws in Ireland, English, 16, 37, 38-41, 60, 65-6, 88, 145

Laws, Brehon, see Brehon Laws
Laws, John, 110
League of Nations, 145
Lecky, William Edward Hartpole, 3, 19-44, 51-4, 84, 149
  on genocide campaign in Elizabethan and subsequent wars, 20-32
  on English atrocities according to:
    Annals of Four Masters, 21; Froude, 22; Holinshed, 21; Leland, 22; Pacata Hibernia, 21; Sir Edward Phyton, 22; Lord Deputy Sidney, 22; Edmund Spenser, 21; Archbishop Usher, 22
  on land confiscations: after Desmond rebellion, 23; during reign of James I, 26; on Discoverers craving for Irish land, 26
  on 'war of extermination' character given by English Parliament to 1641 rebellion, 27; on fanatical speeches of Clotworthy, Pym and Parsons, 27; on scenes of horror all over Ireland, 27-30; on Cole's estimate of slaughter, 30
  on Cromwell's massacres at Drogheda and Wexford, 31-2; on Petty's estimate of numbers killed in Cromwellian campaign, 32; on Petty's estimate of land confiscations under Cromwellian Settlement, 32
  on penal laws: on responsibility of English government for penal laws, 37; on denying Catholics civil rights, 39-40; on placing of all material wealth with Protestant minority, 39-41; on 1719 proposal to castrate unregistered priests, 42; on Protestant aversion to catholics, 42; on description of Irish as 'common enemy', 42-3; on evil and lasting effects of penal code, 43-4; Fitzgibbon's view of code, 44; Burke's denunciation of code, 44
  on Union between Britain and Ireland: Fitzgibbon's view of needs of English garrison, 51-2, 54; Duke of Richmond's arguments for Union, 52; support of Catholic hierarchy for Union, 53-4; Orange Party opposition to Union, 54
Leinster, province of, 27, 28, 50
legal system, British, vii-viii, 65-6
Leland, 22, 26, 28, 29
Liberals, 60, 72-4, 77-8, 139, 159
Limerick: murder of mayors, 90, 142
Lincoln, Abraham, 122
Listowel police station (1920), 87
Livingstone, Ken, 135
Lloyd George, David, 77, 85, 86, 105, 128, 130, 139, 150, 151
Loftus, Sir Arthur, 28, 29-30
Logue, Cardinal Michael, 69, 150
London corporations in Derry, 24
Londonderry, Lord, 75
Long, Walter Hume, 75, 87, 123, 150
Lucas, Frederick, 158
Lynch, John, 90, 118
Lynch, Liam, 95, 150
Lyons, Professor F.S.L., 5, 62
Luby, Thomas Clarke, 6, 150, 157

McAnespie, Aidan, 108
Macardle, 86, 92
MacBride, Major John, 6, 147, 150
MacBride, Seán, 2, 135, 147, 150-1
McCann, Daniel, 109, 111-17
McCracken, Henry Joy, 50, 152
Macready, General, 86, 88, 96
MacCurtain, Tomás, 86, 90, 119, 151
MacDiarmada, Seán, 149, 151
MacDonagh, Thomas, 149, 151
MacDonald, Ramsay, 128

INDEX 175

McDonnell, Sir Anthony, 61, 152
McGrory, Paddy, 115
McKee, Dick, 92-4, 147
MacLellan, Brigadier Andrew, 100-1
McManus, Terence Bellew, 144
MacNamara, Detective, 93-4
MacSwiney, Terence, 151
Maginn, Bishop Dr Edward (Derry), 64, 151
Maginot Line, 142
Magner, Canon, 89-90, 119
Mallin, Michael, 6, 151, 152
Mallow Junction killings, 96
Marie Astrid of Luxembourg, Princess, 41
Markievicz, Countess, 6, 151, 152
Maynooth College, 155, 158
Meath, Earl of, 70
Memorial Arch, St Stephen's Green, 70-1
'men of no property', 4
mercenaries, 71
'middle nation', 16
Millner, Lord, 75, 76
Mitchel, John, 6, 36, 37, 64, 152
Mitchelstown Massacre (1887), 66, 139, 152
Mirabeau, 70
monasteries, 16
Monroe, General, 29
Monroe, Henry, 50
Moore, George Henry, 156
More, Sir Thomas, 25
Moriarty, Bishop David (Kerry), 67, 68, 153
Mountjoy, General, 19, 20, 23, 28
Moylan, Bishop Francis (Cork), 53, 152
Moylan, Seán, 153
   on British army, 97-8, 121
   on political attitudes in rural Ireland, 71-2, 78-9
   on IRA and war of attrition, 129
Mujahedin, 3, 130
Munster, province of, 21, 22, 23, 34, 50, 51, 84
murder as a political weapon, 3, 84, 120

'murder gang', General Sir Henry Wilson's:
   General Crozier on, 88
   Lloyd George's approval of, 121
'murderer, potential', 90
Murphy, Con, 90

Nalson, 28
Nation, The, 145
national liberation movements, 2, 130
nationalism, Irish, 50, 80
nationalists, 71-2, 108
Neilson, Samuel, 46, 48
Nesta, Princess, 12
Newenham, Major, 4
'nits will make lice', 28
non-alignment, Ireland's policy of, 127
Norbury, Lord, 45, 153
Normamby, Lord, 58
Norman Conquest of Ireland, 3, 7-18
Northern Ireland: American pressure on Britain to retain, 128
   birth of partition, 77, 123-4
   Joint Security Committee (1972), 100
   Partition Act (1920), 43, 82, 140
   present state of, 3, 42, 43, 83, 99-108, 122-32
Northern Star, The, 48
nuclear superpowers, 127

O'Brien, Peter, *see* 'Peter the Packer'
O'Byrne sept, 26, 27
O'Callaghan, Michael, 90
O'Connell, Daniel, 61, 63, 153
O'Connell, John, 63
O'Connor, Detective Garda Martin, 120
O'Donnell, Red Hugh, 19, 23
O'Dwyer, Paul, viii
O'Grady, John, 119-20
O'Hanrahan, Michael, 153
O'Hare, Dessie, 119-20
O'Leary, John, 147, 153, 157, 159

O'Leary, Patrick 'Pagan', 146, 153-4, 158
O'Mahony, John, 69, 149, 154, 158
O'Malley, Ernie, 92, 154
O'Neill, Donald, 15, 19, 84
O'Neill, Hugh, 23, 30
'Orange Card', 73
Orange Lodges, Report of Select Committee on (1835), 74
Orangemen, 73-5, 77
Orange Party, 54
O'Reilly, John Boyle, 146
Ormond, James, 1st Duke of, 21, 28, 30, 31
Orr, William, 50, 154
O'Shea divorce case, 144, 154

Pacata Hibernia, 21, 141
Pale, The, 29, 30, 31, 162
Palestinians, 3
papal power, 9-12, 17-18, 159
Parachute Regiment (paratroops), 100-6
Parliament, British, 37, 65, 72-3, 81
Parliament, Irish, 25, 36, 37, 40, 42, 44, 52, 72-3
  see also Dáil Éireann
Parnell, Charles Stewart, 6, 144, 145, 148, 154, 157
Parsons, Lt-Gen. Lawrence, 76
Parsons, Sir William, 26, 27, 28
partition of Ireland: Act of (1920), 43, 82, 140, 150
  birth of, 77, 139
  Dáil Éireann declaration on (1949), 125
  Liberal/Tory/Unionist attitude to, 77-8
  see also Home Rule
Pearse, Patrick Henry, 6, 67, 73, 77, 80, 149, 155
Peel, Sir Robert, 57, 144, 146, 155, 157
Pelham, General, 19, 20, 21
Pembroke, Lord, 42
penal laws, 4, 20, 37-44, 46, 51, 52, 156
Percie, Sir Richard, 21

'Peter the Packer', 66, 155
Peter's pence, 9
Petty, Sir William, 4, 32, 155
Phyton, Sir Edward, 22
Pitt, the Elder, William, 129
Pitt, the Younger, William, 48, 50, 57, 85, 123, 155
Plan of Campaign, 66, 139, 152, 155
  Church's attitude to, 62
plantation schemes, 23-4, 26, 32-3, 145
Plunkett, Joseph Mary, 149, 156
police, see Irish Constabulary; RIC; RUC
'poor and ignorant, the' (Orangemen), 74
Poor Law and Workhouse System, 146
Pope's Brass Band, 156
population of Ireland: census figures, 4, 45, 56
  decimation of, 5, 22, 26, 28-30, 32, 61-2, 71, 84, 155
  nature of, 24
  see also emigration
Portugal, 12, 13
Pounder, Professor Derek, 112-13
Powell, Enoch, 41, 120
Praemunire, 40, 156
Prendergast, 30
Presbyterians, 46, 49, 50, 56, 123
press, British, 2, 62, 85, 116, 119, 120, 135
Preston, General, 29
priests, castration of, 42
Primrose Committee, 61, 152, 156
princes, Irish, 10, 11, 14, 15-17, 19
Privy Council, English, 22, 37
Privy Council, Irish, 42
propaganda, political, 2, 12, 15, 73
Protestants, 26, 33, 36, 38, 39-40, 42-3, 45, 50, 52, 66, 83
Pym, 27

Quarantotti Rescript, 156
Queen's colleges, 155

INDEX 177

racial war, 30
Raleigh, Sir Walter, 35, 141
rebellions: Desmond's, 23
  (1641), 27-31
  (1798/United Irishmen), 50, 55, 123, 144, 146, 152, 158
  (1803/Emmet), 55
  (1867/Fenians), 60, 66-7, 78, 158
  (1916/Volunteers), 148, 149
  (1969- /Northern Ireland), 99-108, 126
Redmond, John, 73, 77, 79, 82, 148, 149, 157
  Woodenbridge speech (1914), 79, 149, 157
Reformation, 7, 25
Registrar-General's reports, 4, 5, 152
Reid, 24
religion, 3-4, 25, 40, 44
Remonstrance, The, 7, 15-18, 84
Repeal Movement, 145, 153
  Church's attitude to, 62
reprisal killings by British military, 95-7
republicanism, 46, 48, 56, 74, 129-30
'resistance beyond constitutional limits', 73
RIC, 60, 66, 78, 79, 85, 86-7, 98, 139, 151, 152, 157
  instructions to, 59, 66, 87
  recruitment, 59, 157
Richardson, Sir George, 76
Richmond, Duke of, 52
'right men/parties, the', 87, 105-6, 118
Rights, Bill of (1689), 41
Roberts, Lord, 76
Robertson, Nora, 34, 76, 84, 157
Robinson, Chief Justice, 36, 38
Royal Anglians, 111, 115
Royal Dublin Fusiliers, 59, 70-1
Royal Irish Constabulary, *see* RIC
Royal Irish Regiment, 59
Royal Munster Fusiliers, 59
Royal Ulster Constabulary, *see* RUC
Royal Veto, 37
RUC, 100
Russell, Thomas, 5, 46, 157

sacking of towns, 94-6
Sadlier, John, 66, 156, 157, 158
Salisbury, Lord, 73, 149
SAS, 85, 111, 113-18, 121
Savage, Seán, 109, 112-17
'scorched earth' policy, 34
Scotland, 23, 28, 74
  colonists to Ireland, 23
Settlement, Act of (1701), 41, 52
Shelley, P.B., 45
'shoot to kill without warning', 114, 131
'shooting by roster', 88
Sidney, Lord Deputy, 22
Sinn Féin, 67, 73, 78, 81-2, 85, 87, 89, 145, 148, 150
  election manifesto (1918), 81-2
Smith, Geoffrey Johnston, 100
Smith, F.E., *see* Birkenhead, Lord
Smyth, Colonel, 87, 105
Solzhenitsyn, Alexander, 1
South African Republics, 70
Spain, 12, 13, 116, 118, 130
Spanish State Security, 116
Special Air Services, *see* SAS
Spenser, Edmund, 15, 21, 24, 35, 84
Stanley, Lord, 64, 146, 151
Stephens, James, 149, 157
Stewart, 23
Summary Jurisdiction, courts of, 60
Supremacy, Act of, 3, 25, 36
Sydney, Sir Philip, 35

Tandy, James Napper, 47, 48, 158
Tenant League, 144, 149, 157, 158
tenants, lack of rights of, 58, 65, 155
terrorism, 3, 85, 97, 98, 121
  see also British army in Ireland: terror tactics
Thatcher, Margaret, 118-19
Tichborne, Sir Henry, 30
Tithe Act (1838), 146
tithe collection, 22, 59
Tone, Theobald Wolfe, 5, 46, 48-9, 65, 80, 157, 158
Tories, 2, 60, 73-8, 123, 139
  Belfast campaign (1912), 74-6, 142

torture of prisoners by Crown forces, 90-4
'transplantation' of Irish, 32
Traynor, Patrick, 91
Treaty Ports, 142
Troy, Archbishop (Dublin), 53, 158
truth, on, x, 1, 2, 13
Tudor, General, 86, 87, 144
'two nations' idea, 15, 36
Tyrone, Earl of, see O'Neill, Hugh

Ulaidh (Ulla), ancient province of, 82
Ulster, province of:
 rebellion in, 27, 30, 50
 1918 General Election, 82
 Elizabethan wars in, 22-3
 home rule and, 68, 74-8
 middle class in, 46
 plantation of, 23-4, 145
 partition and, 139
 republican sentiments in, 46
ultramontanism, 159
Union of Britain and Ireland, 50-67
 Act of (1800), 55, 57, 123, 127, 142, 155
 British reasons for, 50-2, 123
 Church's attitude to, 53-4, 62
Unionists, 70, 72, 75, 79, 82, 139, 141, 150
United Irishmen, Society of, 46-50, 55, 56, 123, 142, 144, 146, 154, 157, 158
 constitution of, 47
United Ireland Party, see Fine Gael
'universality of potential destruction', 127
USA, Irish emigration to, 5, 62
Usher, Archbishop, 22, 84, 159

Valladolid, Agustin, 116
Viceroy, 49
Victoria, visit to Dublin by Queen (1900), 69-70, 147, 159
'violence, acceptable level of', 128
Volunteers: Irish, 67, 78-9, 85, 95, 148, 149
 National, 149
 Ulster, 75-6, 78, 140
Von Clauswitz, Carl, 131
voting rights for Catholics, 48, 49, 56, 147

Watson, Professor Alan, 111-13
Weekly Summary, 89, 90
Wexford, siege of, 31, 32
Whately, Dr Richard, 68, 159
Whyte Knight, 22, 136
Widgery Tribunal (1972), 99, 100, 102, 105, 106
Wilde trial, Oscar, 141
Wilford, Lt-Col. Derek, 100-1, 106
William III, King, 19, 33-4
William the Conqueror, 11
Wilmot, Sir Charles, 21
Wilson, Harold, 126
Wilson, General Sir Henry, 76, 88, 144, 159
 see also 'murder gang'
Wood, Anthony, 31
World War I, 79, 80, 157
World War II, 124, 145
Wyse, Dr, 67

Yeats, William Butler, 6, 67, 69-70, 84, 147, 153, 159
Young, Arthur, 34, 58, 159
Young Irelanders, 65, 145
Younger, George, 118

MORE MERCIER BESTSELLERS

One Day in My Life
Bobby Sands

One Day in My Life is a human document of suffering, determination, anguish, courage and faith. It also portrays frightening examples of man's inhumanity to man.

Written with economy and a dry humour it charts, almost minute by minute, a brave man's struggle to preserve his identity against cold, dirt and boredom. It is the record of a single day and conjures up vividly the enclosed hell of Long Kesh; the poor food, the harassment and the humiliating mirror searches. Bobby Sands and his comrades were often gripped by terror at the iron system that held them and yet their courage never faltered.

Written on toilet paper with a biro refill and hidden inside Bobby Sands' own body, this is a book about human bravery and endurance and will take its place beside the great European classics on imprisonment like *One Day in the Life of Ivan Denisovich* and our own John Mitchel's *Jail Journal*.

'I wish it were possible to ensure that those in charge of formulating British policy in Ireland would read these pages. They might begin to understand the deep injuries which British policy has inflicted upon this nation, and now seek to heal these wounds.' *From the Introduction by Seán Mac Bride.*

Bobby Sands was twenty-seven years old when he died, on the sixty-sixth day of his hunger strike, on 5 May 1981. He had spent almost the last nine years of his short life in prison because of his Irish Republican activities. By the time of his death he was world-famous for having embarrassed the British establishment by being elected as M.P. to the British Parliament for Fermanagh/South Tyrone and having defiantly withstood political and moral pressure to abandon his hunger-strike.

BOBBY SANDS AND THE TRAGEDY OF NORTHERN IRELAND
by **John M. Feehan**

Bobby Sands captured the imagination of the world when, despite predictions, he was elected a Member of Parliament to the British House of Commons while still on hunger strike in the Northern Ireland concentration camp of Long Kesh.

- When he later died after 66 gruelling days of hunger he commanded more television, radio and newspaper coverage than papal visits or royal weddings.
- What was the secret of this young man who set himself against the might of an empire and who became a microcosm of the whole Northern question and a moral catalyst for the Southern Irish conscience?

In calm, restrained language, John M. Feehan records here the life of Bobby Sands, with whom he had little sympathy at the beginning — though this was to change. At the same time, Feehan gives an illuminating and clear account of the statelet of Northern Ireland today and of the fierce guerrilla warfare that is rapidly turning Northern Ireland into Britain's Vietnam.

**THE DISMAL HOUSE OF LITTLE EASE:
A HISTORY OF KILMAINHAM GAOL**
by **Freida Kelly**

Freida Kelly, a guide in Kilmainham Gaol since 1980, unlocks the fascinating and gruesome history of one of Ireland's most infamous landmarks — a place of incarceration where thousands of Irish men and women were shut away not because they were criminals but because they were victims of their time. Today, this unique national monument is restored and open to the public — a surviving statement of the rigid administrative rigours imposed by the British on Ireland.

Kilmainham's history is traced from its foundations in the 13th century as a priory by the Hospitaller Knights of St John of Jerusalem, with a special place for people of 'little ease' of mind, through to the dreadful debtors' prison of the 18th century, to the New County Gaol refurbished in 1796, and finally to the high-security prison of the 19th and 20th centuries, where fourteen of Ireland's finest were executed for their part in the Easter Rising of 1916. James Connolly was the last man to be executed there and Eamon de Valera was the last political prisoner to be held, before the Gaol's doors finally closed in 1924.

Freida Kelly's highly readable account gives a remarkable insight into the unfortunate people who were destined to endure so much within Kilmainham's walls.

Michael Collins and the Treaty
His Differences with de Valera
T. Ryle Dwyer

To Michael Collins the signing of the Treaty between Ireland and Britain in 1921 was a 'Stepping Stone'. Eamon de Valera called it 'Treason'.

The controversy surrounding this Treaty is probably the most important single factor in the history of this country, not only because it led to the Civil War of 1922-1923 but also because the basic differences between the country's two main political parties stem from the dispute.

T. Ryle Dwyer not only takes an in-depth look at the characters and motivations of the two main Irish protagonists but also gives many insights into the views and ideas of the other people involved on both sides of the Irish Sea.

This book is not only the story of Michael Collins' role in the events surrounding the Treaty, but it is also the story of his differences with Eamon de Valera which were to have tragic consequences for the nation.